MW00533072

SOUTHERN LITERARY STUDIES

Fred Hobson, Editor

Peculiar Crossroads

FLANNERY O'CONNOR,

WALKER PERCY,

AND CATHOLIC VISION IN

POSTWAR SOUTHERN FICTION

Farrell O'Gorman

LOUISIANA STATE UNIVERSITY PRESS

BATON ROUGE

Copyright © 2004 by Louisiana State University Press

All rights reserved

Manufactured in the United States of America

FIRST PRINTING

DESIGNER: Andrew Shurtz

TYPEFACE: Whitman

TYPESETTER: Coghill Composition Co., Inc.

PRINTER AND BINDER: Thomson-Shore, Inc.

LIBRARY OF CONGRESS CATALOGING-IN-PUBLICATION DATA

O'Gorman, Farrell.

   Peculiar crossroads : Flannery O'Connor, Walker Percy, and Catholic vision in postwar
   southern fiction / Farrell O'Gorman.

      p. cm. — (Southern literary studies)

   Based on author's thesis (Ph. D.)—University of North Carolina, 2000.

   Includes bibliographical references and index.

   ISBN 0-8071-2988-7 (hardcover : alk. paper)

   1. O'Connor, Flannery—Criticism and interpretation.   2. Christianity and literature—
Southern States—History—20th century.   3. American fiction—Catholic authors—History
and criticism.   4. American fiction—Southern States—History and criticism.   5. American
fiction—20th century—History and criticism.   6. Percy, Walker, 1916—Criticism and
interpretation.   7. Christian fiction, American—History and criticism.   8. Catholics—
Southern States—Intellectual life.   9. Southern States—In literature.   10. Southern States—
Religion.   I. Title.   II. Series.

PS3565.C57Z813   2004

813'.54—dc22

                                    2004011064

The paper in this book meets the guidelines for permanence and durability of the Committee
on Production Guidelines for Book Longevity of the Council on Library Resources. ⊗

Contents

Acknowledgments

I WANT TO THANK my copy editor, Lois Crum, as well as John Easterly, Lee Campbell Sioles, and the editorial staff at Louisiana State University Press for their generous help and encouragement as I prepared this book. My anonymous reader's recommendations have improved its focus considerably, and Margaret Anne O'Connor's stylistic advice was particularly helpful when the work was still being shaped into a manuscript. I am incalculably indebted to my mentors at the University of North Carolina at Chapel Hill—Joseph Flora, Fred Hobson, George Lensing, and Weldon Thornton—for their guidance and encouragement in this and all of my academic endeavors. I also want to extend a general thanks to the faculty of the University of Notre Dame's Program of Liberal Studies for first giving shape to whatever love of books I brought to them.

For their companionship and encouragement—intellectual and otherwise—throughout graduate school, I want to thank especially Bryant Morris, Andrew Harvey, Marti Eads, and Lara Kees. Above all I am indebted to Doug Mitchell and Collin Messer, without whose mulish counsel this study might never have been finished and doubtlessly would not have been so pleasant to compose.

Thanks finally to my parents, who are somehow responsible for all this, and to Natasha, whose love made it complete.

Abbreviations

Page citations are to the reprint editions, where reprints are indicated.

CS   Flannery O'Connor. *The Complete Stories.* Ed. Robert Giroux. New York: Farrar, Straus and Giroux, 1971.

CW   Flannery O'Connor. *Collected Works of Flannery O'Connor.* Ed. Sally Fitzgerald. New York: Library of America, 1988.

HB   Flannery O'Connor. *The Habit of Being: Letters of Flannery O'Connor.* Ed. Sally Fitzgerald. New York: Farrar, Straus and Giroux, 1979.

L   Walker Percy. *Lancelot.* 1977. Reprint, New York: Avon, 1978.

LC   Walker Percy. *Lost in the Cosmos.* 1983. Reprint, New York: Washington Square Press, 1984.

LG   Walker Percy. *The Last Gentleman.* 1966. Reprint, New York: Avon, 1978.

LR   Walker Percy. *Love in the Ruins.* 1971. Reprint, New York: Avon, 1978.

M   Walker Percy. *The Moviegoer.* 1961. Reprint, New York: Ballantine, 1988.

MB   Walker Percy. *The Message in the Bottle.* 1975. Reprint, New York: Farrar, Straus and Giroux, 1976.

MM   Flannery O'Connor. *Mystery and Manners: Occasional Prose.* Ed. Sally and Robert Fitzgerald. 1969. Reprint, New York: Farrar, Straus and Giroux, 1970.

SC   Walker Percy. *The Second Coming.* 1980. Reprint, New York: Ballantine, 1990.

SSL   Walker Percy. *Signposts in a Strange Land.* Ed. Patrick Samway. New York: Farrar, Straus and Giroux, 1991.

TFO   Flannery O'Connor. *Three by Flannery O'Connor.* New York: Penguin, 1983.

TS   Walker Percy. *The Thanatos Syndrome.* 1987. Reprint, New York: Ballantine, 1988.

Peculiar Crossroads

Introduction

The writer operates at a peculiar crossroads where time and place and eternity
somehow meet. His problem is to find that location.
    —FLANNERY O'CONNOR, "The Regional Writer"

If a man cannot forget, he will never amount to much.
    —SØREN KIERKEGAARD, *Either/Or* (epigraph to Walker Percy,
    The Last Gentleman)

MOST TWENTIETH-CENTURY observers of the fabled "mind of the South"
have been inclined to agree with W. J. Cash's 1941 assessment of it as "at
bottom religious."[1] Later thinkers sharing Cash's political sympathies have
perhaps become more sophisticated in describing the nature and sometimes
deleterious effects of southern religiosity (which Cash attributed largely to
the populace's Celtic "blood-strain"), while those of more conservative bent
have praised the region's religious habit of mind; even before Cash, Allen
Tate was noting the South's "convinced supernaturalism" with tacit approval.[2]
Virtually all observers of the region have agreed on the *existence* of its religiosity. But it was largely thinkers of Tate's persuasion who shaped the tradition
of criticism that has until recent years dominated the study of twentieth-
century southern literature, so that an exceptionally strong religious sense—
along with a sense of history, tragedy, family, and place—has long been

1. W. J. Cash, *The Mind of the South* (New York: Vintage, 1991), 54.
2. Allen Tate, "The Profession of Letters in the South," in *Essays of Four Decades* (Chicago:
Swallow, 1968), 521.

1

dubbed one of the most fruitfully enduring characteristics of the region's temperament and, accordingly, of its literature.[3]

Given that understanding, it is curious that many of the traditionalists who established such themes seemed somewhat puzzled—even troubled—by the arrival after midcentury of the two most indubitably religious writers ever to emerge from the region, Flannery O'Connor and Walker Percy. Indeed, in 1975 the authors of *Southern Literary Study: Problems and Possibilities* seemed to betray at least a slight note of anxiety in asking: "Is the introduction of 'alien' philosophical concepts into recent southern literature—O'Connor's Catholicism, Percy's existentialism—indicative of a significant change in the orientation and motivation of southern writing?"[4]

This question and the conditions that produced it provide two of the broadest concerns of my study. For, while the dominant currents of critical discussion have themselves changed considerably in intervening years, today the question remains a vital one in examining a twentieth-century southern literary history that can only now be surveyed completely. At a time when O'Connor has been firmly established as one the major talents of southern—indeed, American—literature, and Percy's now completed oeuvre has received a wealth of ongoing critical attention, the question first posed by Louis D. Rubin Jr. and C. Hugh Holman looms larger than ever before. I want to consider it here not exactly on their terms but rather with the advantage of hindsight, with a larger historical perspective not only on southern letters but also on the transatlantic Christian intellectual milieu in which O'Connor and Percy both immersed themselves, as well as on more recent southern fiction in which their legacies have borne fruit.

This study attempts both to capture the historical context in which the

3. Fred Hobson's *The Southern Writer in the Postmodern World* (Athens: University of Georgia Press, 1991) provides the most recent overview of the problematic endurance of these traditional themes; Michael Kreyling's *Inventing Southern Literature* (Jackson: University Press of Mississippi, 1998) takes to task the critical tradition that shaped the canon in which such themes predominate.

4. Louis D. Rubin Jr. and C. Hugh Holman, *Southern Literary Study: Problems and Possibilities* (Chapel Hill: University of North Carolina Press, 1975), 235. In the first published response to this question, Walter Sullivan identified O'Connor and Percy as symptomatic of the decline of southern literature after midcentury. His work precipitated a series of critical speculations that linked the two as representative of some break with regional literary tradition (see the end of chapter 2 here).

question above was first articulated and to explore the vital commonalities in the philosophically informed Catholic visions that so profoundly shaped the fiction of O'Connor and Percy alike. For Percy's own Catholicism should have been noted in the original question, as well as some qualification regarding the religion's "alien" place in southern letters: Allen Tate, Caroline Gordon, Katherine Anne Porter, John Kennedy Toole, and Cormac McCarthy, to note the most prominent twentieth-century examples, all professed that faith at some point in their lives. But certainly O'Connor and Percy remain both the most profoundly Catholic and the most currently influential members of this group, and today the question might be better stated as follows: How did it come to pass that a woman who spent her days reading Thomas Aquinas and Romano Guardini created such powerful portraits of a rapidly changing—and "Christ-haunted"—South in the wake of World War II? Or that a doctor who became a novelist after reading Jacques Maritain, Søren Kierkegaard, and Ga-briel Marcel set the standard for writing about the postmodern (and "Christ-forgetting") South? How did these two unabashedly Catholic writers come to be among the most influential southern writers of their generation—matched only by Eudora Welty—and what role did their religious faith play in "orient-ing" southern fiction in the second half of the twentieth century? How were O'Connor and Percy related to one another as Christian writers emerging from the American South, and do they have any sort of mutual legacy?

Thus far, there is little substantial scholarship addressing these concerns directly. The only book-length study of Catholic writers in the region is Robert Brinkmeyer's *Three Catholic Writers of the Modern South* (1985), which exam-ines in three separate sections the lives and careers of Tate, Gordon, and Percy, developing the general claim that "all three saw their southern identi-ties as a way to define themselves against the modern world" yet finally "recog-nized that this definition was resistance, not transcendence. They turned to the Church to restore myth, meaning, and mystery to what they saw as a morally irresponsible modern world."[5] Generally perceptive as Brinkmeyer's study is, it overlooks some absolutely crucial distinctions between Percy and the Tates and, furthermore, does not directly address the *interaction* among these three writers (which I unexpectedly found to be one of my major con-

5. Robert H. Brinkmeyer Jr., *Three Catholic Writers of the Modern South* (Jackson: University Press of Mississippi, 1985), xvi.

cerns in this study), let alone their relationship with O'Connor. Accordingly, Brinkmeyer does not concern himself at all with O'Connor and Percy's commonalities or their place in southern literary history. Other critics have touched on such questions, but only briefly, producing a number of scattered articles and chapters in more general studies that place the two writers in a common cultural context and not infrequently suggest their mutual call for a new religious vision that transcends a burdensome regional history.

It is possible to view that vision in a somewhat cynical light, as Michael Patrick Gillespie, not a southern literary specialist but rather a Joyce scholar with a special interest in Catholicism, has done. Considering the broad relationship of O'Connor, Percy, and Toole as postwar writers to their immediate predecessors in the southern tradition, he has argued that "each writer draws on Catholicism to escape the influence of Faulkner and the predictable label of regional writer":

> [A]s Roman Catholics they insinuate into their prose theological perspectives not found in the writings of most Southerners (including many Southern Catholics). At the same time, the ethos forming their attitudes remains relatively close to the Christian temperament of their region. This ethos provides a meaningful counterpoint to their narratives rather than proving an alien commentary on their discourses. Thus each author, in a highly idiosyncratic manner, draws elements of Roman Catholic belief and ritual into various aspects of his or her narratives. As a result, each infuses perspectives into his writings that render them distinct from those dominating the fictional world of the South created by Faulkner.[6]

Such an argument, I contend, is incorrect insofar as it reduces O'Connor and Percy's consistently and soberly professed faith to a mere literary strategy designed to counter "anxiety of influence." I take at face value O'Connor's statement that "belief, in my own case anyway, is the engine that makes perception operate" (*MM*, 109). Indeed, my concern here is first to investigate

---

6. Michael Patrick Gillespie, "Baroque Catholicism in Southern Fiction: Flannery O'Connor, Walker Percy, and John Kennedy Toole," in *Traditions, Voices, and Dreams: The American Novel since the 1960s*, ed. Melvin J. Friedman and Ben Siegel (Newark: University of Delaware Press, 1995), 28, 44–5. By contrast, Styron's work is interpreted here as exemplifying a southern literature utterly in the shadow of Faulkner.

that belief—and the intellectual forces giving it shape—in order to understand more fully the perception, the *vision*, it fostered.

Although Gillespie is mistaken about the motivation behind the Catholic vision of O'Connor and Percy alike, he is essentially correct in his assessment of its effects. Lewis P. Simpson, whose expert perspective on southern letters is a vastly different one, has suggested as much in his succinct observation that both O'Connor and Percy practice an aesthetic of "revelation" distinct from the "aesthetic of memory" that dominated the literary vision of the Southern Renascence.[7] This brief distinction seems to me the single most valuable insight yet achieved regarding the question I concern myself with here, and it profoundly informs my study. What I attempt in this book, however, is not only to provide a broader articulation of exactly what such an aesthetic of revelation might entail (and to speculate on its positive effects— Simpson's assessment is largely negative), but also to present a comprehensive study of the literary relationship of O'Connor and Percy as Catholic writers of the twentieth-century South. For of all the southern writers who might be labeled Catholic, these two alone—O'Connor as a lifelong practitioner and Percy as a convert—somehow balanced a committed and sincere religious faith with authentic and powerful writing about their native region; indeed, by their own accounts, they could not have fully envisioned or written of their time and place without that faith. None of the other successful artists I have mentioned defined themselves so clearly as Catholics. Tate and Gordon, who to a degree mentored the two younger writers, were perhaps equally devout in the wake of their conversions, but the quality of their art declined concurrently. By contrast, the radical religiosity of O'Connor and Percy's vision is precisely what has made them so valuable to the South as original fiction writers and social critics. Furthermore, that vision—even when stripped of its orthodox origins—has in some sense been passed on to a new generation of writers from the region.

My study is informed by consideration of not only southern literary history but also larger twentieth-century literary currents, the cultural climate of the postwar United States, and—most profoundly—O'Connor and Percy's immersion in an often overlooked intellectual milieu of international dimensions.

7. Lewis P. Simpson, *The Brazen Face of History: Studies in the Literary Consciousness of America* (Baton Rouge: Louisiana State University Press, 1980), 246–53.

Tracing the roots of their mature thought in the transatlantic Catholic Revival at midcentury, I place their work—aesthetically and thematically—in an ultimately problematic relationship with both an established modernist southern literature and an emerging postmodern American culture. I demonstrate how their Christian existentialist vision led them to dissent from the historical, tragic mode of the Southern Renascence (as well as from the often absurdist apocalypticism of much postwar American fiction).[8] Despite O'Connor and Percy's devastating satire of both collapsing regional traditions and complacent American consumerism, their "Christian realism" of the "here and now," I argue, finally emphasizes the fundamental promise of the end of the modern world and grounds meaning not in historical consciousness but rather in the potentiality of the present. Such is their distinct legacy to a later generation of writers who attempt to find meaning in a postmodern South wherein historical themes seem increasingly problematic.

I SHOULD SAY a few words about both terminology and methodology. First, let me clarify my use of the always problematic terms *modern* and *postmodern*. Some of my sources, including O'Connor and Percy themselves, at times use the term *modern* in its general sense, to mean "contemporary" or perhaps "twentieth-century." I have avoided doing so myself. I juxtapose the *modern* and the *postmodern* in three different senses here: in referring to broad trends in Western intellectual history; in referring to twentieth-century mass culture in the United States generally; and in referring to twentieth-century Anglophone literature in particular. The appropriate meanings of the terms are implied contextually at different points in my study, but I want to carefully delineate them here.

In the first, broadest usage, *modern* means postmedieval, denoting that period of Western history which has the Enlightenment at its center and is perhaps best characterized by a secular rationalism that culminated in the triumphal scientism—and existential despair—of the middle twentieth century. But Western intellectual life (in the humanities, at least) since that time

8. While O'Connor is not generally deemed an existentialist, I agree with—and, in chapter 2, argue for—Thomas Merton's observation: "I can think of no other American writer who has made a more devastating use of existentialist intuitions" than O'Connor. "The Other Side of Despair: Notes on Christian Existentialism," *Critic* 24 (October–November 1965): 14.

has been marked by a growing sense of the inadequacies of modern rationalism; thinkers in a variety of fields have begun to sense, as historian John
Lukacs has recently argued, "that we in the West are living near the end of
an entire age, the age that began about five hundred years ago." While the
nascent *postmodernism* of our intellectual culture is often associated with radical skepticism, even with a rejection of the entire Western tradition, it may
also take other forms. My own hope is finally similar to that of political philosopher Peter A. Lawler, who rejects the necessary identification of postmodernism with radical skepticism and argues that any such antifoundational view
asserting "the groundlessness of human existence . . . is really hypermodern-
ism, or the exaggeration to the point of caricature of the modern impulse to
self-creation." Postmodernism "rightly understood," by contrast, should entail
"not a rejection of Socratic or Thomistic rationalism" but rather a renewed
recognition of the twofold truth that many influential modern Western intellectuals denied: the fact that human reason is ultimately limited and that it
"exists primarily not to transform reality but to understand and come to terms
with it." Lukacs, similarly, ends his study not in despair but with an understated hope—a carefully qualified Christian hope, no less—regarding the potential for human flourishing in the postmodern era. Insofar as O'Connor and
Percy would have considered themselves open to postmodern thought, this is
surely how they would have done so, much in the spirit in which their mutually favored theologian, Romano Guardini, described what he called "the end
of the modern world" not with dread but with sober and faithful anticipation.[9]

9. John Lukacs, *At the End of an Age* (New Haven, CT: Yale University Press, 2002), 3. Also see
39 for Lukacs's reflections on the term *postmodern*. Lawler, *Postmodernism Rightly Understood*
(Lanham, MD: Rowman and Littlefield, 1999), 2. Lawler briefly links both O'Connor and Percy
with religious humanists Václav Havel and Alexander Solzhenitsyn as "postmodernists rightly
understood"; his study is primarily devoted to affirming the value of the profoundly postmodern
social criticism of Percy and Christopher Lasch as opposed to the essentially modern visions of
Francis Fukuyama, Richard Rorty, and Allan Bloom. For other perspectives on the potential for
religious renewal in postmodernity, see the work of John Milbank and fellow British theologians
associated with "Radical Orthodoxy" (see chapter 3, note 13, here), and also Robert Royal, "Christian Humanism in a Postmodern Age," in *The New Religious Humanists: A Reader,* ed. Gregory
Wolfe (New York: Free Press, 1997), 87–103. Romano Guardini, *The End of the Modern World: A
Search for Orientation,* trans. Joseph Theman and Herbert Burke (New York: Sheed and Ward,
1956).

In their own immediate experience of the post–World War II United States, O'Connor saw the beginnings and Percy the fruition of what influential social observers have called the postmodern in popular culture: that ascendancy of the simulacra and displaced sense of the real that Jean Baudrillard has described as the "hyperreality" of the late-twentieth-century West, a culture characterized by mass consumerism and the all-encompassing prominence of the media in the wake of the communications revolution.[10] This postmodern culture arose even as late modern industrial culture culminated at midcentury, further hastening the erosion of older social structures and mores that— though often having premodern roots—had endured in at least some American settings throughout the brief span of the nation's history. So when I write that O'Connor's and Percy's subject was the postmodern South, I mean the post–World War II South, a South where the stubbornly nostalgic social vision formulated by the Agrarians in the wake of the century's first great war no longer seems even remotely viable. It is also a region where—as in the nation around it—that displacement of the real that Alfred North Whitehead long ago identified as characteristic of the modern scientific mind has been given new impetus by the prevalence of simulacra in the minds of media-saturated consumers. Percy and O'Connor alike write of a South largely under the sway of Madison Avenue and Hollywood, of a time when images of a generic American culture often dominate regional desires but also when, insofar as "the South" itself still exists, shallow, mass-produced images of the region (in advertising, on television, in movies) often seem to have replaced their referent. This is clearly the case in Percy's fiction, and I shall argue that it is a crucial aspect of O'Connor's work as well.

O'Connor and Percy's native region, and their relationship to its past, was thereby fundamentally different from that of the prior generation of southern writers. As Daniel Joseph Singal has argued, those writers who came of age

10. Baudrillard's notion of the simulacrum is developed in *Symbolic Exchange and Death* (London: Sage, 1976) and *Simulacra and Simulation* (Ann Arbor: University of Michigan Press, 1981). In *America* (London: Verso, 1988), he forthrightly declares the United States to be both the progenitor and—in the second half of the twentieth century—the ultimate exemplar of postmodern hyperreality. While O'Connor and Percy would disagree with much in Baudrillard's thought, their work anticipates central aspects of his analysis, perhaps in part owing to their common reading (O'Connor's and Baudrillard's, at least) of renowned Catholic media critic Marshall McLuhan. See chapter 4.

in the South immediately after World War I still clung, often despite themselves, to the seemingly stabilizing ethos of an earlier "Victorian" culture, and even those who finally came to accept "modern" turbulence and uncertainty did so only "by the skin of their teeth."[11] Like that quintessential American literary modernist T. S. Eliot, writers such as Tate and Faulkner largely concerned themselves with confronting the heap of broken images that their culture seemed to have become at the onset of the twentieth century; only in their art, it seemed, could they shore fragments against the ruins of their crumbling civilization, invoke myth to aesthetically order the chaotic wasteland of their contemporary world. But paradoxically, such "modernists" inevitably looked to history—southern or, more broadly, Western—for their myths, and they found the ultimate sources of their art in those shards of the past that still lingered in their present. O'Connor and Percy did not. Although both did write a fiction open to what Michael Guinn has recently called "attenuated modernist methods for scrutiny," they cannot—as I argue extensively in chapter 2—be considered literary modernists. But neither are they easily categorized as literary postmodernists, as both would forthrightly reject the radical narrative and linguistic relativism often associated with the term (and are far from embracing either the naturalism or the "mythoclasm" that Guinn associates with thoroughgoing literary postmodernists from the South).[12] They are transitional figures: writers who live in a postmodern world, to be sure, but best described as Christian existentialists who are finally more optimistic about their culture's future than the modernists and more optimistic about the Truth-telling capacities of language and literature than the postmodernists.

Given the fact that—at least in the mainstream of contemporary criticism—studies of "religion and literature" have in recent years been somewhat out of vogue, if not downright suspect, a few words on my critical approach seem appropriate here. I fully agree with Dennis Taylor's observation in "The Need for a Religious Literary Criticism" that at least a certain sort of such criticism has too often tended to lapse into a "soft discourse" that appeals "to

11. Daniel Joseph Singal, *The War Within: From Victorian to Modernist Thought in the South, 1919–1945* (Chapel Hill: University of North Carolina Press, 1982), 10.

12. Michael Guinn, *After Southern Modernism: Fiction of the Contemporary South* (Jackson: University Press of Mississippi, 2000), ix. See chapter 3 here for more on O'Connor, Percy, and literary postmodernism.

general unexamined values and a pre-converted audience." Taylor has called instead for "religious interpretations that are substantial enough to enter into a productive and competitive relation with the reigning critical discourses" of our time—among which he numbers those expert in discussing dimensions of "historical context."[13] It is precisely such an interpretation that I attempt here. My approach, therefore, is not to read literature and religion alike through a political lens, to reduce both to mere tools for imposing oppressive ideologies in the crude power struggle that some critics take history to be; but neither do I seek to present the sort of old-fashioned formalist reading that—often unfairly—has been caricatured as striving to make literature *into* a religion, to find in fiction the key to absolute, transcendent meaning. My goal has been to render a reading of O'Connor and Percy that is less reductive than the first model and more modest than the second, a reading that reconstructs the period of Catholic intellectual history they were so much a part of and traces how their self-conceptions as artists, as well as their vision of their particular society, were shaped in relation to that milieu.

In doing so I am greatly indebted to southern literary critics from Rubin and Simpson to Fred Hobson and Lewis A. Lawson, but perhaps even more so to recent critics who have shown me new ways to think about the interaction of literature and religion in terms of intellectual and cultural history. Ralph Wood, a distinguished Protestant scholar of religion and literature, was one of the critics whose work I first found to be invaluable in understanding the two Catholic writers I concern myself with here, and his observations inform my study at a number of points. But my reading of Kieran Quinlan's *Walker Percy: The Last Catholic Novelist*—much as I disagree with its ultimate claims about the radically "obsolete" character of Percy's faith—was a watershed for me in thinking about how to approach the particular character of Catholic thought at midcentury; while other studies have informed my understanding of the Catholic Revival since, Quinlan's book first suggested the general direction of this one. Jon Lance Bacon's *Flannery O'Connor and Cold War Culture* provided a broader cultural approach to understanding how Catholicism might have shaped the critique of postwar American society mounted

13. Dennis Taylor, "The Need for a Religious Literary Criticism," in *Seeing Into the Life of Things: Essays on Literature and Religious Experience*, ed. John Mahoney (New York: Fordham University Press, 1998), 3.

by both O'Connor and Percy. And Paul Giles's *American Catholic Arts and Fictions: Culture, Ideology, Aesthetics* has been invaluable in helping me to consider even more broadly how Catholicism has manifested itself in American literature; though I do not share all of Giles's presuppositions, I invariably found his work to be provocative, compelling, and insightful. His "Methodological Introduction: Tracing the Transformation of Religion" should be mandatory reading for anyone concerned with studying the interaction of literature and religion.[14]

Rewarding as these works proved to be, it was not without relish that I turned from studying literary scholarship and intellectual history to reading the contemporary belletristic authors considered in chapter 5 of this study. It was a great pleasure to immerse myself in the work of such writers as Doris Betts, Annie Dillard, Randall Kenan, Josephine Humphreys, and Padgett Powell. It is in my analysis of their work that I hope to have extended the methodology appropriate to the study of literature and religion by suggesting how O'Connor and Percy have passed on to later chroniclers of the postmodern South the language of not history, but rather the mystery that permeates even the most seemingly banal aspects of contemporary life. In the Catholic visions developed by O'Connor and Percy alike, that mystery is rooted in the deeply sacramental sense of a present world that bears witness to an ever-ongoing Creation; and I finally suggest here that the two Catholic writers have somehow bequeathed to even their most unorthodox successors an understated sense of not the lingering presence of the past but rather the possibilities inherent in the present itself, a sense capable of imbuing a postmodern South of shopping malls and interstates with as much meaning as Appomattox—or Yoknapatawpha.

IF SUCH LATE Catholic converts as Tate and Gordon were crucial figures in the first generation of twentieth-century southern writers, O'Connor and Percy are doubtlessly among the most significant of the second generation. Fred Hobson has noted that they are among the most prominent influences

14. Kieran Quinlan, *Walker Percy: The Last Catholic Novelist* (Baton Rouge: Louisiana State University Press, 1996); Jon Lance Bacon, *Flannery O'Connor and Cold War Culture* (New York: Cambridge University Press, 1993); Paul Giles, *American Catholic Arts and Fictions: Culture, Ideology, Aesthetics* (New York: Cambridge University Press, 1992).

on contemporary southern fiction.[15] Given this trend, my initial question—whether O'Connor and Percy via their religious and philosophical concerns brought something significantly new to the "orientation" of southern writing—seems all the more vital. My conclusion, of course, is that they did, in a manner most beneficent to the region's literature. In the autumn of 1952, when the manuscripts of *Wise Blood* and Percy's first novel arrived at Caroline Gordon's door, Percy's lifelong companion Shelby Foote was—along with William Styron and a number of lesser lights—busy writing in the mode of Faulkner (whose own best work was behind him) and puzzling over his friend's new preoccupations as a Catholic novelist and lay philosopher; he would later dismiss O'Connor as a "minor-minor writer."[16] The fact that Percy rather than Foote (who, ironically, became best known as a historian) marked the direction of postwar southern fiction suggests the extent to which the Christian existentialist vision that O'Connor and Percy alike developed in the larger context of the Catholic Revival did indeed entail a profound shift from earlier Renascence concerns. That vision remains their distinct legacy in its insistent focus on not "the past in the present" but rather the essential mystery of a "here and now," no matter how superficially devoid of meaning, in which displaced individuals exercise a profound moral freedom.

So while religion is usually perceived along with history and community as only one of the great abiding themes of southern literature, I finally argue here that O'Connor and Percy's particular experience of Catholicism, which shaped their vision of Western humanity in the second half of the twentieth century, dominated their engagement with those other themes. Neither writer concentrated so much on regional traditions or the burdens of a communal history as on the isolated individual striving toward, or resolutely avoiding, true communion with others in a setting finally sundered from tradition and history. Catholicism gave them in some sense an outsider's perspective on their immediate society (as it could not for a writer like James Joyce), though they did indeed draw on their region's "Christian temperament" in writing about twentieth-century southerners whose experience they saw as in some sense universal. In doing so they joined their great predecessors, but on terms

15. Hobson, 9.

16. Foote to Percy, October 28, 1969, in *The Correspondence of Shelby Foote and Walker Percy*, ed. Jay Tolson (New York: Doubletake/Norton, 1997), 136.

that were finally different from those of the Renascence. O'Connor and Percy's faith shaped their dissent from historical patterns that—though inherently rich—threatened in their own time to become cliché, and thereby their faith enabled them to seek out the depths of the immediate world around them, confident that meaning abided there if only properly seen.

CHAPTER 1

"We Have Had Our Fall"

Malaise and Mystery in the Lives of
Flannery O'Connor and Walker Percy

When Walker Percy won the National Book Award, newsmen asked him why there were so many good Southern writers and he said, "Because we lost the War." He didn't mean by that simply that a lost war makes good subject matter. What he was saying was that we have had our Fall. We have gone into the modern world with an inburnt knowledge of human limitations and with a sense of mystery which could not have developed in our first state of innocence—as it has not sufficiently developed in the rest of the country.

—FLANNERY O'CONNOR, "The Regional Writer"

WHEN FLANNERY O'CONNOR made her claim that the southern writer had some special knowledge of the human condition that the American writer in general lacked, she was interpreting rather seriously a statement Walker Percy made in New York following the National Book Award ceremony in 1962. Given Percy's frequently parodic treatment of the stereotypical southern obsession with the Civil War, it is likely that he in fact spoke to his urbane audience rather wryly—much as Will Barrett, the protagonist of his second novel, would play the appropriate role of "a Southerner in the North, an amiable person who wears the badge of his origin in a faint burlesque of itself"—using the tone (at least partially ironic) in which he and O'Connor herself tended to treat those who sentimentalized that war (*LG*, 50). Yet O'Connor's interpretation obviously touches upon themes that are in fact of the utmost importance to both her own work and that of Percy, themes that just a few years before, in 1960, were given eloquent exposition by historian C. Vann Woodward in *The Burden of Southern History*. O'Connor and Percy alike, because of the long residence of their respective families in the South, were seemingly as well prepared as any twentieth-century writers to confront the "tragic experience and heritage" that Woodward identified as belonging especially to the region, an experience that fell "far more closely in line with the common experience of mankind than the national [American] legends of opulence and success and innocence"; ironically, however, both finally observed that by and large southerners had failed to learn anything from the War, despite having the Christian heritage that O'Connor claimed provided the "means to interpret" their particular fall from grace.[1]

O'Connor might have said more personally, and perhaps more forcefully, that she and Percy in particular had an especially developed "inburnt knowledge of human limitations" and "sense of mystery"—not only because both sprung from families deeply rooted in the common regional experience, but perhaps even more because of their remarkable individual histories. O'Connor and Percy themselves experienced on a deeply personal level something quite like the "Fall" she speaks of here, in ways that were remarkably similar and that finally confirmed both in a means of interpreting their lives and their society that was not only generally Christian but also specifically Catholic. Percy (1916–90) and O'Connor (1925–64) were prepared by a number of common biographical factors to see their world from a similar vantage point: both came from deeply rooted southern families that provided them not only a place in the tragic regional history but also a present sense of decline; both suffered the loss of a father in adolescence, a loss that would strongly affect their view of the world; both spent a brief but significant portion of their young adulthood in New York City and neighboring environs, which left them with a lingering sense of the dislocation of twentieth-century urban life; both suffered from terrible personal illnesses that served to further remind them of their fathers' fates; both matured as World War II and its aftermath changed their region and their larger civilization forever, not only marking the greatest watershed in southern history since Reconstruction but also ushering in what one of their mutually favored European theologians called "the end of the modern world" in the West.

1. See O'Connor's treatment of such Civil War sentimentalists as Sally Poker Sash in "A Late Encounter with the Enemy" and the Grandmother in "A Good Man Is Hard to Find." She praised Woodward's book in a May 1963 letter (HB, 522); I quote here from C. Vann Woodward, *The Burden of Southern History*, 3d ed. (Baton Rouge: Louisiana State University Press, 1993), 24–5.

In grappling with their vocations as writers, both found a mentor in Caroline Gordon, a southerner and a convert to Catholicism, and more general guidance in the writings of the philosophers and theologians of the Catholic Revival at midcentury. Their common experiences granted both a particularly keen vision of the human predicament of isolation and alienation that had become so intensely manifest in their contemporary world. But the religious faith that became for both the means of understanding that predicament confirmed them in a vocation where each believed that seeing their present world as it was and writing about it with a fidelity to the real would necessarily yield meaning. In short, these similar aspects of their lives shaped the way they saw and captured the world that they left, in their fiction, as a legacy to all who care to think about the South—and, as their international critical renown indicates, to all who are capable of seeing in that southern milieu an analogue of twentieth-century Western culture generally.

In what follows I examine their biographies—comparing the experience of each in the specific phases outlined above—with the caveat that I am neither qualified nor inclined to offer a limited psychoanalytical reading of their lives or their work. In fact I, sharing Percy's own reservations about any extreme Freudian view that human beings are not "sovereigns of our own consciousness," think such a project would be positively harmful.[2] Nonetheless, I do believe that it is worthwhile to explore the remarkable similarities in the backgrounds of Percy and O'Connor, experiences that prepared both to see and to write about their South from similar vantage points—for it is surely true that what happens to a writer shapes his beliefs and the way he sees the world. In this view, I agree with Jay Tolson: "the temptation to read a writer's work through his life can lead to reductivism, and even worse distortions. . . . Yet knowledge of [Percy's] life story reveals the remarkable extent to which Percy saw his work as a form of knowledge, an essay toward understanding" his life and his world; and certainly the same is true of O'Connor.[3]

GIVEN THEIR not infrequently ambivalent attitudes about southern history in general and their personal heritage in particular, I doubt that Percy and

2. Lewis A. Lawson and Victor A. Kramer, eds., *Conversations with Walker Percy* (Jackson: University Press of Mississippi, 1985), 223.

3. Jay Tolson, *Pilgrim in the Ruins: A Life of Walker Percy* (New York: Simon and Schuster, 1992), 11.

O'Connor themselves would immediately consider knowledge of their extended family history essential to any understanding of their fiction, but such considerations are a necessary prelude to examining their immediate family setting. And they do have bearing upon Percy's (and O'Connor's) comment about the South's tragic history, however wryly it may have been put. Although the family heritage of Percy and O'Connor may certainly seem less important than the immediate family of each, it is finally impossible to talk about one without the other; Bertram Wyatt-Brown's comprehensive study *The House of Percy* has made this claim so persuasive with regard to the Percys that it deserves consideration with regard to any rooted and traditional family, a category that the O'Connor-Cline-Treanors of Georgia certainly fall into. Each family had remained in one region of the Deep South (with some temporary deviations by the Percys) since coming to America in the antebellum period; both—certainly the Percys—had by the early twentieth century some claim to being "aristocratic"; and both had historically been linked with the Catholic Church, making them paradoxically at home in a supposedly Christian region yet also outsiders in a larger, and occasionally hostile, Protestant culture. Nonetheless, their forebears left to the immediate families of Flannery and Walker a legacy of social success and civic involvement, a sense of obligation to their native communities that the two authors would fulfill in quite a different way. And both families passed down, for better and for worse, a deeply felt concern with the importance of traditional southern manners and mores—an ethos Percy and O'Connor would both frequently satirize as insufficient and obsolete, though only in calling for a return to its "real basis of charity and necessity," the Christian source from which it supposedly sprang (*MM*, 234).

It would be difficult to invent a family more bound up with southern history than the Percys. Bertram Wyatt-Brown has noted: "throughout the generations, the Percys helped to create the Deep South—not just as slave-holding frontiersmen but as agents of change in the post–Civil War years. They belonged as much to the New South of heavy industry and plantation agribusiness as to the Old South of large-scale land speculation and cotton-growing."[4] While the first American Percy acquired land in what is now southern Mississippi and Louisiana, later antecedents of Walker Percy would settle

4. Bertram Wyatt-Brown, *The House of Percy* (New York: Oxford University Press, 1994), 4.

in northern Alabama and the Mississippi Delta. In each place, Jay Tolson points out, "they have felt obliged to do more than tend to their own gardens. They have served—not without self-interest but also with a real sense of obligation to the commonweal."[5] Traditionally paternalistic and therefore condescending to African Americans, Walker Percy's ancestors nonetheless vigorously opposed the more savage racism of the Ku Klux Klan (and perhaps thereby acquired their reputation for having Catholic "leanings," though in fact they were at most sporadically so, generally belonging to Protestant churches).

Charles Percy was, it seems, one of the few Catholics in the Percy fold, though from what little is known of the life of Walker Percy's great-great-great-grandfather, it appears that he practiced the faith primarily as a means of winning favor in Spanish West Florida, the region (not yet part of the United States) where he established a foothold for the Percys. Charles was born in 1740 somewhere in the British Isles, probably southern Ireland; he married and fathered a son while serving in the British army but left his family for the New World. After spending 1775 and 1776 with a mistress in Bermuda and wandering through North Carolina and the Caribbean, he left the Dutch island of St. Eustatius—bringing along "nine dependents, doubtlessly slaves"—and, Thomas Sutpen–like, settled in British West Florida on land granted him as a result of his military service.[6] He thrived as a planter, acquiring three plantations in what is now Mississippi and Louisiana and adjusting pragmatically to the acquisition of West Florida by the Spanish; he married a local woman, Susannah Collins, and started the line from which Walker Percy would descend. His success, however, did not prevent him from fits of melancholy and eventual suicide—a family legacy remembered well into the twentieth century, recorded by William Alexander Percy in *Lanterns on the Levee,* and made a fictional part of Tom More's heritage in Walker Percy's *The Thanatos Syndrome.*[7]

One of Charles Percy's sons by his second marriage was Thomas George Percy, Walker Percy's great-great-grandfather, who attended what would become Princeton University and eventually settled in Huntsville, Alabama, at

5. Tolson, 24.

6. Wyatt-Brown, 28.

7. My primary source here is Wyatt-Brown, 26–33.

the urging of a college friend named John Walker. A successful banker, he soon married and named a son John Walker, thereby establishing his friend's surname in the Percy lineage. When he died in 1841, his widow Maria moved to Washington County, Mississippi, where her husband had owned land. By 1853 she and her sons had established Percy Plantation not far from Greenville, Mississippi, which would become the home of Percys for the century to come.[8]

One of those sons was William Alexander Percy, whose life spanned the middle years of the nineteenth century and who would move the Percys into Greenville—and into Mississippi history—for good. After graduating from Princeton and earning a law degree from the University of Virginia, he served with the Army of Northern Virginia at the Wilderness and in General Jubal Early's march up the Shenandoah Valley to Washington. Colonel Percy returned home to become a state political leader; Walker Percy's great-grandfather, the "Gray Eagle of the Delta," served in the Mississippi state legislature and as Democratic Speaker of the House of Representatives, a champion of the Delta planter interests.[9] From his day forward, all the males of the Percy line would labor under the weight of a legacy of noblesse oblige—a weight none would be able to bear lightly, and some would not be able to bear at all.

One of the sons of the "Gray Eagle" was John Walker Percy, grandfather of the novelist, but another was almost as important to his sense of the family history: LeRoy Percy, who would become an ardent opponent of the Ku Klux Klan and father of the second William Alexander Percy, later "Uncle Will" to Walker Percy. LeRoy Percy graduated from the University of the South and the University of Virginia law school before returning home to marry, in 1883, Camille Bourges, a Catholic woman whose family was long established in New Orleans. When his father died in 1888, LeRoy assumed the Percy mantle of community leadership with vigor, not only improving his own lot but also aiming to advance that of his neighbors. Patrick Samway has said that LeRoy Percy "could be considered the Henry Grady of the Delta; he wanted to bring order and wealth to an impoverished region of the country."[10] He did so partly by serving on the levee committees—vital to the interests of his region—as

8. Patrick H. Samway, *Walker Percy: A Life* (New York: Farrar, Straus and Giroux, 1997), 424–5.

9. Wyatt-Brown, 173; Samway, 426.

10. Samway, 427.

his father had, a role that brought him into conflict with the racist demagogue James K. Vardaman. When one of Mississippi's seats in the U.S. Senate was vacated by the death of the sitting senator in 1909, LeRoy Percy vigorously opposed Vardaman's campaign and was ultimately awarded the seat himself in 1910. He lost to Vardaman in the 1911 election after a vicious campaign, but he continued to battle the interests represented by his opponent for the rest of his life (his history is conflated with that of Percy's direct antecedents in *The Last Gentleman* and *The Second Coming*). He was particularly active in fighting against the Ku Klux Klan during its revival in the 1920s and so earned the Percys some public association with Catholicism despite the fact that LeRoy Percy, like his father before him, was an Episcopalian. Only one devout Roman Catholic could be found in Walker Percy's direct family line prior to his own conversion—LeRoy's son William Alexander Percy, who practiced the faith of his mother with zeal before he lost it forever while in college. But I will say more of "Uncle Will" and his creeds later, for his influence on young Walker Percy was more direct.

LeRoy Percy's brother John Walker, another graduate of Sewanee and the University of Virginia Law School, also lived a successful life in the Percy tradition, though in Alabama rather than Mississippi. Knowing that LeRoy, as the eldest, would inherit the family land outside Greenville, he came to the newly founded and apparently promising city of Birmingham in 1886.[11] Settling into a career as a corporation lawyer, in 1888 Walker married Mary Pratt DeBardeleben, a member of a wealthy Alabama family that had invested heavily in Birmingham's industries. He not only prospered financially—he worked as a banker in addition to continuing his legal career—but also lived up to the family legacy of public service, eventually winning election to the Alabama state legislature. They also bore a son LeRoy, in 1889, and a daughter, Ellen, in 1893.[12] Yet despite every appearance of success and social adjustment—Walker was a member of numerous clubs and was considered good, gregarious company—all was not well. He suffered a nervous breakdown in 1911 and, despite a seemingly complete recovery, shot himself in 1917. There was no immediately apparent reason for the suicide; but certainly it revealed

11. Jay Tolson provides a useful overview of the origins of the "Magic City," so different from older Greenville, in the first chapter of *Pilgrim in the Ruins*.

12. Samway, 430–3.

in Walker a streak of the melancholy that had first been manifested in Charles Percy (and had been borne out in other members of the Percy family off the main line traced here, as Wyatt-Brown has demonstrated at length). His body was found by his son LeRoy, whose young wife Mattie Sue had given birth to Walker Percy's grandson—likewise named Walker—less than a year before. Neither son nor grandson would forget their progenitor's failure to find satisfaction in apparent worldly success.

THE MOTHER of the novelist Walker Percy had been born Martha Susan Phinizy of Athens, Georgia, and came from a family nearly as significant in her own state's history as the Percys were in their region; her sister would marry into the similarly distinguished Spalding family and raise a son, B. Phinizy Spalding, who would later become a distinguished historian at the University of Georgia. As a graduate student in the 1950s, this first cousin of Walker Percy became intensely interested in the fiction of a fellow Catholic living down the Oconee River from his Athens home, outside of the small city of Milledgeville. When he wrote to Flannery O'Connor and mentioned his pending master's thesis on the poetry of William Alexander Percy, she responded with her usual directness: "when I answered him I asked who was Wm. Alex. Percy . . . a return postcard announced the arrival of Mr. Phinizy Spalding to take place the following Monday, [and,] he being horrified to learn that I didn't know who W. A. P. was, was bringing himself and a copy of Percy's masterpiece, *Lanterns on the Levee,* now in its 16th printing." Not only did O'Connor accept his visit graciously—"anybody with a name like that could not but be welcome," she told a friend—but the brief connection would have reverberations in later life (*HB,* 236–8).

One of Spalding's mature academic accomplishments was serving as editor of the *Georgia Historical Quarterly,* and in the very last issue printed under his cognizance, Sally Fitzgerald outlined the most comprehensive extant history of the families—the O'Connors, the Clines, and the Treanors of Georgia—who contributed to the heritage of the woman he had met nearly a quarter century before.[13] If O'Connor's family had been in the South a shorter period of time

13. Sally Fitzgerald, "Root and Branch: O'Connor of Georgia," *Georgia Historical Quarterly* 64:4 (Winter 1980): 377–87. This was Spalding's last issue as editor, and he signs off aware that he has been accused by some readers as being "too pro-Jewish, too pro-Catholic, and too pro-Negro" (375).

than Percy's (though on all sides hailing from Ireland, an impoverished and defeated agrarian society whose historical experience has been likened to that of the South by the Fugitives and C. Vann Woodward), in that time they had nonetheless taken steps to establish themselves firmly in its history.[14] Their scale was certainly smaller, more modest, than that of the Percys, but O'Connor's Irish Catholic ancestors eventually rose from their yeoman roots to serve the interests of their state, especially in Milledgeville and Savannah but also on behalf of the Catholic community throughout Georgia. They had a less romantic beginning than that afforded by Charles Percy—more that of the typical American immigrant, except that it took place in the relatively small community of Irish Catholics in the South. By the late nineteenth century they could lay claim to being at least small-town gentry, much like W. J. Cash's prototypical "[Scotch-]Irishman" who rose from frontier roots to become an "aristocrat"—though the O'Connors clung to their native faith, rather than joining the Scotch-Irish Calvinists who surrounded them.[15]

Doing so was a more difficult proposition in Georgia than in the Percys' Mississippi Delta. Fitzgerald describes Georgia's traditional anti-Catholicism—which had its roots in the bloody history of seventeenth-century Great Britain—in some detail, noting that "under the Trust in 1733," Roman Catholics were the only religious group forbidden in the colony, along with "rum, lawyers, and blacks."[16] Anti-Papist sentiments were initially strengthened by the proximity of Spanish Florida and French Louisiana; legal restrictions against settlement were dropped later in the eighteenth century, but Catholics were forbidden from holding office in Georgia until 1871, and remnants of the original sentiment against them remained through at least the Klan revival in the 1920s.

14. Wyatt-Brown suggests that Charles Percy's line was originally Irish as well. He relates the story of Jane Percy Sargent Duncan, a wealthy member of a northern branch of the Percys who, caught up in the genealogical craze of the late nineteenth century, hoped to establish her family's good Anglo-Saxon roots and perhaps even a link to the famous Northumberland Percys immortalized by Shakespeare. She soon stumbled upon a disturbing legal document in which Charles Percy referred to Ireland as his "home"; still hoping that he would turn out to be "an Anglo-Irish gentleman and not merely a peasant," she dug further, only to uncover records of his service in Ireland confirming that he "was neither an officer nor a gentleman—and he was a lowly Irishman besides" (346–7). Jane Percy Sargent Duncan kept her findings to herself.

15. W. J. Cash, *The Mind of the South* (New York: Vintage, 1991), 14–17.

16. Fitzgerald, "Root and Branch," 378.

The first Catholic settlement in the state was at Locust Grove, a small community in Taliaferro County. Founded in 1790 by English families from Maryland, its numbers were first supplemented by refugees from the French Revolution, but in the early and middle years of the nineteenth century, Irish emigrants—fleeing oppressive laws, famine, and war in their homeland—became the main source of growth for the settlement. One of these was Patrick Harty, Flannery O'Connor's first ancestor in America, who brought his family from County Tipperary to Locust Grove in 1824. Little is known of their economic state, but given the general condition of Catholics in Ireland at the time, it seems fair to assume that they came with no great material or social advantages. He was likely a humble yeoman farmer at best; historian Dennis Clark has noted that "Irish landholders in the South did not usually hold slaves themselves" and points specifically to "fifty families from Tipperary in Taliaferro County, Georgia, [who] worked their own land successfully without slaves."[17]

His daughter Johannah Harty eventually married another Tipperary immigrant, Hugh Donnelly Treanor; the couple, who later became the great-grandparents of Flannery O'Connor, moved to Milledgeville, then capital of Georgia, in 1848. Hugh Treanor had previously purchased and improved a grist mill there, on the Oconee River, and made a good living from it; he died a "well-off, well-read" man, and his widow Johannah donated a portion of their newly acquired land to build the present-day Catholic Church of Milledgeville (the first mass in the town had been celebrated in their hotel apartment some years earlier).[18] Their daughter Margaret Ida married Peter James Cline, the Augusta-born son of yet another Tipperary immigrant, who had been sent to a Catholic school in Pennsylvania but returned to Georgia in 1865 at the age of twenty to begin selling silks and broadcloths out of the back of a wagon that he drove through the Carolinas. He soon acquired a partnership in an Augusta store, opened another shop in middle Georgia, and finally settled as a successful merchant and farmer in Milledgeville. In 1888

17. Ibid., 380; Dennis Clark, "The South's Irish Catholics: A Case of Cultural Confinement," in Catholics in the Old South, ed. Randall M. Miller and Jon L. Wakelyn (Macon, GA: Mercer University Press, 1983), 208.

18. Fitzgerald, "Root and Branch," 380; Sally Fitzgerald, "The Invisible Father," Christianity and Literature 47:1 (Autumn 1997): 12.

he was elected the first Catholic mayor of the former Georgia capital. As Sally Fitzgerald has noted, the Cline-Treanor families had initially lived "in a kind of tribal phalanx, protecting their faith from erosion in an ambiance of more or less passive hostility and misapprehension among their neighbors as to their supposed 'foreign' Popish practices"; but they alleviated the fears of their neighbors by engaging "in a pursuit that could be recognized as 100% American—getting rich" and thereby certifying their worthiness as honorary members of "Mr. Calvin's Elect."[19] Regina Cline, one of the daughters of the newly respectable Peter Cline and Margaret Treanor, would become the mother of Mary Flannery O'Connor.

At least one of Regina's cousins on the Treanor-Harty side had risen to even greater heights than the Clines, in a city more cosmopolitan and less rigorous in religious distinctions than Milledgeville. Mary Ellen Norton, a granddaughter of Patrick Harty, had married John Flannery, an accomplished citizen of Savannah. In 1851, at the age of sixteen, Flannery had left a famine-devastated Ireland and arrived at Charleston. He worked briefly as a clerk in Atlanta, becoming a Savannah bookkeeper by the end of the decade. Having escaped the nightmare of Irish history, in 1861 he found himself saddled with the burden of Southern history; he joined Confederate Savannah's Irish Jasper Greens regiment as a junior officer, serving with a distinguished record at Lee Battery on the Savannah River and later under General John Bell Hood in his ill-fated Tennessee campaign. Suffering from malaria, he was discharged from the Confederate Army with the rank of captain and returned to Savannah. There he flourished as a business and civic leader: he was a founder and president of a major Georgia bank, a factor in the Savannah Cotton Exchange, and director of several railroad companies. Moreover, he was a philanthropist who "took an active role in civic and cultural activities, until almost no enterprise in the city failed to include him as a participant." He contributed generously to the building of the first cathedral of the Diocese of Savannah (which then oversaw the entire state of Georgia) in the 1870s, and when it was destroyed by fire in 1898, he chaired the building committee for the present Cathedral of St. John the Baptist. His presence would remain strongly felt in the life of the young Mary Flannery O'Connor—who received his surname as her baptismal name—when her family lived literally in the shadow of the

19. Fitzgerald, "Invisible Father," 13.

great home he built in Savannah (and which had been inherited by his daughter Katie Flannery Semmes, married to a nephew of the Confederate admiral and Maryland Catholic Raphael Semmes).[20]

Savannah was also home to the O'Connors and the place where Regina Cline would meet Flannery's father. His grandfather Patrick O'Connor had been born in Ireland in the mid-1830s, later emigrating to Savannah and establishing himself as a wheelwright; he eventually opened a livery service as well as a carriage and wagon factory. His son Edward Francis O'Connor, born in 1872, became a successful businessman, working comfortably in the city's fairly large Irish community as a wholesale grocer and eventually serving as president of the People's Bank and director of the Hibernia Bank—small but respectable ventures.[21] One of his sons, Edward Francis O'Connor Jr., met Regina Cline in 1922. After a short courtship they were married, and in 1925 she gave birth to their only child, Mary Flannery.

BOTH WALKER PERCY and Flannery O'Connor came from families that had lived in the South for as long as they had been in America. As children and adolescents they found themselves in the same society where their forebears had achieved success and won the respect of those around them; they very much "knew their place," in the best sense of that phrase, and were the beneficiaries of an intricately interwoven network of family relationships. Although as mature writers they would become somewhat ambivalent about their heritage, they very much knew where they came from and what their native society was. Ted Spivey, who has written on both Percy and O'Connor, suggests as much when he claims that "in my first meetings with both, they presented themselves as very deeply Southern in their sense of place, of family, and of hierarchy," as befitted "Southerners who had deep roots in what is traditionally called the Southern 'aristocracy.'"[22]

Such a sense of rootedness must have contributed greatly to the feeling of security ideally associated with childhood, and by all indications both did spend their preadolescent years in homes where parents were generally lov-

20. Ibid., 14. Also see Fitzgerald, "Root and Branch," 383–4.

21. Fitzgerald, "Invisible Father," 14; Fitzgerald, "Root and Branch," 385.

22. Ted Spivey, *Flannery O'Connor: The Woman, the Thinker, the Visionary* (Macon, GA: Mercer University Press, 1983), 41.

ing. Their fathers were hardworking businessmen like their forebears—though dwelling more exclusively in urban settings, as befitted men of the twentieth century—and dutifully carried on the family legacy of public service. But each underwent a period of decline about the time the children entered their teenage years: Percy's father, beset by an ever deepening and inexplicable depression, took his own life when Walker was twelve (his mother died in a car accident two years later); O'Connor's father, struggling financially in the throes of the Great Depression, was diagnosed with lupus erythematosus when she was twelve and died when she was fifteen. Both Percy and O'Connor saw an early end to their years of childhood stability, and they carried the effects of it—however reticently—for the rest of their lives.

The year O'Connor was born in Savannah, Walker Percy was nine years old and living with his parents at the pinnacle of Birmingham society. LeRoy Percy had not only the Percy name but also perhaps the most distinguished education of any of his line: after graduating from Princeton in 1910, he proceeded to Harvard Law School, where he made the Law Review before spending a postgraduate year abroad at the University of Heidelberg. During a summer vacation in these hectic years he met Mattie Sue Phinizy, and after he returned to Birmingham (and his father's law firm) in 1914, the couple continued their courtship and married in September 1915. Their first son, Walker, was born a year later; he would be followed by two other boys. After the elder Walker Percy's suicide, LeRoy assumed virtually all of his late father's responsibilities: in the law firm, on business councils, and even as president of the Country Club of Birmingham. Except for a brief interlude with the Army Air Corps during World War I—he was so skilled a pilot that he was, to his great disappointment, assigned to instruct others in Texas rather than being shipped to Europe—LeRoy Percy was firmly settled into the routine of Birmingham life; indeed, he seemed to be living the life of his father.[23]

Such was, of course, not in all regards a good pattern to follow. If both men were alike in their business success, "their charming manners, their ease with people, and their humor," LeRoy was also like his father in being "prone to depression, a tendency that grew more pronounced with the years, to the concern of friends and family." Though engaged in all manner of community

23. Tolson, 36.

activities, including deaconship in the theologically liberal Independent Presbyterian Church of Birmingham, LeRoy Percy seems to have felt that he was not living up to the family legacy of public leadership.[24] Some insecurity regarding his personal worthiness is perhaps indicated by his intense sense of individual honor—a burden for many upper-class southerners of the time, yet particularly pronounced in the Percy line—as was made evident in LeRoy's near involvement in a pistol duel with another lawyer in the early 1920s. A lingering fascination with his father's act of self-destruction further suggests that he was also obsessed with family heritage in the worst sense; after the elder Percy's suicide, LeRoy moved his young family into the very house where the deed had occurred, a large Victorian home that Walker Percy later described as "spooky . . . like the Munsters' house on TV."[25] The fact that LeRoy Percy had actually been in the house when his father shot himself could only have made it more so for him.

Young Walker and his two younger brothers actually found life there, in the bustling Five Points area of Birmingham, pleasant enough, and they settled easily into the routine of school years. Walker established a reputation as a serious student but also as a quiet one with a wry sense of humor. Their father would soon—in 1924—take them out of the city, however, to an ostensibly more pleasant environment: Shades Valley, an isolated development across a mountain from Birmingham, where the Percys became "pioneers of suburban living." The Birmingham Country Club golf course was soon to follow (and this home would be echoed in the description of the Vaught family's "castle fronting on a golf links" in *The Last Gentleman*). Such a move perhaps suggests a longing for a more traditional rural life, but—in keeping with Tolson's assessment of the Percy experience in Birmingham as "a charged symbolic encounter between an archetypal 'Old South' family and a prototypical 'New South' city"—Walker Percy's family here did not so much affect a return to the

24. Ibid., 33–5. Tolson cites a curious letter from LeRoy Percy to his uncle in Greenville wherein he describes rising nativism in Birmingham (leading to an "open season" on Catholic priests, one of whom he reports shot by "a jack-legged Methodist minister"); yet he seems to do so only in order to indirectly accuse himself of doing nothing to oppose it, suggesting that he has failed to live up to the family code (35).

25. Quoted ibid., 33.

Old South as anticipate the newest of New Souths, a subregion of postmodern America. They had moved to the suburbs.[26]

Their new home did not, however, provide happiness as advertised; in fact, family life for the Percys steadily got worse in the second half of the 1920s. LeRoy Percy's occasional bouts of depression became more frequent and more extreme. Though often kind and generous to his family, he began having occasional outbursts of temper and drinking regularly. In the face of his mood swings, Mattie Sue—herself affectionate if somewhat delicate—withdrew from both her husband and her sons; though they later recalled her fondly, she seemed almost "otherworldly" to them. In these years especially, Walker's brother Roy has recalled that "it just wasn't a happy family."[27] LeRoy seemed to recognize his increasing problems, and in 1925 he committed himself to the psychiatric clinic at the Johns Hopkins Hospital in Baltimore. The doctors there found him generally stable and successfully adjusted to life, as his continued participation in the whirlwind of upper-class Birmingham social life seemed to indicate, yet subject to occasional depressive moods. Finally the "cure" affected there was no more lasting than his father's 1911 recovery had been. On July 9, 1929, alone at the house in Shades Valley, LeRoy Percy shot himself "with the same gauge and type of gun that his father had used a dozen years before."[28]

In an interview more than a half century later, Walker Percy downplayed the effect that his father's suicide had on him at the time: "Well, you know how kids are—they don't take that sort of thing too seriously. You don't think too much about it."[29] But this claim seems grossly misleading, especially given the evidence of Percy's ongoing thematic concern with suicide—and with the missing father—in his novels from *The Moviegoer* on. Whatever its immediate effect, LeRoy Percy's suicide had a tremendous effect on Walker Percy over the course of his life; indeed, to some degree it explains his obsessions as a "philosophical" novelist, one who was readily influenced by such existentialists as Albert Camus, who claimed that "there is but one truly serious philo-

26. Ibid., 38, 25.
27. Quoted ibid., 42.
28. Wyatt-Brown, 238.
29. Lawson and Kramer, 254.

sophical problem, and that is suicide. Judging whether life is or is not worth living amounts to answering the fundamental question of philosophy."[30] Certainly Percy gave a more accurate account of the significance of his father's death when, while teaching at Louisiana State University in 1974, he called out to a passing student in an uncharacteristically confessional moment: "I guess the central mystery of my life will always be why my father killed himself. Come here, have a seat."[31] Such a comment suggests an ongoing struggle with the appeal of the "Roman option" that Percy himself—as numerous critics have suggested—perhaps considered.

Walker Percy at age twelve was far from being able to articulate such thoughts, but he immediately experienced a concrete sense of uncertainty in the wake of the suicide. As the nation headed into the Great Depression, Mattie Sue uprooted her orphaned children and took them east, to her hometown.[32] There Walker spent his first year of high school as a seemingly normal student, but one already privately seeking out the intellectual experiences that might ultimately help him to understand better the events of the preceding summer: there, as he later recalled, he read *The Brothers Karamazov*, "and how can I disconnect Ivan and Mitya from reading about them sitting in a swing on my grandmother's porch in Athens, Georgia, in the 1930's? Should I?"[33]

AT THE TURN of that decade, the young Flannery O'Connor was spending her summers about seventy miles due south of Athens, visiting her Cline relatives in Milledgeville (*CW*, 1237). But her parents were settled in Savannah and would remain so until events beyond their control changed their plans. Her father was happily at home among the extended and comfortable (if not quite elite) O'Connor clan and working at building his own business. Such was a new responsibility for Edward O'Connor Jr., who had a happy youth behind him: growing up among his seven siblings in Savannah, he had attended private parochial schools and graduated from Mount Saint Mary's College in Emmitsburg, Maryland, a popular educational institution among

30. Albert Camus, *The Myth of Sisyphus and Other Essays* (New York: Knopf, 1967), 3.

31. Quoted in Tolson, 396.

32. Wyatt-Brown, 255.

33. Walker Percy, introduction to *Walker Percy: A Comprehensive Descriptive Bibliography*, by Linda Whitney Hobson (New Orleans: Faust, 1988), xvii–xviii.

Catholics of the southern Atlantic states at the time. After failing to obtain an appointment to the U.S. Naval Academy, he joined the army in 1916, at age twenty, and served in France during World War I as a lieutenant in the American Expeditionary Force. Returning to Savannah, the young veteran began working in the real estate business and enjoying his native city. Sally Fitzgerald has described him as "naturally exuberant, full of *joie de vivre* as a youth": "he was a member of the Junior Hussars and a dashing young-man-about-town. He loved, his sister told me, to put on his white linen suit, tilt his straw boater over his eye, and go out to Tybee Island dancing of a summer evening."[34] Such bachelor pleasures came to an end in 1922, when he attended his sister Nan's wedding to a young man from Milledgeville named Herbert Cline; there he met the groom's sister Regina, and they themselves were married within the year.

Sally Fitzgerald has indicated that from the very beginning of their marriage, Regina Cline felt that her husband's lineage was not quite as distinguished as that of the Clines and the Flannerys and that she therefore hoped for much from him in the way of entrepreneurial zeal. Ed O'Connor found himself suddenly diminished in comparison with the legacy that his new wife saw as her own; such a sense was given concrete expression when, after Mary Flannery's birth, Regina's cousin Katie Flannery Semmes provided the young family with a townhouse adjoining her own mansion on Lafayette Square. Ed O'Connor paid a nominal rent to her, but he and his family were essentially dependent, an arrangement that could not have been entirely comfortable for a man of his era. Nonetheless, Katie Flannery Semmes's generosity proved invaluable in many ways. In honor of the newborn child, she also gave the family a financial gift that enabled Ed O'Connor to found his own business, the Dixie Realty Company, in 1926; by 1927 he added a construction company to it (*CW*, 1237).

Despite his apparent initiative, Flannery's father never flourished in the business world, though not necessarily through any fault of his own—the timing was certainly not fortuitous for any new enterprise. Consequently, the O'Connors lived in a fine house in a wealthy section of Savannah, but only in a sort of shabby gentility. Flannery later recalled "with some amusement, that during the Depression they had eaten ground round steak and turnip greens

34. Fitzgerald, "Invisible Father," 15.

every day." But she enjoyed attending parochial schools during the academic year—taking special pleasure in drawing and writing—and visits to her mother's family in Milledgeville during the summers. An only child, she was doted on by both parents, but especially by her father; as he entered into his years of responsibility, "she was the real—and perhaps the only—joy of his life, and he was very proud of her."[35]

Despite his financial struggles, Ed O'Connor found time for one activity he took great pleasure and pride in: the American Legion. He saw such service as a promising and effective means of public leadership and succeeded there as nowhere else. Elected commander of a Chatham County post in 1935, he became commander of the Legion for the entire state the following year; he consequently devoted himself to traveling throughout Georgia, earning himself a name in the state newspapers as he presented speeches and launched new programs for the organization. Sally Fitzgerald has described those speeches as "quite well-written, clear and cogent, free of any jingoism of tone or content."[36] Flannery herself "read over some of the speeches he made and . . . was touched to see a kind of patriotism that most people would just laugh at now, something childlike, that was a good deal too good and innocent for the Legion. But the Legion was the only thing provided by the country to absorb it" (*HB*, 166). Inconsequential as such an organization may seem, it was for the essentially gregarious and charitable Ed O'Connor a way of contributing to his community (and later it perhaps inspired his daughter, despite her illness, to travel and give lectures, an aspect of her life that has not been fully appreciated).[37]

In 1937, however, such success could be little consolation for Ed O'Connor or his family. That year, when Flannery turned twelve, his business reached its nadir. But an even more significant blow came at the same time. Ed O'Connor had been in failing health for a year or so (he resigned his Legion position as a result of it), and what had initially been diagnosed as arthritis was discovered to be lupus erythematosus, a disease that was then untreatable and fatal. Courageously, he paid little heed to his own predicament and sought employ-

35. Ibid., 16–17.

36. Ibid., 17.

37. See Jean Cash, "Flannery O'Connor as Lecturer: '. . . a secret Desire to Rival Charles Dickens,'" *Flannery O'Connor Bulletin* (1987): 1–15.

ment to support his family. In March 1938 he accepted a position as a zone real estate appraiser for the Federal Housing Authority and moved the family to Atlanta. The transition was a jarring one for Flannery and her mother, who after six months left the city to live in the sprawling Cline house in Milledge-ville. There Flannery began school for the fall term while her father worked in Atlanta, living in a boarding house and traveling home on the weekends. He did so until 1940, when his deteriorating health compelled him to resign from the FHA and be taken in by his wife's family. In a condition of total dependency in the last months of his life, he died on February 1, 1941, when his daughter was fifteen years old.

The immediate effect on Flannery was devastating. In an undated journal entry that Sally Fitzgerald places after her father's death, the young O'Connor wrote: "The reality of death has come upon us and a consciousness of the power of God has broken our complacency like a bullet in the side. A sense of the dramatic, of the tragic, of the infinite, has descended upon us, filling us with grief, but even above grief, wonder. Our plans were so beautifully laid out, ready to be carried to action, but with magnificent certainty God laid them aside and said, 'You have forgotten—mine?'"[38] Her father's death was perhaps not the central mystery of her life in the same sense that Percy's father's suicide was for him, but her description here suggests that it was to her the earliest manifestation of the ultimately religious mystery she would explore so powerfully in her own fiction. O'Connor would also differ from Percy in that she would not return to the character of her father in her fiction in any remotely recognizable fashion. Nonetheless, she would see herself writing *for* him in a sense. In 1956, fifteen years after his death, she wrote to a new friend: "my father toted around some of my early productions [writing and drawing]. . . . [he] wanted to write but had not the time or money or training or any of the opportunities I have had. . . . Anyway, whatever I do in the way of writing makes me extra happy in the thought that it is a fulfill-ment of what he wanted to do himself" (*HB*, 168). In 1960 she would dedicate her final novel, *The Violent Bear It Away*, to him. Above all, she would remem-ber him and his fate during her own affliction with lupus, but that marked a significant chapter in her own life, one deserving full consideration in and of itself.

38. Sally Fitzgerald, "Rooms with a View," *Flannery O'Connor Bulletin* (1981): 17.

Both Percy and O'Connor, then, lost their fathers in manners that would continually engage their thought and would ultimately shape their understanding of themselves as writers in mature life. Such a loss can certainly be investigated in terms of general psychiatric theory (though, again, Percy himself would point out the limitations of any such theory with regard to understanding the individual). In light of such theory, Bertram Wyatt-Brown has explored the manner in which Percy's loss of his parents might have affected him, and to some extent his observations might be extended to O'Connor. Wyatt-Brown cites analyst Felix Brown on the effects of such a loss on children in general and the creatively gifted in particular; though the effect is obviously a depressive one, "the mourning process may lead the orphan, if gifted, to develop his or her own resources and imagination."[39] Brown himself writes that the effects of the death extend far beyond the immediate bereavement: "[I]t is probable that the traumatic influence is not so much the actual bereavement as the family disruption which may follow it. Frequently the whole family is disorganized by the death of a parent resulting in children being moved from place to place among strangers."[40] For both Percy and O'Connor, though neither quite ended up among "strangers," a change in place was indeed occasioned by the circumstances of each death, as we have seen. In Percy's case, his father's suicide caused a physical uprooting, a move from Birmingham to Athens and, ultimately, Greenville—or from New South to Old, as Jay Tolson has characterized it; for O'Connor, her father's diagnosis resulted in a move from relatively cosmopolitan Savannah to rural Milledgeville, with a brief, uncomfortable stay in Atlanta. Such sudden changes for these two adolescents only foreshadowed their more drastic experiences of travel and urban life in the coming years, as they moved toward their final vocations.

FOLLOWING THE DEATHS of their fathers, O'Connor and Percy alike—under the influence of various mentors—took indirect routes to settling on their life's work. O'Connor, much earlier than Percy, committed herself to becoming a literary artist, though she, like him, studied a modern "science" in college (sociology, as opposed to chemistry) and initially leaned toward

39. Wyatt-Brown, 297.

40. Felix Brown, "Bereavement and Lack of a Parent in Childhood," in *Foundations of Child Psychiatry*, ed. Emanuel Miller (London: Pergamon, 1968), 439.

journalism rather than fiction. Both left the South upon completion of their undergraduate studies and spent significant time in the North, gaining experiences that influenced their earliest fiction and their sense of contemporary urban life in general. These years were crucial precursors to the seemingly cataclysmic experiences of illness that shaped the manner in which they finally settled into practicing their art; there are, of course, significant differences to be noted here, but the generally similar patterns are once again striking.

Whereas O'Connor's father had provided her with early encouragement and an incentive toward her final vocation, Walker Percy's model was found not in LeRoy Percy but rather in the guardian who adopted him and became his second father: William Alexander Percy, or "Uncle Will." In the year following LeRoy Percy's suicide, when Walker was thirteen, Will Percy came to Athens and offered to take in Mattie Sue and her three sons; it was the first time Walker had laid eyes on his cousin, though he had heard much of him. When the family did move to Greenville, tragedy soon struck again when Mattie Sue died in a mysterious car accident.[41] From then on the boys had but one guardian in the world, and they were fortunate to have found such an exceptional one.

Walker Percy's essay "Uncle Will" is the best testimony of what this lawyer-planter-poet who regularly opened his house to wandering intellectuals and artists did for him. Will Percy devoted himself so much to what he perceived as his inherited obligations to his family and the Greenville community that he had little time in mature life to devote to literature; but he did not fail to share his passions with his three charges, not only recounting the family history—particularly his father's battles with the Klan—but also playing classical music and reading Shakespeare aloud to them. In staying with him, the mature Percy reflected, "I gained . . . a vocation and in a real sense a second self; that is, the work and the self which, for better or worse, would not otherwise have been open to me" (*SSL*, 55). In a very real sense, Walker spent the rest of his life reacting to Uncle Will, finally rejecting the ultimately bleak Stoic vision that his mentor espoused in his autobiography, *Lanterns on the*

41. My consideration of Percy's personal history follows most of the available scholarship in being admittedly patriarchal in focus. It certainly seems that much more work can be done with Percy's mother in light of, for example, the "Our Lady of the Camellias" reverie in *Lancelot*.

Levee, and embracing the Catholicism that Will Percy had discarded as a youth. But finally, Walker wrote, "he was the most extraordinary man I have ever known and I owe him a debt which cannot be paid" (*SSL,* 62). Walker Percy always regarded his guardian as a fixed point to look back upon, as a model of a certain species of integrity—limited but admirable nonetheless—that he continually responded to both in life and in fiction.[42]

Uncle Will's proselytizing on the Stoic values of the Old South aristocracy was given an added flavor by the locale. In Greenville, ancestral home of the Percys, Walker and his brothers were immersed in a culture very unlike that of protosuburban Birmingham. The boys generally adjusted well to their new life in the Delta, that subregion of Mississippi that historian James C. Cobb has called "the most southern place on earth." While his uncle entertained distinguished guests (including William Faulkner, who arrived drunk for a brief and disastrous tennis game), Walker excelled at school and displayed some playful skill in his writing for the high school paper. But the most important milestone of his Greenville life was a personal one: here he met and established a friendship with Shelby Foote, who would encourage Walker in a sort of informal literary education—and an engagement with southern history—for the rest of his life.

Whatever specifically literary ambitions were kindled at the house in Greenville, where he continued to live at least sporadically through his twenties, would have to wait, however. When in 1933 Percy enrolled not at Sewanee or Princeton but the University of North Carolina at Chapel Hill, he chose to major in chemistry; he was already breaking from the pattern that his ancestors, almost all of whom had been lawyers, had established. In doing so he was perhaps establishing himself firmly as a man of the twentieth century, which would be so characterized by its rapid technological advances;

42. William Alexander Percy's own curious relationship with the Catholic Church remained important for Walker Percy. Not only had his guardian been intensely devout as a youth, but he also apparently lost a teaching position he briefly held at Sewanee because of his prior affiliation with the Catholic Church (see Samway, 433–4). Almost two decades after Will's death, and one decade after joining the Church himself, Walker commented in a 1957 letter to B. Phinizy Spalding that William Alexander Percy "used to speak often in admiration of the Catholic Church—of her wisdom, noble tradition, esthetic beauty, etc.—but he would not have regarded himself as a believer. . . . [H]e regarded the Catholic Church as a purely human institution with a noble history and a great store of wisdom." Quoted in Samway, 120.

but he was also by his own account making an attempt to study a discipline the "elegance" and "beauty" of which lay in its "simplicity," in "ordering the endless variety and the seeming haphazardness of ordinary life" (*SSL*, 187). The appeal of such a discipline to a young man who had found his own early life so mysterious and troubling is clearly suggested by the protagonist Percy created in *The Moviegoer* nearly thirty years later: Binx Bolling remembers how in his youth he "stood outside the universe and sought to understand it" by reading books such as "*The Chemistry of Life*," books that explained the universe in such a way as to "dispose" of it (*M*, 59).

Such an understanding of the universe ultimately proved inadequate to Percy, but its strong appeal was suggested in one of his few literary ventures of this period. The 1937 fragment "Young Nuclear Physicist" was written in the summer after Percy's undergraduate career and at the beginning of the next phase of his life: medical school at Columbia University in New York City. If Chapel Hill had placed Percy in close proximity to yet another vision of the South (that of Howard Odum and the progressive Regionalist school), Percy was embarking on an altogether new journey in the urban North, and the literary fragment, which concerns a frustrated southern science student relocated to New York, clearly reflects some of his own ambivalence about the move. Patrick Samway has described Percy at this juncture of his life as "uprooted, without family or friends," and his protagonist is in the same situation.[43] Secure in his career hopes but lonely and dislocated in his new urban life, he muses: "I have been a fool. My error is simply a failure to apply method. I apply method with competence and success to mathematical and physical problems. Why should I imagine that my personal life is exempt, that it should work itself out with no conscious direction?"[44] He then proceeds to make a list of possible ways to meet women. Even at this stage of his life, then, Percy introduces some irony and humor into his treatment of the objec-tive-minded scientist, though not to the extent that he committed himself to later. For the moment, any literary venture was a distraction for Percy. He threw himself into his medical studies, even as he underwent psychoanalysis and enjoyed the diversions of the city. None of these experiences were wasted on the later writer. One of his earliest fictional efforts, *The Gramercy Winner*,

43. Ibid., 89.
44. Walker Percy, "Young Nuclear Physicist," *Oxford American* 25 (January–February 1999): 32.

drew heavily on both medical culture and the urban North, as *The Last Gentleman* did to a lesser degree. But Percy finished medical school and his life took a radically different turn before he undertook any serious attempts at fiction.

During Percy's medical school years, O'Connor's life took a radical turn of its own. Following her father's diagnosis with lupus in 1937, the family was uprooted from their old townhouse, with O'Connor and her mother finally settling in Milledgeville while her father worked on in Atlanta. The Cline family home that they came to was markedly impressive. Built in 1820 using slave labor, it had been used as the interim governor's mansion when Milledgeville was the state capital; acquired by Peter Cline in 1886, it symbolized the extent to which the modest Irish immigrant family had bought into the legacy of the Old South.[45] Young Flannery was, of course, already familiar with the house (where her mother had been born) from summer visits, and she knew most of the extended family that lived or regularly visited there. O'Connor now settled in for what would be a seven-year stay at the house. This period was punctuated with visits to the family farm outside of town, a place that became even more familiar to her later in life.

Having always attended Catholic parochial schools, O'Connor found the local public high school, which was an "experimental" one run by the Education Department of Milledgeville's Georgia State College for Women, an unsettling change. O'Connor later derided her education there: "I went to a progressive high school where one did not read if one did not wish to; I did not wish to." But nonetheless she did well in classes, also taking time to write and draw cartoons for the school paper (and reading for pleasure on her own—mainly Edgar Allan Poe). She continued these extracurricular activities when in 1942 she enrolled as an undergraduate at the college itself, majoring in English and sociology. The disdain she acquired for the latter discipline came out clearly in later correspondence: "In college I read works of social-science, so-called. The only thing that kept me from being a social scientist was the grace of God and the fact that I couldn't remember the stuff but a few days after reading it" (*HB*, 98).

Her reaction to this education not only drove her to a new career, as it

45. Robert Fitzgerald, "Flannery O'Connor: A Memoir," in *The Third Kind of Knowledge: Memoirs and Selected Writings of Robert Fitzgerald,* ed. Penelope Laurans Fitzgerald (New York: New Directions, 1993), 106.

were, but also provided the impetus for much of her fiction. Much as Percy's novels were largely concerned with the limitations of the scientific view of the world in which he had been trained, hers mercilessly satirized the secular pseudoscientific "schoolteachers," such as Rayber of *The Violent Bear It Away*, who attempt to reduce individual human beings to rationally comprehensible types. It is difficult not to see in her dubious experience with modern education—as opposed to her earlier training at Catholic schools—the roots of her major theme. Furthermore, going back and forth from the cold analytical study of social science to conversations at the ancestral family home, where now she lived with her mother and two aunts (and at the farm, where she saw and heard the local hands), doubtlessly fostered an awareness of the tension between the abstract claims of the former realm and the more concrete concerns of the latter, a tension reflected in the very language of the inhabitants of each. As Robert Coles, himself a psychiatrist and a keen writer on social issues, and an ardent admirer of both O'Connor and Percy, has observed, O'Connor disliked social science precisely because of "the prideful excess of generalization to be found in some of the sociological and psychological journals. She fought hard for the concrete, the particular—to the point that, thereby, her point of view as a writer of fiction was shaped."[46]

As she neared graduation, O'Connor was fortunate enough to find a new faculty mentor, Dr. George Beiswanger; recognizing her talent as a writer, he encouraged her to apply to the graduate school of journalism at Iowa and played a large role in securing a scholarship for her there in 1945. While it is intriguing to imagine what sort of journalism O'Connor might have produced (and it is certainly possible to see her impulse toward cartooning in her later fiction), her teachers—specifically Paul Engle, the director of the Iowa Writers' Workshop—saw her great promise as a fiction writer, and she transferred to the Workshop in 1946. There she not only wrote prolifically but also, under Engle's direction, began reading extensively in modern fiction (including Joyce, Franz Kafka, and Faulkner) for the first time.[47]

She was by all accounts at the head of her class. When prominent writers

46. Robert Coles, *Flannery O'Connor's South* (Baton Rouge: Louisiana State University Press, 1980), xxviii.

47. Sally Fitzgerald, "Flannery O'Connor: Patterns of Friendship, Patterns of Love," *Georgia Review* 52:3 (Fall 1998): 412.

such as John Crowe Ransom, Robert Penn Warren, and Allen Tate visited the Workshop, they invariably singled out her stories for praise. Of course, there were clear affinities between her preferred subject matter and that of these former Agrarians. As Percy had the advantage of spending his late teens and young adulthood with a minor southern poet, O'Connor had the advantage of direct instruction under Andrew Lytle when he taught at the Workshop in her last year there (and, of course, she benefited from the friendship of Tate and his wife later). A classmate observed: "In my opinion Andrew Lytle worked more, and more closely, with Flannery O'Connor than any staff member at Iowa. . . . His relationship with Flannery was very special. . . . [Both] Andrew and Flannery were in a strange land, outside the South, deep in the Yankee territory of—my God, they must have thought—Iowa. But his outlook was Southern and so was Flannery's. . . . Such was the emotional basis of their master-apprentice relationship."[48] A quiet student in the classroom, she worked hard on her own and won a class award for the six stories that formed her master's thesis. The first to be published was "The Geranium," in 1946, about a homesick Georgian in New York, a topic she was soon to learn more about.[49]

For if Iowa had seemed alien to O'Connor, she was on her way to even stranger surroundings. Accepted to Yaddo, the prestigious writers' colony near Saratoga Springs, New York, she moved there in the summer of 1948; she spent the next two years there, in New York City, and in Connecticut, while she worked on the novel that would become Wise Blood. During this period she met some of the elite literary society of the day, including the poet Robert Lowell and one academic couple, Robert and Sally Fitzgerald, with whom she would remain friends for life. These friends were also Catholics, and they provided intellectual encouragement in the faith that was increasingly important to her. O'Connor had never rebelled against the Church she was raised in, but since leaving Georgia she had become increasingly devout; in 1945 she began attending Mass daily in Iowa City, and at Yaddo she regularly joined "the Irish domestic staff" at Mass in Saratoga Springs.[50] It is not difficult to

48. James B. Hall, quoted in Jean Cash, "O'Connor in the Iowa Writers' Workshop," Flannery O'Connor Bulletin (1995–96): 70.

49. O'Connor wrote of "The Geranium": "[it was] no experience of mine as far as old men and slums went, but I did know what it meant to be homesick" (HB, 204).

50. Fitzgerald, "Patterns," 414.

imagine that the Church provided the one thread of continuity with her earlier life as she moved into a more impersonal and potentially disorienting world.

Her personal faith, however, was still not integrated with her literary sensibility; her first six stories show virtually no sign of the intense religious concern that mark her mature work. Nonetheless, her literary career seemed to be moving along smoothly. By age twenty-five, she had secured a permanent literary agent and a publisher and was thriving as she lived with the Fitzgeralds at their farmhouse outside of Ridgefield, Connecticut (disenchanted with the city after a brief stay in New York itself in 1949, she had begun boarding with them that fall). She seemed poised to begin a successful literary career. But she had not yet truly found her mature voice or her major theme; both would come soon, with the final drafts of *Wise Blood* and with other, more irrevocable changes in her life.

BOTH PERCY and O'Connor, then, had some initial attraction to scientific disciplines in their first years of intellectual inquiry. The attraction of modern science as a means of fully understanding human beings wore off for O'Connor much more quickly than it did for Percy—who always remained seriously engaged with science, and particularly the broadly "anthropological" sciences—but it provided both with fodder for their often satirical fiction in mature life. Likewise, their experiences with twentieth-century urban life proved disorienting enough to these displaced southerners to suggest the larger metaphors of homelessness that pervade their fiction. Ted Spivey has claimed with regard to O'Connor's late story "Judgment Day" (a reworking of "The Geranium") that she considered "New York, like Atlanta, to be primarily a megalopolis where individualism seemed to disappear," as characters such as Hazel Motes and Francis Marion Tarwater discover; and Percy is likewise concerned with the loss of identity in twentieth-century society in his fiction from *The Moviegoer* on (though his later protagonists tend to live suburban rather than urban lives).[51] Both writers sensed that neither modern science itself nor an advanced technological society—despite the obvious material advantages attendant upon each—necessarily fosters adequate recognition of the individuality and mysterious dignity of each human being. Percy and

51. Ted Spivey, *Revival: Southern Writers in the Modern City* (Gainesville: University of Florida Press, 1986), 163.

O'Connor would come to sense this problem most strongly in events that involved not leisurely intellectual reflection but rather their own suffering and isolation.

O'Connor had found her vocation early in life, but she was strengthened and deepened in it by her affliction with lupus at age twenty-five; the illness was not only profoundly life-changing in itself, but it also served to remind O'Connor of her link to the father who had departed from her life so mysteriously a decade earlier. For Percy, it took an extended period of illness to turn him away from medicine (and his unsatisfactory "faith" in scientific method) toward the Catholic faith and his ultimate vocation of exploring the human condition through language. It was tuberculosis that occasioned the initial turn in Percy's life, but he eventually spent much of his adult life struggling with the disease that killed his father: depression. For both, the experience of illness was inescapably bound up with their own mature self-awareness, their experience of religious faith, their sense of vocation, and, accordingly, their fictional vision of the particular world they inhabited.

In June of 1941, Walker Percy received his M.D. from Columbia and made arrangements to begin an internship in pathology at New York's Bellevue Hospital the following January. During the interim he worked at a clinic in Greenville, a period that served to introduce him to his future wife and enabled him to spend extended time in the company of Uncle Will. Undoubtedly he here renewed his consideration of his guardian's almost classical understanding of the human condition, the Stoic view that in some ways complemented the cold, objective stance of the modern scientist toward reality. Such philosophical considerations took on a sense of urgency when Will, who had been diagnosed with acute exhaustion and high blood pressure, suffered a cerebral hemorrhage shortly before Christmas.[52] As the new year approached—and the United States entered World War II—Walker Percy headed back to New York knowing that he was not likely to see his second father ever again.

Percy had undergone several years of psychoanalysis as a medical student (this was a necessary prerequisite for becoming a psychoanalyst), but he finally entered a specialty at the opposite end of the medical spectrum: pathology. For all his interest in plumbing the depths of the self, he yearned for the

52. Samway, 114–6.

detached simplicity of the pathologist examining "the mechanism of disease" through his microscope (SSL, 187). Again, the seeming certainty afforded by the scientific method in an often uncertain world—an uncertainty reinforced when Uncle Will died in late January of 1942—attracted Percy; as Robert Coles, who knew Percy in later life, has said, he eventually chose to enter residency in pathology rather than psychiatry because he somehow thought that the more "objective" discipline could help him "get to the bottom of things."[53]

Ironically, however, Percy's decision to do so ultimately led him to abandon medicine altogether. Assigned to work with tuberculosis victims, he became careless in following the necessary sanitary procedures and by March had contracted pulmonary tuberculosis himself: he found himself infected with "one of these elegant agents of disease, the same scarlet tubercle bacillus I used to see lying crisscrossed like Chinese characters in the sputum and lymphoid tissue of the patients at Bellevue. Now I was one of them" (SSL, 187). Before, he had stood apart from the disease, admiring its "beautiful mechanism" through a microscope; now he and the disease were one. Percy spent the next two years as an enforced invalid at a sanatorium at Saranac Lake in upstate New York, and while there he began reading the authors who would awaken him to a new understanding of the world: Fyodor Dostoyevsky, Kierkegaard, Jean-Paul Sartre, Camus, Marcel. He would later deem this period of isolation and confinement, which at the time seemed such an inconvenient distraction from his larger purpose, the most fortunate of his life, indeed as crucially enabling him to choose the life he ultimately led.

Up to this time he had learned to see the world entirely mechanically, had disdained religion, had enjoyed literature but seen it merely as a diversion, and had sought to understand himself through psychoanalysis. He saw the world as the modern rationalist does. But now he realized that there was a phenomenon his prior paradigm for grasping the real had failed to account for: "Did my eyes deceive me or was there not a huge gap in the scientific view of the world (scientific in the root sense of the word, knowing)? If so, it was an oversight which everyone pretended not to notice or maybe didn't want to notice. . . . After twelve years of a scientific education, I felt somewhat like the Danish philosopher Søren Kierkegaard when he finished reading

53. Robert Coles, lecture, Duke University Center for Documentary Studies, April 15, 1997.

Hegel. Hegel, said Kierkegaard, explained everything under the sun, except one small detail: what it means to be a man living in the world who must die" (*SSL*, 188). The European existentialists brought home to Percy the realization that modern science could not explain his individual self, nor could it construct an adequate anthropology of man in general. He did not lose respect for the scientific method; in its proper place, it remained a valuable way of seeking a kind of truth. However, Percy had stumbled onto a clue here, noting an anomaly that the currently dominant paradigm for grasping the real failed to recognize, and his discovery changed the rest of his life. He began to believe that art, specifically the novel, was a means of approaching a sort of truth that positivistic science could not touch. Furthermore, he began to understand that, despite crude materialist claims to the contrary, the human self was radically different from any other phenomenon in the cosmos and must be understood as such if it was to be understood at all.

In later life Percy was quite forthright about the crucial role that his encounter with tuberculosis played in shaping his life and thought. He was less so about his ongoing battle with depression, which he was not comfortable reducing to a physiological illness, but which certainly surfaces in his fiction—most significantly, perhaps, in Will Barrett's confrontation with the legacy of his "death-dealing" father in *The Second Coming*.[54] Whatever their particular experiences, the characters in Percy's fiction tend to undergo suffering and isolation as preludes to personal awakenings, thereby echoing his own life. Discussing both his own sense of the shortcomings of contemporary psychiatry and the specific plot of *The Second Coming*, Percy said in a 1981 interview: "You have to define [the] self through ordeal, which the psychologists don't tell people. And God knows, it takes an awful lot of ordeal . . . it takes an awful lot these days to come to a sense of self." And relating the Christian philosophy of Kierkegaard to his fiction, he could say in 1974 that "suffering is an evil, yet at the same time through the ordeal of suffering one gets these strange benefits of lucidity, of seeing things afresh"; hence in his novels suffering becomes "an asset, a cognitive avenue toward knowledge, or grace."[55]

54. See Wyatt-Brown, 334–5. Percy jokes about being a "manic depressive" who is never manic, but he is clearly ambivalent about limiting depression to something that can be explained by a "gene for manic depressive psychosis" such as Wyatt-Brown suggests he has inherited.

55. Lawson and Kramer, 219–20, 121.

The latter comment suggests the path Percy's own life was to follow. After a period of intense reflection, including a tubercular relapse that briefly sent him to a Connecticut sanatorium in 1945, the young agnostic doctor had by 1948 returned to the South, married, entered the Catholic Church, and begun a new life devoted to both philosophy and fiction. But his experience with medicine and personal illness would remain with him in the years to come, only broadened in his consideration of "not the physiological and pathological processes within man's body but the problem of man himself . . . specifically and more immediately, the predicament of man in a modern technological society"; as a writer he would be a "diagnostician," exploring the "pathology" of just such a society, specifically as it manifested itself in the rapidly changing South after World War II (SSL, 189, 194).

Percy later traced his original inspiration in his new vocation to his second father, Uncle Will; O'Connor linked hers to her first, and that link was emphasized by the path her life took after 1950. Again, she had clearly already settled on her own vocation as a writer after her undergraduate days, and so she was much less forthright in her essays about the effect of lupus on her life and work. Not only was the illness less fundamentally transformative of her life's ambition than Percy's tuberculosis was of his, but the fact that it was a permanent rather than a temporary affliction gave O'Connor a horror of being seen as driven by bitterness or self-pity; she respected what she saw as the mysterious power of fiction too much to allow her own to be so simply—and safely— interpreted. But some of her personal remarks, in letters to friends, are clearly revelatory of the disease's impact, not only on the basic conditions under which she practiced her craft but also on the way she understood her faith, and thus on her most fundamental theme.

Throughout 1950 O'Connor was contentedly settled in the Fitzgeralds' Connecticut home and working on a preliminary draft of Wise Blood. As the end of the year approached, however, she began to experience unexpected physical ailments, beginning with a heaviness in her arms while typing. Then, as she took the train to visit Milledgeville for Christmas, came the completely unexpected. Sally Fitzgerald has described the results of this trip: "When I put Flannery on the train for Georgia she was smiling, perhaps a little wanly, but wearing her beret at a jaunty angle. She looked much as usual, except that I remember a kind of stiffness in her gait as she left me on the platform to get aboard. By the time she arrived she looked, her uncle later said, 'like a shriveled old woman.' A few nights later her mother called to tell us that Flannery was dying of lupus" (*HB*, 21–2). O'Connor herself did not believe that death would come quite so soon, and she was right. Taking cortisone treatments and visiting an Atlanta doctor, she recovered and soon was able to resume her work. But she nonetheless assessed her new condition realistically, in light of the only previous experience she had with the disease: at the time immediately following O'Connor's diagnosis, "she expected to live no more than the three years her father had survived after falling ill."[56] Her life during those years would, she knew, have to change radically from what she had become accustomed to after college. For reasons of practicality, she had to stay in Milledgeville and live with her mother, at first in the Cline house but soon—after she became too weak to negotiate the stairs in the big house—at the family farmhouse, Andalusia, where she settled into a room on the ground floor. Though she traveled often enough, she spent most of her remaining life here.

Fitzgerald claimed that "in this precarious *vita nuova* . . . her chief aim became to produce as much good fiction as she could in the time allotted to her."[57] If Percy's tuberculosis had given him a new vocation, O'Connor's lupus intensified and focused the one she already had (as was first indicated when a reworked *Wise Blood* was published in 1952). She adapted as gracefully as she could to her new life on the farm, even when her physical ordeal worsened. The very medical treatment that enabled her to live longer than her father had would eventually cause her hip bones to degenerate so that she finally had to use crutches; but she took the pain and increasing limitations to her freedom as best she could: "There was no way out of this checkmate, so she adapted herself to it, as she had to in her relative isolation, with a willed acceptance grounded in her ever-deepening faith, and the sardonic humor that was so much a part of her personality and her mind. She had begun to realize that her forced return to the South had not signaled the end of her writing life, but rather what she could regard as a benevolent redirection of her course that would greatly enrich it."[58]

The seemingly providential nature of the affliction was perhaps empha-

56. Fitzgerald, "Patterns," 418.

57. Ibid., 419.

58. Sally Fitzgerald, introduction to *TFO*, xvii.

sized by one factor Fitzgerald does not mention here—its obvious connection of Flannery's fate to that of Edward O'Connor. Though she rarely spoke of her father explicitly, O'Connor clearly thought of her own disease as bringing her closer to him. In 1958, long after her diagnosis, she could write to a new friend with her typical deflating humor: "You didn't know I had a DREAD DISEASE didja? Well I got one. My father died of the same stuff at age 44 but the scientists hope to keep me here until I am 96" (*HB*, 266). But in more serious moments she would suggest that she owed both her life's work and her debilitation to him. In a 1956 letter wherein she credits her father with encouraging her artistic nature while she was young, she adds "I am never likely to romanticize him because I carry around most of his faults as well as his tastes. I even have about his same constitution. I have the same disease" (*HB*, 168). And, she implied, she had a vocation made possible by him.

The term *vocation* would have held a very particular meaning for both Percy and O'Connor: in the Catholic Church, the term applies to those "called" to religious life, though also to the layman whom God has called to specific work and obligations. Fitzgerald wrote of O'Connor's acceptance of her disease and the spiritual growth that ensued as her response to a call of the deepest sort, flatly comparing her with the Trappist monk and writer Thomas Merton by claiming that "both practiced simultaneously not one but two vocations, each to the enrichment of the other."[59] O'Connor held a less hagiographical view of her own character, but it is certain both that her illness added something to the character of her religiosity and that such religiosity gave her fiction its great power. She had a clear sense that her personal limitations and the discipline they entailed somehow fostered sharper vision: "I have enough energy to write with and as that is all I have any business doing anyhow, I can with one eye squinted take it all as a blessing. What you have to measure out, you come to observe closer, or so I tell myself" (*HB*, 57). What she observed was not God, as the mystic might, but rather the God-haunted region that she thought she had left for good. Her unplanned return was a fortunate fall, according to Fitzgerald:

Had Flannery O'Connor been able to continue in her planned self-exile from the South and permanently join her literary colleagues in the North,

59. Fitzgerald, "Rooms with a View," 7.

she still might have left her mark on contemporary literature by reason of sheer talent, but probably in a less interesting and lasting way. The result of extended expatriation might well have been a watered-down religious sensibility and almost certainly a dulled ear. The struggle to learn thoroughly enough any other region and language than those ingrained in her, which she used so effectively in giving incarnate life to her characters, would have consumed her energies, I think, with considerably less interesting results.[60]

When she gave life to those characters, they were not infrequently grotesques—a characteristic that has been linked to her illness's effect on the specific religious vision she developed in her fiction. Kathleen Spaltro has argued that "O'Connor understood her disability and her consequent death as necessary precipitants of her spiritual growth. This perception also governed her fictional use of disability and of the grotesque to depict spiritual deadness and awakening."[61] More specifically, O'Connor's discovery of her mature religious theme can be traced to the first years after her diagnosis, the period Fitzgerald has called O'Connor's "dark night of the soul," when she was working on the final version of her first novel.[62] Virginia Wray has traced the multiple versions of the novel's opening chapter and persuasively argues that "what is surprisingly different from O'Connor's apprentice pieces [from her M.F.A. thesis] is the presence in *Wise Blood* of a mature functional form of the religious theme that was to inform everything she wrote in the remaining thirteen years of her life." Her early drafts are in the "flat, realistic mode" of her thesis story "The Train," whereas the later drafts show "radical growth toward the multidimensional, metaphorical fiction that, with *Wise Blood*, became synonymous with O'Connor's name."[63]

Wray notes more specifically that in the final drafts "talk of home has come to take on a double-edge clearly absent in the thesis version of the story and in the previous multiple revisions of the opening chapter of the novel."[64]

60. Ibid., 46.

61. Kathleen Spaltro, "When We Dead Awaken: Flannery O'Connor's Debt to Lupus," *Flannery O'Connor Bulletin* (1991): 33.

62. Fitzgerald, "Rooms with a View," 15.

63. Virginia F. Wray, "'An Afternoon in the Woods': Flannery O'Connor's Discovery of Theme," *Flannery O'Connor Bulletin* (1991): 45.

64. Ibid., 46.

O'Connor had written of homesickness as early as "The Geranium," but now—back in Milledgeville—she came to understand it on a deeper and ultimately religious level that she had not before. Even in coming home, she would remain somewhat apart, experiencing a sense of alienation that she herself saw as fundamentally spiritual: "In a sense, sickness is a place, more instructive than a long trip to Europe, and it's always a place where there's no company, where nobody can follow. Sickness before death is a very appropriate thing and I think those who don't have it miss one of God's mercies" (HB, 163). Like Percy, she would see in her own illness a metaphor for the condition of her age and would connect it with the disorientation and displacement of twentieth-century humanity and more particularly of the contemporary southerner.[65] But also as with Percy, the displaced persons and wayfarers that populate her fiction are ultimately bound toward a homeland beyond their own imagining; she shows them—and their earthly home—incomplete only so that her readers might recognize themselves and thereby have hope of being made whole.

PERCY AND O'CONNOR can both be characterized as broadly satirical writers whose religious faith granted them a rich perspective from which to evaluate and criticize a southern society in the midst of rapid change after World War II, and the striking similarities in their personal histories clearly account to some degree for their similarities in vision. Each one's own "inburnt knowledge of human limitations" and accompanying "sense of mystery," as O'Connor would have it, might be seen as the result of personal rather than more broadly regional experience. It is crucial to understand that Percy and O'Connor themselves would not categorize their experiences of decline, illness, and mortality as psychological trauma that led to a neurotic obsession with death; such a categorization would reduce understanding of their individual lives to the realm of modern rationalism. Rather, they understood their own seemingly burdensome histories as opportunities for a more fundamentally philo-

65. For a convincing argument that O'Connor viewed her illness-induced isolation as eremitic in a specifically Christian sense, see Richard Giannone, *Flannery O'Connor, Hermit Novelist* (Urbana: University of Illinois Press, 2000). Giannone also briefly suggests that Percy (along with Don DeLillo) joins O'Connor in drawing on the tradition of the "desert monastics" to shape his own "rigorous" moral critique of late-twentieth-century American culture (2–3).

sophical realization of personal mortality and, consequently, a heightened need to seek the eternal. As Percy implied, his personal experience of illness awakened him to the question of "what it is like to be a man living in the world who must die" and caused him to see the world around him in light of that question—one frequently overlooked in technological societies such as his South was becoming. Hence he would take as his model in fiction those novelists who have "an explicit and ultimate concern with the nature of man and the nature of reality where man finds himself," novelists of a "philosophical" or "religious" bent: "I use the word 'religious' in its root sense as signifying a radical *bond*, as the writer sees it, which connects man with reality—or the failure of such a bond—and so confers meaning to his life—or the absence of meaning. Such a class might include writers as diverse as Dostoevsky, Tolstoy, Camus, Sartre, Faulkner, Flannery O'Connor" (*MB*, 102–3).

O'Connor would indeed agree as to the central importance of such questions in any individual life, and she would, like Percy, see the fiction writer as fundamentally well suited to explore them; in her essay "The Regional Writer," immediately following the quotation that serves as the epigraph for this chapter, she notes that the writer's vocation is to find "where time and place and eternity meet" and capture it in the written word (*MM*, 59). Her and Percy's peculiar experiences in that most peculiar of American regions would eminently qualify them to do so, by marking them as wayfarers never completely at home in the place where their ancestors were at home, as pathologists whose diagnoses of their contemporary South were fundamentally spiritual. They were prepared for such work not only by their raw experiences, of course, but also by their intellectual formation, which for each was largely grounded in the thought of European Catholic philosophers and theologians at midcentury. Such thought, in conjunction with the support of two southern converts to Catholicism, Allen Tate and Caroline Gordon, would prepare both O'Connor and Percy to become Christian existentialists whose vision of the South would be not only profoundly original but also particularly well suited to capture the changes in the region in the second half of the century. But for Percy and O'Connor, whose immersion in serious philosophical and religious thought matches or surpasses that of any other writers from the region, such questions of intellectual formation deserve lengthy consideration in themselves.

CHAPTER 2

South to Rome

*Four Southern Writers
and the Catholic Revival*

The South has no tradition without the Church; for the thing we all still cherish in the South was originally and fundamentally Catholic Christianity. . . . Twenty years ago I knew that religion was the key to the South (as it is to everything else) but I didn't see far enough then.

—ALLEN TATE TO WALKER PERCY, January 1, 1952

When Flannery O'Connor began to write . . . the last word in attitudes was the Existentialist one, resting on the perception that beyond any immediate situation there is possibly nothing—nothing beyond, nothing behind, nada. Now, our country family in 1949 and 1950 believed on excellent grounds that beyond the immediate there was practically everything, like the stars over Taulkinham—the past, the future, and the Creator thereof. But the horror of recent human predicaments had not been lost on us. Flannery felt that an artist who was a Catholic should face all the truth down to the worst of it.

—ROBERT FITZGERALD, "Flannery O'Connor: A Memoir"

AT THE END of 1951, Caroline Gordon, a generous editor as well as an accomplished writer of fiction herself, received at her Minneapolis residence the manuscripts of two apprentice novels: O'Connor's *Wise Blood* and Percy's *The Charterhouse*. Her reaction to these works was overwhelmingly positive. She wrote to her friend Brainard Cheney: "It's no accident, I'm sure, that in the last two months the two best novels I've ever read have been by Catholic writers. The Protestant *mystique* has worn out, but people [such as Truman Capote] would have gone on forever writing those curiously dry novels . . . if something new hadn't come along. And Walker's novel and Flannery's novel are IT. They are both so damned good!"[1] Read out of context, her enthusiasm for her new protégés seems not only excessive but also utterly puzzling in its emphasis on their religious vision; yet given the preoccupations of Gordon and her husband, Allen Tate, both exiled southerners who had recently joined the Catholic Church themselves, her attraction to O'Connor and Percy is more readily understandable. Together, these four writers would mark the postwar confluence of a tradition of southern thought with the seemingly alien Catholic intellectual tradition, a confluence that Tate and Gordon had been moving toward for a quarter century. Although their personal interaction was limited—Gordon was the primary link, writing extensively to Percy and even more so to O'Connor—the Tates provided the younger writers with encouragement and intellectual sustenance regarding religion and region alike at this crucial juncture in their careers and on into the next decade.

They did so in the midst of a much larger rediscovery of traditional Christian thought by American intellectuals, one fueled not only by the belletristic and critical writings of such transatlantic literary figures as T. S. Eliot and W. H. Auden but also by philosophers and theologians—those of the European Catholic Revival in particular, at least for these four southerners. Percy and O'Connor first came to these thinkers, however, largely on their own and with their own preoccupations, which were finally quite different from those of the Tates. Their Catholic visions differed from those of their southern mentors primarily in their embrace of what has been called "Christian existentialism," and as a result the pupils rather than the teachers marked the direction of postwar southern fiction. For it was largely the disappearance—and inherent shortcomings—of the older agrarian South as a social order that eventually led the exiled Tates to the Catholic Church, and their postconversion writings had little bearing on the contemporary region; but it was an intensely religious sense of the immediate predicament of the individual in the nascent postmodern world that led Percy and O'Connor to write about that predicament in the concrete place they knew and lived in, and hence they became the foremost chroniclers of life in the South after World War II and, almost incidentally, the most gifted satirical observers of southern mores since Mark Twain.

In exploring this crucial phase of Percy and O'Connor's development, as

1. Caroline Gordon to Brainard Cheney, December 31, 1951, quoted in Ann Waldron, *Close Connections: Caroline Gordon and the Southern Renaissance* (New York: G. P. Putnam's, 1987), 286.

well as that of southern literary history, several distinct issues must be considered. Given the tendency to lump Gordon and Tate together with Percy and O'Connor as "southern Catholic writers," it is important to distinguish not only similarities and possible patterns of influence but also essential differences between the older pair and the younger.[2] I do so by initially considering the path that Tate and Gordon followed to the Church, one necessarily taken in relation to their long-standing concerns both as literary modernists and as associates of the southern Agrarian movement. Such abiding concerns shaped their engagement with the thinkers of the Catholic Revival, whom—I will argue—O'Connor and Percy encountered from the very different perspective of individual thinkers first coming to maturity in the 1940s, on the brink of the postmodern world. The younger writers' libraries contained identical works by Jacques Maritain, the celebrated French thinker who grew close to the Tates at Princeton and whose rearticulation of medieval Thomism influenced all four writers, but they also included works by thinkers such as Romano Guardini and Gabriel Marcel, who more particularly conveyed to O'Connor and Percy a vision of life in the contemporary Western world. Tate and Gordon did play an ongoing role in fostering the thought of the two young writers they first encountered in 1951, one that has not yet been as fully chronicled as it might be. Finally, however, the "Catholic" literature of the younger writers is radically different from that of the older; and despite the

2. Robert Brinkmeyer's *Three Catholic Writers of the Modern South: Allen Tate, Caroline Gordon, Walker Percy* (Jackson: University Press of Mississippi, 1985) has, in its effort to establish a common pattern of conversion among Tate, Gordon, and Percy, overlooked some of these essential distinctions. Its claim that all three shared "the heritage of Old South tradition and community" (ix) is generally accurate, but the younger writer did not grow up in the same "Old South" as Tate and Gordon did, as we have seen in his Birmingham years as well as in his scientific studies at Chapel Hill. Furthermore, Brinkmeyer's argument that "all three [initially] saw their southern identities as a way to define themselves against the modern world" (xvi) seems much more true of the older writers than of Percy, who as a youth turned so eagerly to modern science. The subsequent claim that each saw Catholicism not as yet another means of "resistance" against modernity but rather as a means of "transcendence," on the other hand, seems more true of Percy than of Tate or Gordon—though I will claim that Percy's "transcendent" perspective on southern culture led him neither to resistance nor to withdrawal, but rather to *engagement* with his own milieu. Finally, Brinkmeyer does not emphasize the fact that Percy's conversion had no relation to the experience of literary modernism that informed Tate and Gordon's movement toward the Church.

apparently radical differences between Percy's and O'Connor's own fictions in terms of style and character, they are fundamentally similar in their setting in the postwar South and in sharing what Thomas Merton called an "existential insistence on grace as event, as an ever-renewed encounter with God and one's fellow man *now,* in present reality. . . ." It is precisely their common refusal to "evade the present and fly from it into a safe and static past, preserved . . . in a realm of ideal essences"—or even to *consider the real possibility of* such a past at all—that distinguishes O'Connor and Percy from both the Tates and southern modernists in general (a group that might include figures as diverse as Faulkner, Jean Toomer, and Katherine Anne Porter).[3] Herein lies the nature of their most fundamental contribution to southern letters, one that is inherently bound up with their peculiar vision as highly educated and self-aware Catholic artists in the postwar South.

RICHARD KING has written that "aside from such intellectuals as T. S. Eliot and Henry Adams, the South . . . has clearly been the *locus classicus* of Catonist intellectuals. Pessimistic about the future, the Catonist looks with longing toward a past heroic age. In Nietzsche's terms he is a despairing 'monumentalist'" who longs to repeat the past though he realizes that this is impossible.[4] King outlines this rubric specifically in regard to a thinker we have already considered: William Alexander Percy, the Mississippi planter who would have been glad to see himself associated with Cato (the Roman aristocrat who—in a manner all too familiar to the Percys—killed himself after his conservative cause collapsed). Yet King further suggests the appeal of the Catonist view to Allen Tate, who finally found the southern "heroic age" inadequate and whose movement toward the Catholic Church can be understood at least partially as a search for a more satisfactory mythology.

It is difficult to analyze succinctly Allen Tate's relationship with the Catholic Church, not because of a shortage of material, but because of a surplus. Although Tate did not formally join the Church until 1950, he had at that

3. Thomas Merton, "The Other Side of Despair: Notes on Christian Existentialism," *Critic* 24 (October–November 1965): 22. Merton's definition of Christian existentialism draws directly on O'Connor's work but uses language reminiscent of Percy at a time when Merton was corresponding with him (see further discussion of this essay in subsequent text).

4. Richard King, *A Southern Renaissance: The Cultural Awakening of the American South, 1930–1955* (New York: Oxford University Press, 1980), 90–1.

time been moving toward it for a quarter century. John Gould Fletcher, who met Tate in 1927, later observed that Tate "had by instinct always been a Roman Catholic"; but if so, a great deal of intellectual work was necessary to move his thought in line with his instinct, and Tate's essays from the mid-1920s on bear witness to this struggle.[5] Tate was finally a programmatic social—even political—thinker and cultural critic as much as a poet and literary critic.[6] His central artistic concern was with formulating and practicing an aesthetic appropriate to the fallen modern culture that he concerned himself with both in his essays and his poetry. Hence his longstanding attraction to and emulation of T. S. Eliot not only as literary critic and poet but also as cultural critic, and hence his appropriate placement in the modernist milieu of Eliot, W. B. Yeats, and Ezra Pound, all of whom ruminated on the fragments of Western culture in the twentieth century while casting a backward glance toward a former era of wholeness. Tate's sentiment "that the modern age lacked an overarching myth by which to order itself" suggests his essential kinship with these poets.[7] He is distinguished from them primarily in his particular fixation on the culture of the Old South (as opposed to, for example, Yeats's on that of Celtic Ireland), which steadily broadened to include that of all European civilization. Even in his conversion it can be argued that he remained essentially the literary modernist, seeing an idealized version of medieval European society as a basis for social order and Catholic theology as the basis for a universal aesthetic—as did Caroline Gordon, though her social concerns were never expressed as discursively as those of her husband. This claim seems particularly plausible upon examination of the well-documented development of Tate's intellectual concerns—which, to oversimplify a bit, generally progressed from artistic to social to religious—and is crucial in distinguishing his Catholic vision from that of Percy and O'Connor.

Tate has been said to possess the greatest sheer intellect among all the

5. Radcliffe Squires, *Allen Tate: A Literary Biography* (New York: Pegasus, 1971), 94.

6. Hence Tate's prominent place in Eugene Genovese, *The Southern Tradition: The Achievements and Limitations of an American Conservatism* (Cambridge, MA: Harvard University Press, 1994), a study of the political tradition espoused by the Agrarians, Richard Weaver, and M. E. Bradford. The names of Percy and O'Connor are conspicuously, and appropriately, absent, despite Genovese's frequent comparison of "southern conservative" critiques of capitalism to those offered by the Catholic Church.

7. Brinkmeyer, 8.

writers associated with the Agrarian movement, and any brief attempt to do justice to the scope of his thought regarding literature, culture, and religion is bound to be inadequate. But taking his early years at Vanderbilt among the Fugitives as a given (and even there he was forcing the elder John Crowe Ransom and Donald Davidson to confront the cosmopolitan currents of literary modernism in a manner not altogether to their taste), it is crucial to remember that Tate leapt more fully into the intellectual and social milieu of American and European modernism than any other writer of the Southern Renascence. As an undergraduate at Vanderbilt in 1922, he was reading T. S. Eliot, corresponding with Hart Crane, and chafing at the limits of his southern milieu, as indicated when he wrote to a little magazine that he was twenty-two and lived in Nashville, "of which two facts . . . the latter is perhaps the more damning."[8] From 1924 to 1928, together with his new wife Caroline Gordon, he was living in New York in the close company of Crane and other prominent literati. From 1928 to 1930 he ventured even farther afield, living in Paris and meeting Eliot, Ernest Hemingway, F. Scott Fitzgerald, Gertrude Stein, Ford Madox Ford, and others. He was attuned to the prevailing revolutionary techniques and often despairing cultural sentiments of the great literary modernists as none of his Nashville colleagues were (though he did bring something of Vanderbilt to Paris with him; he interpreted all reports about the wasteland of the modern West in the light of his excellent classical education, one that Eliot himself praised in observing that such was, regrettably, no longer available at Harvard).[9] As a result of this period of intellectual formation, Tate, more fully than any other member of the Agrarians, brought the larger context of Western civilization (larger both geographically and chronologically) to the "southern" problems his Nashville colleagues later considered.

During his formative period in the 1920s, Tate not only wrote his own poetry but also largely made his living from freelance reviews, and he immersed himself in the literature of the day. In his essays of this period, primarily literary criticism, we see recurring ideas on art, culture, and finally religion that support one another and which are usually not explicitly connected with

8. Quoted in Squires, 38.

9. Louise Cowan, *The Fugitive Group: A Literary History* (Baton Rouge: Louisiana State University Press, 1959), 33.

the South, though they were repeated in that context in Tate's later Agrarian period (Tate finally wrote even "Ode to the Confederate Dead" in New York, then traveled to Paris on a Guggenheim fellowship only to write a biography of Jefferson Davis; he carried his regional heritage with him wherever he went).

Robert Brinkmeyer has claimed that even "by the early 1920s . . . three important traditions had surfaced in Tate's life: Old South order and community, Roman Catholicism, and Modernism."[10] But it seems more accurate to say that literary modernism was his dominant concern, finally shaping his vision of both his native South and, in a perhaps unforeseen way, the Church he eventually joined (Brinkmeyer bases his claim about Tate's early religious concern only on the one year he spent at a Catholic parochial school in Washington). Tate, who had been raised by a Laodicean mother and a free-thinking father, primarily concerned himself in the 1920s with formulating and practicing the proper aesthetic for modern poetry; for example, his first published essay, "Whose Ox," in the fourth issue of the *Fugitive,* tentatively suggests that traditional and modern modes can coexist in the twentieth century.[11] This literary concern later led him to cultural criticism and, ultimately, to religious questions. Such a starting point for moving toward the Catholic faith was radically different, as we have seen, from that of Percy, and it was even more alien to O'Connor's experience as a "cradle" Catholic.

Peter A. Huff has traced Tate's search for what the poet himself called "the right kind of modernism" in matters both literary and social and found in his writings a clear debt to T. S. Eliot. Huff argues that Tate was inspired by Eliot's *The Sacred Wood* (1920), the collection of critical essays that included "Tradition and the Individual Talent," to "embark on what amounted to a lifelong crusade against the Emersonian-Whitmanian cult of expressionism in literature—the popular notion that art is the expression of an artist's emotions."[12] One paradigmatic assault in this "crusade," it seems to me, occurs in Tate's essay "Hart Crane" (which O'Connor later admired [*HB*, 149, 178]). Here Tate derides the lingering nineteenth-century romanticism he saw em-

10. Brinkmeyer, 6.

11. Squires, 15–16, 45.

12. Peter A. Huff, *Allen Tate and the Catholic Revival: Trace of the Fugitive Gods* (New York: Paulist Press, 1996), 35.

bodied in the work of his friend, deeming it not only inappropriately optimistic in its tone toward twentieth-century American culture, but also profoundly reflective of that culture's shortcomings in its "vagueness of purpose" and a "locked-in sensibility" removed from "the ordinary forms of experience."[13] It was largely in relation to his felt need for a "new emphasis on classical formalism" in literature that Tate's ideas about culture developed; like Eliot, Huff claims, Tate found that his ideas about poetry "carried distinctly social overtones. The recovery of tradition in aesthetic theory matched a search for hierarchy and order in the chaotic modern social realm."[14]

If a concern with aesthetics led Tate to a concern with culture, both pointed to an ultimate concern with religion. In his essay on Crane, for example, Tate referred to the *Divine Comedy* as the aesthetic antithesis of the romantic project of *The Bridge:* "we not only know that the subject is personal salvation, just as we know that Crane's is the greatness of America: we are given also the complete articulation of the idea down to the slightest detail, and we are given it objectively apart from anything that the poet is going to say about it." Dante's "perception" of an "idea" is only extended in relation to the concrete "groundwork" of the poem, whereas Crane's "sensibility" is fundamentally ungrounded.[15] Such an argument clearly suggests the appeal to Tate of Catholicism's sacramental vision of reality—whereby the transcendent is found in the immanent—as the basis for an aesthetic, one that he developed more fully in the years to come.

In Tate's rejection of *The Bridge* and embrace of *The Divine Comedy,* we might see implicitly the pattern of his ideas about culture as well. Whatever its form, no poem by an Ohioan singing "the greatness of [modern] America"—using the Brooklyn Bridge as a symbol, no less—could have gone over well with Tate, who was as early as 1926 inspired by New York City to write poems such as "Retroduction to American History" and "The Subway" in condemnation of the urban wasteland of the twentieth century. The inherent relationship that he sensed between the state of modern culture, most fully

13. Tate, *Essays of Four Decades* (Chicago: Swallow, 1968), 313. This essay was not published until the 1930s, but it clearly bears witness to concerns in Tate's mind during his friendship with Crane while both were actually engaged in the writing of poetry in the 1920s.

14. Huff, 36.

15. Tate, *Essays,* 316.

realized in the United States, and the problems of the modern artist was clearly suggested in his 1929 essay "Humanism and Naturalism." Here he claims that the limpid "humanism" espoused by most twentieth-century intellectuals "is not enough," and he further asserts that "if the values for which the humanist pleads are to be made rational, even intelligible, the background of an objective religion, a universal scheme of reference, is necessary." Modern culture not only is lacking in values but also threatens the realm of art—allegedly Tate's primary concern—precisely because art is not a religion:

> The humanists quarrel with literature because it cannot give them a philosophy and a church; but they keep turning to literature because they cannot find these things elsewhere. You cannot have the sense of literature without the prior, specific, and self-sufficient sense of something else. Without this you expect too much of literature; you expect of it a religion and a philosophy; and by expecting of it the wrong thing, you violate it, and in the end you get from it less than it is meant to yield; you get neither literature nor religion, nor anything that is intelligible. You destroy literature without constructing a religion.[16]

This essay was published in Eliot's *Criterion*, again suggesting Tate's essential affinity with the then newly converted Anglican poet, who, Tate confessed to Donald Davidson as early as 1925, "writes up my own ideas much better than my poor skill permits me to do for myself." But whatever the source of his ideas, Tate was seeing that his own concerns with art were bound up with a culture that seemed directionless without a religious tradition. And the tradition he was most actively investigating as "a universal scheme of reference" for culture and art alike was older even than that which Eliot had recently embraced. Although Tate stated in "Humanism and Naturalism" that "this essay urges the claim of no special religion, and it is in no sense a confession of faith," his presentation of Dante as a poetic ideal, his call for a proper sense of authority in philosophy and religion, and his remarks regarding the deleterious effects of the Reformation mark the piece as Tate's first public step toward the Roman Catholic Church. Such a step was made more explicit in his personal correspondence. "I am more and more heading towards Ca-

16. Tate, *Memoirs and Opinions, 1926–1974* (Chicago: Swallow, 1975), 190, 194.

tholicism," he wrote Davidson in 1929; "we have reached a condition of the spirit where no further compromise is possible."[17]

To Davidson's dismay, such sentiments marked Tate's contribution to the collection that largely provided the context for his cultural thought in the early 1930s: the Agrarian manifesto *I'll Take My Stand*. Tate had remained in close contact with his Vanderbilt colleagues while abroad and, upon his return to the United States in 1930, joined them in responding to the crisis they saw implicit in the national ridicule of southern culture following the 1925 Scopes trial in Tennessee. The trial and its aftermath, as Davidson said, "broke in upon our literary concerns like a midnight alarm" and precipitated for him and Ransom a shift to larger cultural concerns such as Tate underwent in Europe.[18] Tate found the old Fugitives ready to embrace a form of the social conservatism he himself was espousing, and a form with an allegedly religious underpinning, but one profoundly different from that Tate had ruminated upon in Paris:

> The Agrarians chose the new religious movement of fundamentalism as the religious symbol to embody their critique of modernity. Despite the fact that the main exponents of Agrarianism were generally unaffiliated with traditional Protestantism (and some were openly hostile to organized religion), the Agrarian movement recognized fundamentalism as a powerful mode of protest against oppressive currents in modern culture. While rejecting the world view of theistic supernaturalism, they nevertheless admitted that the fundamentalist objection to the cherished assumptions of modern America possessed a measure of moral validity.[19]

17. Ibid., 190. Also see Huff, 9. Tate to Davidson, July 8, 1925; February 18, 1929, in *The Literary Correspondence of Donald Davidson and Allen Tate*, ed. John Tyree Fain and Thomas Daniel Young (Athens: University of Georgia Press, 1974), 141, 223. Tate's increasing interest in cultural criticism generally parallels that of Eliot, who in the coming decade would write such works as *After Strange Gods: A Primer of Modern Heresy* (1934), *The Idea of a Christian Society* (1939), and *Notes toward the Definition of Christian Culture* (1940). Percy and O'Connor obviously admired certain aspects of Eliot's thought as well but never studied or embraced his social views to the degree that Tate did.

18. Donald Davidson, *Southern Writers in the Modern World* (Athens: University of Georgia Press, 1958), 40.

19. Huff, 39.

Such a claim seems borne out by the generally ambiguous place of religion in *I'll Take My Stand*. Though initially motivated by northern mockery of a "primitive" southern religiosity and in theory attracted to an old-fashioned notion of a God with "thunder" rather than a modern god without (as Ransom would have it, in his *God without Thunder* [1930]), the Agrarians were by and large not interested in endorsing any particular religious position. Ransom's "Statement of Principles" sets the tone for the general Agrarian attitude toward religious faith: the fact that "religion can hardly expect to flourish in an industrial society" is presented as just one of the many negative effects of industrialism, finally no more—and probably less—significant than the fact that the arts do not have "a proper life under industrialism, with the general decay of sensibility which attends it."[20] Ransom's own attraction to a "fundamentalist" sense of mystery is, it seems, largely a function of the desirability of a religious "sensibility" for the artist, regardless of the creed's truth. Huff has observed insightfully that "much as a poet takes on a fictive persona in the creation of lyric verse, the Agrarians borrowed the alien voice of fundamentalism in polemical prose to express their antimodern social criticism," a borrowing that "reflects the deliberate attempt of 'lost-generation' critics of modernity to foster an intellectual affinity with the ultimate outsiders in early-twentieth-century America."[21] Yet *I'll Take My Stand* in general endorsed no particular dogma, and one might go so far as to observe that it only implicitly belongs in the Judeo-Christian tradition.

Tate was less content to use religion consciously as a means to an end, as it were, and more committed to thinking through the nature of a religion that was actually "proper" both in itself and in its relation to what southern culture *should* have been, as his "Remarks on the Southern Religion" reveals. Although Brinkmeyer suggests that Tate did not join the Catholic Church in 1929 "mainly because he came to see such a step as a repudiation of his own heritage—that is, his southern identity" and "was at this point too much the provincial and too much the poet to join the Church," this essay reveals a profound attempt to think through precisely what the shortcomings of his heritage were.[22] If in "Ode to the Confederate Dead" Tate had portrayed the

20. Ransom, "Statement of Principles," in Twelve Southerners, *I'll Take My Stand* (Baton Rouge: Louisiana State University Press, 1977).

21. Huff, 40.

22. Brinkmeyer, 25.

predicament of the modern southerner who was detached from the heroic deeds of the past, here he took to task that past itself.

"Remarks on the Southern Religion" is famously dense and obscure, particularly in its half-developed use of a horse as a figure for contemplating the proper role of religion in a society; Tate's purpose in offering the analogy is to reject the twin temptations to see religion either as a utilitarian means to ordering society or as pure abstraction, as one possible myth that might be readily replaced with any other. After this problematic analogy, however, Tate is fairly straightforward in his presentation of southern society's religious shortcomings, which, as he sees it, are inevitable given its historical circumstances. Beginning with an implicitly Catholic account of the unity of faith and reason in medieval Europe, Tate locates the origins of the South in a period when the two had been separated; paradoxically, however, the South, unlike the rest of the United States, developed a social order more appropriate to the older, Catholic era than to the age in which it was founded. The Old South was "a feudal society without a feudal religion" and "stood thus for a certain stage in the disintegration of the European religion." Indeed, "its religious impulse was inarticulate simply because it tried to encompass its destiny within the terms of Protestantism," which was "in origin, a non-agrarian and trading religion; hardly a religion at all, but a result of secular ambition."[23]

Largely ignoring the concrete differences between feudal Europe and the essentially modern southern slavocracy, Tate went on to claim that despite the fact that "the South never created a fitting religion," it was in one sense "a profoundly traditional European community." It was so precisely in its unconsciousness of being severed from the European tradition. The southern mind, "simple" and "unintellectual," was unaware of its radical break with the past in the New World, whereas "in the nineteenth century New England confessed her loss of the past by being too much interested in Europe": "there is the tragedy of the 'Education of Henry Adams,' who never quite understood what he was looking for."[24] Yet, ironically, Tate is playing a southern version of Henry Adams here himself. Certainly his own approach is neither simple

23. Tate, "Remarks on the Southern Religion," in *I'll Take My Stand,* 166–8. As Huff notes, Tate's denigrating description of Protestantism here seems to owe something to Max Weber's *The Protestant Ethic and the Spirit of Capitalism.*

24. Tate, "Remarks," 168, 171–2.

nor unintellectual, and he is radically self-conscious in his own sense of severance from tradition. For this reason, despite his earlier awareness of the "danger" of perceiving religion in a utilitarian sense or of confusing it with myth, he falls prey to these very temptations himself: his remark about "creating" the proper religion, as well as his observation that the Old South "had a religious life, but it was not enough organized with a right mythology," bears witness to his own inability to discuss religion in any other terms. He himself cannot experience religious faith in the holistic manner he acknowledges as proper to the believer but instead is trying to recover "by violence" the proper tradition that he believes he and his region have been separated from by history. What is superficially an essay about religion becomes in a very real sense an essay about history and the necessity of finding the proper "myth."[25]

The essay is also a clear early example of Tate's tendency to posit medieval Europe as an ideal in both religious faith and social structure, a tendency that differentiated him from the Agrarians in their understanding of society (and, later, from Percy and O'Connor in their understanding of religion). A number of Tate's colleagues shared his concern with the South's relation to Europe, but only to a degree. Whereas Ransom and Davidson affirmed that the values of the South were in fact those of Western civilization, Tate claimed that those values were present in the southern tradition only in decayed form and had to be recovered more fully. As he wrote to Davidson in 1929, he believed that "[p]hilosophically we must go the whole hog of reaction, and base our movement less upon the actual Old South than upon its prototype—the historical social and religious scheme of Europe. We must be the last Europeans."[26] This attraction to the Old World—which entailed in Tate's mind a critique of intellectual history and social order since at least the sixteenth century—would continue to characterize his thought despite the fact that it was virtual heresy to at least some of his Agrarian colleagues. Increasingly, Tate "saw the history of the nation more in terms of a conflict between East and West than between North and South. The East, for Tate, represented the European heritage, the seat of classical-Christian values; the West embodied the unbridled impulse to explore and expand, to push back the frontier."[27] In "Remarks on

25. Ibid., 173–4.
26. Tate to Davidson, August 10, 1929, in Fain and Young, 230.
27. Brinkmeyer, 23.

the Southern Religion" Tate had reinterpreted the southern heritage that he had sometimes seen as the possible source of mythic inspiration in light of this new orientation, as a locus where the "East" endured in the New World, but only in a profoundly problematic manner. In doing so, he bordered on undermining the entire Agrarian project.

Though he never followed Eliot's example and left America for good, Tate briefly returned to Europe in 1932 (Gordon had won a Guggenheim) and there resumed writing poems, including one of his best, "The Mediterranean." This meditation upon Aeneas's quest to found a new society that carries on the traditions of vanquished Troy obviously reflects the cultural themes that were uppermost in Tate's mind. Though "We've cracked the hemispheres with careless hand!" the speaker passes through "the Gates of Hercules" and

> Westward, westward, till the barbarous brine
> Whelms us to the tired land where tasseling corn,
> Fat beans, grapes sweeter than muscadine
> Rot on the vine: that land where we were born.[28]

In this most actively political period of Tate's life, such overtly European interests continued to bear fruit that often distinguished him from his Nashville colleagues. Tate was strongly attracted to the English Distributist movement, which, led by such Catholic intellectuals as G. K. Chesterton and Hillaire Belloc, presented anti-industrialist arguments similar to those of the Agrarians and was chief organizer of the 1936 joint Agrarian-Distributist publication *Who Owns America? A New Declaration of Independence*. In the 1930s, Tate increasingly found such Catholic forms of social thought, including that of the Catholic Worker movement led by Dorothy Day, whom Tate and Gordon had known in New York prior to her conversion, more attractive than southern forms.[29]

In part this attraction might be interpreted as a continuation of the impulses made evident in Tate's earliest European literary sojourns. As Paul Giles has noted in a study of literary modernism and American writers of Catholic persuasion, such writers might easily sense "the links between the universalist impulse of the Catholic Church and the internationalist impulse of modern-

28. Tate, *Poems, 1922–1947* (New York: Scribner's, 1948), 4, lines 31–6.
29. See Huff, 64–71.

ism" while, conversely, "modernism's hostility to the notion of separatist provincial culture could be seen as a correlative to Catholicism's universalist subversion of the idea of national identity."[30] "The Profession of Letters in the South" (1935) supports this observation, for here Tate specifically suggests his problems with the particular "provincial" culture in which the Agrarians based their critique of modern capitalism. And, again, in doing so he points to medieval Europe as a social ideal. In the Old South, he claims, "the distance between white master and black slave was unalterably greater than that between white master and white serf after the destruction of feudalism. The peasant *is* the soil. The Negro slave was a barrier between the ruling class and the soil. . . . All great cultures have been rooted in peasantries, in free peasantries, I believe, such as the English yeomanry before the fourteenth century: they have been the growth of the soil." Despite his continuing interest in such cultural criticism, Tate was by the mid-1930s not only more explicitly dissatisfied with the southern tradition than before but also growing wary of overt political activism generally. He warned at the end of "The Profession of Letters in the South" that presently "the prevailing economic passion of the age once more tempts, even commands, the southern writer to go into politics"—but this can "become a pretext for ignoring the arts."[31]

When Tate himself focused on the arts during this period, he articulated an aesthetic that showed a deepening affinity with Catholicism. For example, in the preface to *Reactionary Essays on Poetry and Ideas* (1936), Tate speaks of poetry as "the art of apprehending and concentrating our experience in the mysterious limitations of form." Giles sees such a perspective, with its emphasis on *mystery,* as standing "in sharp contrast to that of traditional classical humanism, which associates formal control with what is eminently knowable and so susceptible to human reason." In this sense the statement represents a progression in Tate's aesthetic views, reflecting not only his consistently antiromantic concern with form but also a seemingly antithetical concern

30. Paul A. Giles, *American Catholic Arts and Fictions: Culture, Ideology, Aesthetics* (New York: Cambridge University Press, 1992), 121. In Tate's later essay "The New Provincialism" (1945), he attacked a "picturesque" but shallow "regionalism of local color" as "a mere byproduct of nationalism," demonstrating his own ongoing participation in the internationalist impulses Giles speaks of. *Essays,* 536. In Tate's case, at least, such impulses were finally chronologically as well as geographically "universalist."

31. Tate, *Essays,* 525, 534.

with mystery, a significant component of what Giles calls Tate's "analogical imagination," one that reflects a sacramental conception of reality.[32] In Tate's case this imagination was shaped profoundly, beginning in the 1930s, by the thinkers of the Catholic Revival.

For Tate's attraction to the Catholic Church must finally be understood not merely as an attraction to the reactionary social and political forms with which it was popularly associated (and as the Catholic Worker movement, which in American political terms was radically liberal, illustrates, such associations were themselves oversimplified), but rather as an engagement with a seemingly all-encompassing and unified philosophical system that stood in marked contrast to the apparent intellectual disorder of the day. It was, furthermore, a system that was newly vigorous in the early part of the twentieth century, though not immediately so in the United States. Tate was in fact first exposed to the cultural fruits of a revitalized European Catholicism as early as the 1920s, during his Guggenheim stay in Paris, where (when not writing on Jefferson Davis) he read such recent and contemporary Catholic literary lights as Charles Péguy, Léon Bloy, and François Mauriac.[33] The imaginative possibilities he glimpsed in their work, like the social structures he associated with Catholicism, were appealing to Tate but seemingly lacked a more comprehensive philosophical underpinning—or at least one that had been articulated in terms appealing to the twentieth-century mind. He would wait another decade to find such a philosophy. As Huff has observed, Tate was "already Catholic in spirit by the 1930s," but had he "not discovered the enticing system of Neo-Thomism, his interest in Catholicism would have remained perverse spiritual flirtation."[34] One of the primary architects of this new articulation of the philosophy of Thomas Aquinas, Jacques Maritain, later crossed the Atlantic himself and met the exiled southerner in Princeton. Fittingly, when Tate finally joined the Church in 1950, the Frenchman served as his godfather—for the philosopher had in fact been guiding the poet toward the Church for more than a decade. Maritain's ideas about literature, expressed

32. Ibid., 613; Giles, 195. Such views later resonated with O'Connor, not only in her essays but also in such formally rigorous yet profoundly mysterious stories as "Greenleaf."

33. Tate, Memoirs, 50.

34. Huff, 72.

in such works as *Art and Scholasticism* (1930), confirmed Tate's earliest instincts about poetic form, provided him with the "universal scheme of reference" he longed for, and finally convinced him to join the Church whose seemingly moribund tradition he had long admired from afar.

Tate's encounter with the Catholic Revival in the middle decades of the century, though it must be understood in concert with the ongoing intellectual concerns already discussed here, raises the question of the nature and effects of the Revival in general, which directly involves Percy and O'Connor as well and for that reason is best deferred until they have been introduced into this milieu. First, however, Caroline Gordon's movement toward the Church should be briefly considered. Her conversion is in itself no less important than Tate's, of course, but there is simply less of a written record of her interest in the Catholic Church prior to her 1947 conversion, especially in comparison with the "Catholic" theory of fiction she vigorously outlined in following years, partially in communication with O'Connor and Percy. Whatever attraction she had to the Catholic Church before that time was simply not a matter of public record, making it both less accessible to the scholar and less potentially influential on her two protégés.

Precisely for this reason Gordon's conversion seems at once simpler and less readily explicable than Tate's. She shared his history as a child of the turn-of-the-century Upper South and as an exiled literary modernist in New York and Europe. The two romans à clef she wrote following her conversion, *The Strange Children* (1951) and *The Malefactors* (1956), suggest the subdued sense of anguish she felt during those years, the latter in particular as it chronicles the experience of a married couple whose bohemian years in Europe have left them unfulfilled. But even her earlier works had focused on figures attempting to find a suitable code for living in a decaying world—specifically, the historical South. As one study of Gordon's work has noted, her "five early novels— *Green Centuries* (1941), *Penhally* (1931), *None Shall Look Back* (1937), *Aleck Maury, Sportsman* (1934), and *The Garden of Adonis* (1937)—can be ordered to show the decline of southern society and culture from the mid–eighteenth century to the Depression," and each illustrates that "in every age there are few who become heroes and none whose heroism is uncomplicated by some selfish motive or by pride." The stoic code advocated by Gordon during this period might be compared to that of Hemingway; the supreme example of such heroism is, appropriately, the southern outdoorsman, Aleck Maury.[35] In the representative short story "The Last Day in the Field" (perhaps Gordon's best-known), an aging Maury continues to hunt despite the onset of illness and intimations of coming death. That the shortcomings of such a code, its final pessimism, eventually disposed Gordon to search for something more is, it seems, not an implausible claim.

Despite her interest in southern historical settings and her constant self-identification with her native region, Gordon was never a programmatic social thinker like her husband and steadfastly avoided his forays into "politics." When she and Tate were living in Tennessee in the 1930s, "Gordon could not take Tate's Agrarianism very seriously and could not but speak of the Agrarians (who often visited the farm and whom she often referred to in her letters to Sally Wood as 'the boys') in a vein of jest."[36] The rigorous cultural criticism and longing for a "proper" social order that characterized her husband's thought was never of central concern to her. Later in the 1930s, Gordon's reaction to the recently converted "lost generation" bohemian whom she had originally known in Greenwich Village in the 1920s is indicative of this essential difference: "The Tates each responded to Dorothy Day as they would to their conversions to Catholicism over a decade later. Allen was impressed by her theoretical grasp of the similarities between Agrarianism and the Catholic Worker movement. . . . Characteristically, Caroline seemed more interested in how Catholicism affected her character and her way of life."[37] Nonetheless, Gordon did, like her husband, show some attachment to Catholicism as an Old World religion, as indicated in her comments citing the significance of specific events in her life abroad—such as her encounter with a French "peasant woman"—in her movement toward the Church.[38] Such events are reflected in *The Malefactors*, where, despite the presence of a Dorothy Day figure, the Claibornes are presented with a very European Catholicism, one replete with French peasants and Irish priests, as they move toward conver-

35. Rose Ann C. Fraistat, *Caroline Gordon as Novelist and Woman of Letters* (Baton Rouge: Louisiana State University Press, 1984), 37–8. Also see Brinkmeyer, 73.

36. Brinkmeyer, 79.

37. Veronica Makowsky, *Caroline Gordon: A Biography* (New York: Oxford University Press, 1989), 133.

38. Waldron, 258.

sion. Indeed, much of the novel is concerned with revisiting what seem to be the Tates' own experiences with the lost generation in Europe.

Gordon's entry into the Church seems finally to have been prompted by her interaction with individual Catholics, not only with Day but also, and most importantly, with other artists. The example of Eliot as "Anglo-Catholic" had been set for some time, of course, but in the 1940s more examples were to follow. She and Tate spent the winter of 1942–3 in Monteagle, Tennessee (not far from a cabin owned by the Percy family), with Robert Lowell and Jean Stafford, "in the period of Lowell's greatest fervor, soon after his conversion to Catholicism."[39] In the wake of World War II a number of other American writers followed Lowell into the flock, and when Gordon began seriously to contemplate joining the Church in 1947, she did so as a "literary" convert: she arranged a meeting with Robert Fitzgerald, then living with his wife Sally in New York City, saying that "she had decided to become a Catholic and wanted to talk to a Catholic writer."[40] Her desire to do so signaled the direction her thought would take in the years to come, linking her faith with literary aesthetics. In retrospect she described her conversion in such terms: "I am a Catholic, I suspect, because I was first a fiction writer. If I hadn't worked at writing fiction for so many years I doubt if I'd have made it into the Church, but working at writing fiction all those years taught me how god-like a trade it is. We are actually trying to do what God did: make our word flesh and make it live among men."[41] The Joycean resonance in this comment is unmistakable and strongly suggests the view of "Catholic" fiction that Gordon would articulate in the years to come. Even if Joyce—or, more precisely, Stephen Dedalus—had gotten the "jesuit strain . . . injected the wrong way," as Buck Mulligan put it in *Ulysses*, his image in *A Portrait of the Artist as a Young Man* of the writer as "a priest of eternal imagination, transmuting the daily bread of experience into the radiant body of everliving life" provided a worthy model that Gordon and Tate alike later drew on in their attempt to synthesize a modernist literary sensibility with their newfound faith.

It is possible to view their decision to do so through a political lens. Thomas Haddox has recently argued that Tate's and Gordon's conversions

39. Makowsky, 176.
40. Waldron, 257.
41. Ibid., 259.

should be understood as "part of a deliberately 'southern' literary and theoretical strategy" that was "prompted in large part by the failure of Agrarian politics." Claiming that the clear establishment of industrial capitalism in the South after 1945 drove the Agrarians to take refuge in English departments, "where, as New Critics, they sought to preserve their authority and their ideology through the construction of a southern literary canon," he portrays the Tates as following a slightly different path: "[N]either Tate nor Gordon abandoned the 'resistance' of a southern identity when they migrated to Catholicism. On the contrary, they suggested that they were better able to realize an Agrarian artistic vision because they did not confuse religion with history or myth. Their work constitutes an alternative to the New Critical retreat into the universities, an attempt to preserve the iconicity of southern literature beyond all historical change by investing it with the authority of an absolutist faith." Although I do not share Haddox's overarching political approach, he is right in his claim that Tate and Gordon's postconversion notions of "Catholic" literature must be understood in light of their connections to Agrarian social thought and the essentially modernist aesthetic ideals that came to be associated with the New Criticism. He is certainly right to refrain from considering Percy in this light. But his subsequent claim that "O'Connor's achievement is best seen as part of this [political] effort to base southern literature on a[n apparently] transcendent foundation" is, I believe, fundamentally incorrect.[42] I take O'Connor at her word when she "reversed" Gordon's statement about the relationship between faith and fiction: whereas Gordon claimed that she became a Catholic because she was an artist, O'Connor claimed, "because I am a Catholic I cannot afford to be less than an artist" (*MM*, 146).

But the fundamental distinctions that must be made among the Catholic imaginations of O'Connor, Percy, Tate, and Gordon can only be made in the context of the intellectual milieu that all four shared as informed religious thinkers in the postwar era. For this reason we must briefly consider the nature of the Catholic Revival, its leading thinkers, and the degree of their influence on these four writers as a necessary prelude to the question of their

42. Thomas Haddox, "Contextualizing Flannery O'Connor: Allen Tate, Caroline Gordon, and the Catholic Turn in Southern Literature," *Southern Quarterly* 38:1 (Fall 1999): 173–4. Haddox specifically takes issue with Brinkmeyer's portrayal of Tate's, Gordon's, and Percy's "struggles with modernity and faith only as individual attempts to discover how to live."

final relationship with one another and their places in southern literary history.

FIRST, THE TERM *Catholic Revival* itself demands more accurate definition. Intellectual historians have characterized the revitalized Catholic culture of late-nineteenth- and early-twentieth-century France, Germany, and England as the "Catholic Renaissance" or the "Catholic Revival" in Europe; in an American context, the term refers more precisely to what Arnold Sparr has labeled the "Catholic literary revival" of 1920–60. The latter phenomenon, of course, drew heavily upon European sources, not only literary but also philosophical and theological. Sparr locates the height of the revival in the United States during 1940–55, crediting it largely to the post-1935 impact on American Catholic intellectuals of contemporary European thinkers, specifically Jacques Maritain, Etienne Gilson, and others forging the "neo-scholastic synthesis" that "creatively adapted the thought of Thomas Aquinas to modern times."[43] Their writings laid the foundations for an approach to literature that influenced committed Catholic writers and literary critics at midcentury, many of whom were converts. There was indeed what Anne Waldron has called a "boomlet" in Catholicism after World War II, and in certain circles it was almost "chic" to join the Church: prominent national figures such as Henry Ford II and Clare Booth Luce joined the "literary" converts, which included Heywood Broun and Frances Parkinson Keyes as well as Stafford, Lowell, Merton, Gordon, and Tate.[44]

These distinctions may help to clarify some of the observations made previously: while Tate may have admired some of the fiction writers of the Renouveau Catholique in 1920s Paris, it took the newly articulated neo-Thomist philosophy he read in America in the late 1930s and 1940s to finally lead him into the Church. Furthermore, he and Gordon developed a close friendship with Maritain and his wife, beginning at Princeton in the late 1940s; for this reason alone it is plausible to call Maritain the single greatest influence on the Tates' postconversion thought. O'Connor and Percy were similarly en-

43. Arnold Sparr, *To Promote, Defend, and Redeem: The Catholic Literary Revival and the Cultural Transformation of American Catholicism, 1920–1960* (New York: Greenwood Press, 1990), xi–xiii.

44. Waldron, 257–8. See also Kieran Quinlan, *Walker Percy: The Last Catholic Novelist* (Baton Rouge: Louisiana State University Press, 1996), 36 and passim.

thralled by this Frenchman's work. O'Connor called *Art and Scholasticism* "the book I cut my aesthetic teeth on"; Percy drew heavily on Maritain—whom Jay Tolson calls "the living philosopher [Percy] most admired"—in writing his own essays on language in the 1950s. Maritain's work is in fact the single most significant common influence on all four writers both aesthetically—insofar as each attempted to articulate a "theory of fiction," or even of language itself, that was consonant with neo-Thomism—and perhaps even thematically, especially with regard to his concept of "angelism" as a behavioral peculiarity of the modern era.[45]

To some degree O'Connor and Percy drew upon Maritain by way of Tate and Gordon, but in the main they read and interpreted him on their own, coming to him as they did with backgrounds and concerns that were finally very different from those of the older couple. Such would shape not only their reaction to the neo-Thomists but also their reading of other Catholic Revival writers who did not directly influence the Tates, the theologian Romano Guardini and various thinkers articulating a Christian approach to existentialism in particular. O'Connor and Percy's differences with their mentors were borne out in the character of their fiction in the coming decades, which brilliantly captured the postwar South even as the exiled Tates' literary output declined.

It is, for example, not unreasonable to categorize Tate's interest in Maritain as at least partly a function not only of his purely philosophical and artistic interest in formulating an aesthetic but also of his long-established interest in a proper social order. For the neo-Thomists could be read both as philosophers addressing eternal truths and as historically inclined propagandists for the lost order of the medieval world. Kieran Quinlan has observed with regard to Maritain, Gilson, and Christopher Dawson that "T. S. Eliot had long sympathized with their thought, particularly with their nostalgia for the lost cultural and religious unity of the European Middle Ages," and, as we have already seen, Tate was likewise inclined to such sentiments.[46]

Paul Giles takes this observation one step further and provocatively claims that "the idealization of the medieval order by Maritain, Gilson, and other

---

45. See O'Connor, *HB*, 216; Jay Tolson, *Pilgrim in the Ruins: A Life of Walker Percy* (New York: Simon and Schuster, 1992), 244. See chapter 3 here for more regarding Maritain's influence.
46. Quinlan, 39.

Catholic scholars at this time can be seen as a counterpart to the idealized utopias concocted by Yeats, Eliot, and Pound" in its attempt to postulate "an imaginative (not to say fanciful) global synthesis." In this way "neo-scholasticism eventually came to offer its own parallel version of [literary] modernism" to Tate, who was thereby presented with vast imaginative resources not only for literary purposes but also for taking the measure of the twentieth century.[47] Huff's assessment of Tate in 1958 seems to support this view:

> Like Maritain, he invested medieval society with paradigmatic status and appropriated from it criteria for the criticism of modern culture. Though he repeatedly denied that his admiration for the Middle Ages entailed reversion to an ideal past, he shared the Catholic Revival's affection for the period and used it as the reference point for discussion of a restored Christian civilization. The organic unity of the culture, the agrarian pattern of its economy, and the common mythic structure shaping its vision were stock features of the Revival's interpretation of the Middle Ages, but they appealed to the same instincts in Tate that drove him to reject much of what he found mediocre and destabilizing in modern culture. For most of his career, Dante figured as the icon of the fully developed artist in Christian society, and the medieval university served as his model for the understanding of genuine religious humanism.[48]

Such an explanation for Tate's conversion, considering it essentially continuous with his earlier modernist tendencies as cultural critic, perhaps does not do justice to his personal struggles in moving toward the Catholic faith, but it certainly seems at least partially convincing in light of the public writings that reveal his interest in the Church as a source of social order. As Giles notes, Tate maintained such latently political sentiments despite the fact that the Vatican actually condemned such thinking—using medieval Catholicism as a "metaphor" for ordering society—as heretical.[49] On the other hand,

47. Giles, 123, 207.

48. Huff, 31.

49. See Giles, 124, 200–1. Maritain himself had been marred in the Church's eyes by his brief association in the 1920s with the *Action Française* movement to restore the French monarchy; Pope Pius XI excommunicated the movement's leader, Charles Maurras, an agnostic who used nostalgia for Catholic order to his purposes, in 1926. Yet Tate continued to express admiration for Maurras's "historical insight" into the value of Catholicism as late as 1950, in his contribution to a symposium titled "Religion and the Intellectuals" in *Partisan Review* 17:3 (March 1950): 250.

Giles's claim does not fully account for Tate's interest in the Catholic sacramental imagination as literary resource. As we shall see, he and Gordon alike would in their postconversion years elaborate discursively on that imagination, though again in terms that often echoed their long-standing concerns as literary modernists, and to some degree they would impart their understanding of it to Percy and O'Connor.

But Percy and O'Connor were finally thinkers of a very different order from the Tates. Chapter 1 emphasized the extent to which O'Connor and Percy approached their faith in a radically personal manner and to some extent independently of the "chic" intellectual milieu that Tate and Gordon moved in so confidently. As a young Catholic girl, O'Connor had seen the hand of God in the death of her father; though her faith was bolstered and integrated with her vocation as artist by the writers of the Revival, it was lived before it was thought through or applied to her art. And Percy, as Jay Tolson has noted, came to the Church by a far "more idiosyncratic and peculiar path than that of the literary converts"; the questions the young doctor struggled with were first worked out in the isolation of his sanatorium in the Adirondacks, where he read Aquinas not under the instruction of a French philosopher but in preparation for debate with Arthur Fortugno, a Catholic "college boy" from Jersey City, New Jersey, "a likeable companion but a feisty debater well-versed in Catholic apologetics."[50]

Accordingly, the radical faith they came to was professed in neither literary nor social terms, as when O'Connor wrote, "for me the meaning of life is centered in our redemption by Christ and what I see in the world I see in its relation to that" (MM, 32). And surely such a sentiment underlies Percy's description in Lost in the Cosmos of a man who chooses not to commit suicide and is thereby free to contemplate "the comic mystery" of his own existence, even to accept the "preposterous eventuality that news did come from the God of the Cosmos, who took pity on your ridiculous plight and entered the time and space of your insignificant planet to tell you something" (78). Though O'Connor and Percy might occasionally make passing reference to

50. Tolson, 171, 174. Tolson explicitly describes Percy as quite different from the "literary converts" on 198. Quinlan, by contrast, is at pains to emphasize that Percy's decision to convert "was by no means unique . . . his was simply one of a 'tidal wave' of conversions among writers and intellectuals" (36).

the wholeness of the Middle Ages—usually by way of explaining their own reticence in writing a "celebratory" twentieth-century Catholic literature—statements such as these reveal the extent to which they saw the Catholic faith as profoundly personal and contemporary, in a manner not readily apparent in most of Tate's work. They were not primarily intellectuals in search of a "tradition" or an aesthetic theory. They were believers first and artists second, both in biographical fact and in mature self-perception.

Such inclinations marked their reading of the Catholic Revival thinkers, which they did in the relative isolation of Milledgeville and Covington, far from the academic centers of intellectual ferment—not infrequently northern or midwestern—frequented by the nomadic Tates. As Percy remarked with regard to O'Connor, Faulkner, and Poe, such isolated southern locales are "Crusoe's island for a writer and there's the good and bad of it"; their very "lack of a literary community" and tradition "makes for great originals" (*SSL,* 402). Percy became such an original himself, however, partly through his reading of many of the same authors preferred by O'Connor. And whereas Tate and Gordon were rather set in their ways as writers at this time and necessarily drew upon the Revival in relation to their earlier thought, Percy and O'Connor were more amenable to new influences, truly establishing the foundations of their intellectual interests in their at times idiosyncratic readings of Revival thinkers.

O'Connor gave a relevant account of her own rediscovery of her native faith in a letter to fellow southern writer Cecil Dawkins (who was also raised Catholic) about the difficulties of connecting with the Church's intellectual tradition when one is in a lonely parish in Georgia or Alabama: "Anyway, to discover the Church you have to set out by yourself. The French Catholic novelists were a great help to me in this—Bloy, Bernanos, Mauriac. In philosophy, Gilson, Maritain, and Gabriel Marcel, an Existentialist. They all seemed to be French for a while and then I discovered the Germans—Max Picard, Romano Guardini and Karl Adam. The Americans seem just to be producing pamphlets for the back of the Church (to be avoided at all costs) and installing heating systems—though there are a few good sources like *Thought,* a quarterly published at Fordham . . ." (*HB,* 231). This statement provides a good overview of some of the authors preferred by both O'Connor and Percy. He was not so taken with the earlier French novelists as she was, but like O'Connor he often expressed a preference for European fiction writers, whom both considered to have a generally more mature religious understanding than American writers (both, for example, had the highest regard for the Orthodox Dostoyevsky). More important is their mutual admiration of not only Maritain and Gilson but also Marcel, whose engagement in both philosophy and literature—so appealing to Percy—was typical of the existentialists, even though his interpretation of the movement most often associated with the unbelieving Sartre and Camus was distinctively Christian. And the German theologian Guardini was virtually revered by both writers throughout their careers (Percy referring to his continuing influence, on *The Second Coming*, as late as 1983).[51] A strong interest in the work of these latter thinkers would most clearly differentiate O'Connor and Percy from the Tates in their reading of the Catholic Revival: the existentialists encouraged each of the younger authors to focus intently— and virtually ahistorically—on the situation of the radically free individual self in an often apparently absurd world, while Guardini imparted to O'Connor and Percy alike a specifically Catholic understanding of the predicament of the lonely believer in the post-Christian era that he saw beginning with "the end of the modern world" in the wake of World War II.

I expand upon this claim in the two chapters that follow, but a brief overview of these different ways of reading the Revival seems appropriate here. Ralph Wood, a distinguished Protestant scholar of religion and literature with a long-standing interest in both Percy and O'Connor, has given an insightful assessment of O'Connor's reaction to the main Catholic Revival thinkers through his examination of the nearly one hundred book reviews she wrote for her small diocesan newspaper between 1956 and 1964, an assessment that succinctly addresses the issues I am concerned with here. Wood argues persuasively that O'Connor's reviews finally "imply a certain critical distance from the central Catholic tradition of Thomistic humanism."[52] Although she "acclaims Jacques Maritain's *The Range of Reason* for its insistence that faith and rationality do not contradict one another" and generally "assents to the Thomistic thesis that finite reason can attain a certain knowledge of the Infinite when it carefully examines the created world," O'Connor is finally not as

51. *Conversations with Walker Percy*, ed. Lewis A. Lawson and Victor A. Kramer (Jackson: University Press of Mississippi, 1985), 280.

52. Ralph Wood, "The Heterodoxy of Flannery O'Connor's Book Reviews," *Flannery O'Connor Bulletin* (1976): 4.

comfortable as Maritain in espousing such "delicately poised Catholic human-ism" (14). Rather, "she seems finally to have regarded the modern secular world as spiritually too moribund a place ever to be resuscitated by an infusion of well-tempered Catholic humanism" (4). For this reason she ultimately pre-ferred the vision of Guardini (though Wood finally considers him a classic Christian humanist as well), "for in his work she detects a salutary tension between traditional certainties and modern perplexities" (15).

Whereas Maritain was apt to point to the medieval mind as having achieved a wholeness that might be recovered if the modern world would only listen to reason—albeit a reason more broadly conceived than the post-Enlightenment West was generally comfortable with—Guardini held a bleaker vision of the difficulties of attaining such wholeness in the twentieth century. As O'Connor herself wrote of his *Prayer in Practice:* "He discusses the problem of those whose faith is so insufficient that they cannot pray with sincerity. His concerns are very much for the problems of modern man, in whom faith is often no more than a possibility. It is, in part, the realization of the modern condition that makes all of Monsignor Guardini's work so vital." Furthermore, O'Connor claims, "one feels that these difficulties are [Guardini's] own, that he does not stand on a height above the modern mind, that his is the modern mind coping with its own agonizing problems but infused with grace."[53] Like Percy and O'Connor themselves, Guardini knew the difficulties of achieving real Christian belief in the twentieth century and addressed this issue in terms focused on the predicament of the individual.

Although Wood does not explicitly address this issue, I would contend that what he identifies as O'Connor's sense that "something more radical [than Catholic humanism] was required—a darker reading of human misery, a more startling revelation of transcendent hope" explains not only her attrac-tion to Guardini but also her engagement with the existentialists.[54] That en-gagement has not yet been as extensively acknowledged as it might be, but Thomas Merton's claim that "no other American writer . . . has made a more devastating use of existentialist intuitions" than O'Connor is persuasive enough to merit further recognition and investigation. Placing her work at

---

53. Flannery O'Connor, *The Presence of Grace and Other Book Reviews,* comp. Leo J. Zuber, ed. Carter W. Martin (Athens: University of Georgia Press, 1983), 53, 17.

54. Wood, 4.

the center of his 1965 essay "The Other Side of Despair: Notes on Christian Existentialism"—itself in part an attempt to define Christian existentialism—Merton chastises unnamed traditionalist theologians for immediately writing off all existential thought as heresy, then proceeds to discuss the possible virtues of the movement by pointing to the fiction of O'Connor. He affirms that Tarwater's argument with Rayber in *The Violent Bear It Away* presents "the existentialist case against the scientism and sociologism of positivist society. It is a brief for the person and for personal, spiritual liberty against determinism and curtailment," whereas Rayber reduces the human being to a "function." Existentialism is valuable to the Christian thinker, Merton argues, precisely because in considering the human being, it raises the question of *"who"* as opposed to not only the positivist *"how"* but also the metaphysical *"what"* of traditional Thomism.[55] Merton goes on to provide an overview of the worthy focus on the individual—particularly on the isolated and alienated individual in contemporary society—found in the work of all the major existential thinkers, even as he affirms that a truly Christian existentialism must not embrace such isolation as the ultimate destiny of humanity.

Merton's intuition here is supported by evidence in O'Connor's letters and elsewhere as to specific existential influences. Her reading of Kierkegaard, the nineteenth-century Danish Protestant who has been considered the progenitor of existentialism, was certainly never so rigorous as Percy's; but her relationship to the French playwright and philosopher Marcel, a profound influence on Percy, is another story. Percy himself seemed to sense some affinity between the two, claiming that O'Connor would agree "that the great virtue of the novel [form] is that it describes man in transit, what Marcel would call *homo viator*."[56] That essential affinity has been further developed by Stephen L. Tanner, who argues convincingly that "these two Catholic artist-philosophers" share not only "parallel temperaments and spiritual orientations" but also a conviction that "concrete human experience is the only avenue to the mystery of being." More specifically, he documents the substantial extent to which "the concepts and even the terms of Gabriel Marcel echo through *Mystery and Manners*" and thereby firmly establishes O'Connor's debt

55. Merton, 14–15.
56. Lawson and Kramer, 231.

to him, a debt clearly suggested in her library holdings and letters in *The Habit of Being*.[57]

What might be easily overlooked is the fact that such interest in existentialism could in fact be consistent with O'Connor's—and Percy's—reading of neo-Thomism. The existentialists' quarrel with modern philosophy was that it tended to deal in abstractions, to focus on systems that vaguely dealt with human nature rather than with the situation of individuals in a concrete world (hence their proclivity for espousing their own philosophy in the form of literature, as in Sartre's *Nausea*). Thomistic philosophy, itself rigorously systematic and inclined to speak of the "essence" of human nature, was in one sense kindred to the modern systems the existentialists attacked; yet certain neo-Thomists favored by O'Connor and Percy saw the two modes of philosophy as potentially consistent precisely because they read Aquinas as emphasizing both the priority of existence over essence and the roots of human knowledge in sense experience.[58]

For example, the noted Catholic philosopher James Collins, whose *The Existentialists* (1952) was owned by both Percy and O'Connor and heavily annotated by Percy, examined Kierkegaard, Friedrich Nietzsche, Edmund Husserl, Sartre, Karl Jaspers, Marcel, and Martin Heidegger from "the critical standpoint . . . of a philosophical theism and realism" characteristic of neo-Thomism, noting that even Maritain and Gilson "have spoken of their doctrine as the only authentic existentialism or, at least, as the only philosophy of being in which existence receives its rightful place."[59] And in O'Connor's

57. Stephen L. Tanner, "Flannery O'Connor and Gabriel Marcel," *Literature and Belief* 17 (1997): 151.

58. Indeed, Aquinas's Christian sense of creation ex nihilo enabled him to emphasize the "gift" of individual existence in a manner that Aristotle—for whom essence, or form, was an abstract idea imposed upon a preexistent but inchoate matter—could not. See Kenneth L. Schmitz, *The Gift: Creation* (Milwaukee: Marquette University Press, 1982). Quinlan downplays Percy's debt to the comparatively "irrational" existentialists and instead emphasizes his attraction to the rigorous system-building of the neo-Thomists (see 33–5 especially), failing to explore the potential compatibility of the two schools—though he does briefly acknowledge that such mainstream Catholic thinkers as James Collins and Frederick Copleston treated existentialism "with surprising sympathy" (57–8). Quinlan finally presents Percy himself as attempting to reconcile existentialism and Thomism in his essays on language but implies that he was a lone traveler in this regard (63–5).

59. James Collins, *The Existentialists: A Critical Study* (Chicago: Regnery, 1952), x.

copy of *Introduction to Saint Thomas Aquinas*, editor Anton Pegis's introduction spoke of "what it is now fashionable to call the existentialism of St. Thomas Aquinas." O'Connor herself underlined the following passages, passages that implicitly criticize post-Cartesian philosophy's failure to take into account what it is like to be an individual human being:

> [W]hat we call the decline of medieval philosophy was really a transition from man as a knower to man as a thinker—from man knowing the world of sensible things to man thinking abstract thoughts in separation from existence. What is thinking but dis-existentialized knowing? . . . Man as a knower must be such that he can give existence, within his knowledge, not to abstract essences, but to sensible beings. That is why man as a knower needs a body; for, through the senses of his body he can give sensible existence in the order of knowing to that which is sensible in the order of being.[60]

Such an understanding clearly supports Percy's oft-repeated claim that the most profound shortcoming of modern science, itself a product of the Cartesian mind, is that it cannot account for what it is like to be an individual who lives in the world and that the novel by contrast allowed him to consider "a man in a concrete situation." In the work of Revival thinkers such as Collins and Pegis—as well as Frederick Copleston, another common influence—it is clear how Thomism, despite its own "abstractedness" as a philosophical system, could precisely because of its Christian foundations be seen by Percy and O'Connor as compatible with existentialism's emphasis on the predicament of the individual in the world.

What neo-Thomism itself does not convey is the perceived bleakness of the human predicament that is usually associated with existentialism. Insofar as such bleakness is characteristic of O'Connor and Percy's fiction—though both would argue that even their darkest works, Percy's *Lancelot* and perhaps the bulk of O'Connor's oeuvre, are finally comic—its intellectual roots can be

60. Anton Pegis, ed., *Introduction to St. Thomas Aquinas* (New York: Modern Library), xvi, xxiv, xxvi. For O'Connor's annotations, see *Flannery O'Connor's Library: Resources of Being*, ed. Arthur F. Kinney (Athens: University of Georgia Press, 1985), 71–2. For other comments on the compatibility of neo-Thomism and existentialism, particularly from O'Connor's perspective, see Sparr, 133, 165.

traced at least partially to the confluence of the Catholic Revival with what Auden deemed "the Age of Anxiety" in the wake of World War II. Writers such as Sartre and Camus were not only critiquing the insufficiency of modern analytic philosophy for understanding what it is like to be a human being: they were positing the fundamental loneliness, anguish, and terrifying freedom of that condition. Serious Christian writers at the time felt compelled to confront such a possibility largely because of what Robert Fitzgerald, in the epigraph to this chapter regarding O'Connor, called the undeniable "horror of recent human predicaments." For example, Auden himself attributed his conversion to Christianity largely to the profound sense of evil he gained in witnessing the Spanish Civil War and the rise of the Nazis. As a result of such experience, and of closely reading Kierkegaard, he wrote in Partisan Review's 1950 symposium "Religion and the Intellectuals" of the necessary role of existentialism in contemporary religious thought: "All of us have suffered in recent history the experiences of what can happen when mathematical quantitative notions of mass and number or biological notions like species or class are applied as absolutes to human life. No reader of PR, I imagine, is going to accept any religion, naturalistic or otherwise, which does not allow and account for our experience of ourselves and our friends as being, not only individual members of a class, but also persons, each a member of a class of one, i.e. no religion is credible today which lacks an existentialist aspect."[61]

Here Auden actually makes two separate observations. First of all, existentialism, at least as it manifested itself in the 1940s and 1950s, could in part be understood as a reaction to the Holocaust and the moral vacuum that precipitated it. For Percy and O'Connor such an understanding would be emphasized by their reading of the German Guardini, never associated with existentialism per se but nonetheless possessed of a strong sense of what he called the terrible "loneliness in faith" of the Christian in a century where love seemed to absent "from the face of the public world"; his The End of the Modern World was introduced by its editor as "the most somber book to come out of Germany since the Third Reich died in the bomb-pocked gardens of the Wilhelmstrasse."[62] Second, existentialism could be seen in a positive light as

61. W. H. Auden, Partisan Review 17:2 (February 1950): 123–4.

62. Frederick Wilhelmsen, introduction to The End of the Modern World, by Romano Guardini (Chicago: Henry Regnery, 1956), 3; Guardini, 132. Likewise, Guardini's The Faith and Modern Man

emphasizing the plight of the individual person in danger of being subsumed in contemporary mass society. Percy and O'Connor found explicit Catholic support for this sort of existentialist reading in Marcel, who in *The Mystery of Being* (owned and admired by both) warned of the advent of the "Moloch state" in which "the general bureaucratization of life" contributes to the wane of real human identity and intimacy.[63]

It is precisely Marcel's emphasis on human intimacy, however—what he formally called "intersubjectivity"—that distinguished him from Sartre (who famously posited in *No Exit* that "hell is other people") and finally led him to dissociate himself from existentialism. Insofar as the term was associated with Sartre's atheistic convictions and suggested the radical loneliness of the individual in an essentially meaningless universe, it was obviously profoundly unacceptable to Marcel, O'Connor, and Percy alike. As Auden noted, "a purely existentialist attitude, since it has no conception of the universal or the eternal, cannot be Christian, to whom the existential is only one, admittedly very important, aspect of his situation."[64] But insofar as it suggested the loneliness of the individual in contemporary mass society—where he was necessarily detached from any sort of meaningful religious tradition—yet emphasized his radical freedom to choose an authentic or inauthentic life, existentialism *was* compatible with a Christian vision, precisely because it emphasized the bleakness of such a society.

Such "Christian existentialism," stark but finally hopeful, might—despite Marcel—seem fundamentally Protestant rather than Catholic in its emphasis on the will, on the necessity of the individual choice that Kierkegaard catego-

---

(New York: Pantheon, 1952)—owned by O'Connor and Percy alike—was originally a collection of booklets written and secretly circulated in wartime Germany, "when the Christian life was deeply threatened by hostile doctrines"; hoping to elude "the tightening thought control" of the Nazis, Guardini sought to provide "a restatement, in terms of contemporary life and experience, of the eternal spiritual and humane verities" (vii). The Holocaust itself eventually reverberated in O'Connor's and Percy's work as well. See Sue Mitchell Crowley, "*The Thanatos Syndrome*: Walker Percy's Tribute to Flannery O'Connor," in *Walker Percy: Novelist and Philosopher*, ed. Jan Nordby Gretlund and Karl-Heinz Westarp (Jackson: University Press of Mississippi, 1991). Also, John Desmond, "Flannery O'Connor, Walker Percy, and the Holocaust," in *At the Crossroads: Ethical and Religious Themes in the Writings of Walker Percy* (Troy, NY: Whitston, 1997).

63. Gabriel Marcel, *The Mystery of Being* (Chicago: Regnery, 1950–1), 30–1.
64. Auden, 124.

rized so memorably as the "leap of faith." As we have seen, Ralph Wood suggests that O'Connor sympathized with such a radical vision rather than solely with a "Catholic humanism" that emphasizes the role of reason and a communal tradition in approaching faith. And Percy's attraction to the comparative irrationalism of Christian existentialism, as opposed to the rational structure of Thomism, is clear in his selection of dueling epigraphs to "The Message in the Bottle," to give just one example: Aquinas's claim that "the act of faith consists essentially in knowledge" is juxtaposed with Kierkegaard's that "faith is not a form of knowledge" (*MB*, 119). Of course, the Catholic tradition itself is not limited to Thomism or "humanism"; Pascal—who has been called an antecedent of the existentialists—and Augustine, for example, are more akin to Kierkegaard than to Aquinas. With regard to our particular concern, however, one thing is certain: Tate and Gordon's attraction to Catholicism and their notion of a Catholic literature owed nothing to "Christian existentialism," however broadly conceived. Percy and O'Connor's owed a great deal to it. Their work, and the vision of the postwar South found there, was profoundly shaped by Christian existentialism's sense of the lonely individual in a society where traditional moral codes had collapsed and history did not seem even a potential guide to meaning.

Such, for now, is a sufficient overview of the Catholic Revival and its various readings by the four southern writers who immersed themselves in it. I have not yet addressed at length any of the significant thinkers introduced above; some others I have left entirely unmentioned. What I hope to have established at this juncture is simply the fundamental difference in the approaches to the Revival of the Tates on the one hand and O'Connor and Percy on the other. Allen Tate's engagement with the Revival was in a sense limited to his engagement with Maritain and neo-Thomism generally, and, as we have seen, his reading of such thinkers was done in the context of a larger historical—at times forthrightly political—concern that was entirely alien to the thought of Percy and O'Connor. Gordon, as we shall explore more fully, largely adapted neo-Thomism to her modernist (and New Critical) aesthetic concerns, which were only partially communicated to O'Connor and Percy. And perhaps the most important distinction of all lies in those Revival thinkers whose works focusing on contemporary life were scoured by both Percy and O'Connor but not drawn upon by the older and established Tates.

* * *

NONETHELESS, the Tates themselves did play a significant role in O'Connor and Percy's development. Although I explore some of the commonalities in aesthetic theory and possible patterns of influence between the two pairs more fully in the next chapter, the essential biographical facts regarding their interaction fit well here. For at the same time that all four were reading deeply in the largely European thinkers of the Revival, Gordon was encouraging and advising the two younger writers, who primarily drew on Tate from a distance, almost entirely through his published work. The intensive, detailed advice that Gordon gave them was perhaps finally less significant in its specific effect upon their finished manuscripts than it was to their general notion of what the Catholic literary imagination was and should strive for. Most important of all may have been simply the generous interest and support she showed to O'Connor and Percy alike, who, though they did not meet or correspond directly until the 1960s, first became aware of each other through Gordon in 1951.

Percy first briefly met the Tates in 1936, when he was a college student on summer break at the family cabin at Monteagle, near Sewanee, Tennessee, in circumstances not particularly conducive to literary or theological discussion: his "first recollection of Tate was of him playing tennis, perhaps with Uncle Will." He did not become particularly close to Tate or Gordon, but in 1939 he felt comfortable taking a weekend off from medical school to visit them in Princeton. His distinguished hosts were also entertaining Maurice Coindreau (who was then translating Faulkner into French) and were embarrassed by their young southern friend when he asked their European guest, "Why bother with Faulkner?"[65] Percy was a considerably different young man when, still recovering from his bout with tuberculosis, he encountered the Tates again in Tennessee in 1945. Tate, who had hosted Lowell and Stafford at Monteagle not long before, was editing the *Sewanee Review* at the time and having serious marital problems with Gordon; by the middle of 1946 they had divorced, remarried, and moved to New York City, but they visited Percy and his own new wife at Sewanee again near Christmas of that year. No record of their conversations during these visits remains; but Percy, who had decided

65. Samway, *Walker Percy: A Life* (New York: Farrar, Straus and Giroux, 1997), 85, 111. See also Percy to Shelby Foote, September 18, 1978, in *The Correspondence of Shelby Foote and Walker Percy*, ed. Jay Tolson (New York: Doubletake/Norton, 1997), 246. Coindreau later translated *Wise Blood* into French as well.

not to practice medicine and was contemplating a life devoted to literature, and the Tates alike were on their way into the Catholic Church: in 1947 Percy and Gordon both converted, he in New Orleans in November and she in New York in December.

That same year Tate met Flannery O'Connor during a visit to the Iowa Writers' Workshop. His first encounter with the young Georgian was professional rather than personal; he later recalled reading a few short stories and a fragment of *Wise Blood* in Iowa, not knowing what to make of "the flat style, the cranky grammar, the monotonous sentence structure." He "hadn't the vaguest idea of what she was up to" at the time and even offered to correct her grammar, but he sensed a power that he would later come to appreciate fully. O'Connor was reminded of Tate in the coming years when she worked with his longtime colleague Andrew Lytle (who was also an acquaintance of Percy's at Monteagle) at the Workshop, and again when she associated with Lowell at Yaddo and Sally and Robert Fitzgerald in and around New York. Tate saw her again "in 1949 or 1950" at the Fitzgeralds' country house in Connecticut, where he thought they "had made her a member of the family, and the role of niece or younger sister suited her very well."[66]

It seems likely that O'Connor met Gordon at the same time, but their friendship did not begin in earnest until 1951, when on Robert Fitzgerald's advice, O'Connor—by now diagnosed with lupus and at home in Milledgeville—forwarded the manuscript of *Wise Blood* to her. Gordon admired the novel immediately, even extravagantly; but she suggested revisions, and O'Connor implemented them. From that time forward, Gordon, not her husband, became the younger writer's primary consultant in the writing of fiction. As Sally Fitzgerald has suggested, the two of them conducted a "master class" by mail, maintaining their correspondence—which usually concerned direct discussion of the younger writer's manuscripts—for the rest of O'Connor's life. Indeed, Gordon read and suggested revisions for "Parker's Back," the last story her "pupil" worked on, even as O'Connor approached her death in 1964.[67]

66. Tate, untitled memorial to Flannery O'Connor, in *Critical Essays on Flannery O'Connor,* ed. Melvin J. Friedman and Beverly Lyon Clark (Boston: G. K. Hall, 1985), 67.

67. Unfortunately, the bulk of these letters are privately held and remain unavailable. Three appear in *The Habit of Being* and several others in Sally Fitzgerald, "A Master Class: From the Correspondence of Caroline Gordon and Flannery O'Connor," *Georgia Review* 33:4 (Winter 1979): 827–46. See also Tamara O'Hearn Christenbury, "The Literary Relationship of Flannery O'Connor and Caroline Gordon" (M.A. thesis, James Madison University, May 1989).

One of Gordon's first letters, in late September or early October of 1951, introduced O'Connor to her other new protégé: "I had a letter yesterday from Will Percy's nephew, Walker Percy, who lives at Covington, Louisiana. He says he has written a novel which he guesses is 'a Catholic novel, though it has no conversion or priests in it.' I don't know that your paths are likely to cross, but if they ever should I imagine you'd find it interesting to know each other. He has been in the Church about five years."[68] Likewise, when Gordon received the manuscript of Percy's first attempted novel, *The Charterhouse*, she wrote back to him not only thirty pages of commentary but also the closing remark that she had high hopes for the future of Catholic fiction (a previously disappointing category), given what she had seen from him and one other writer: "I don't know how far Covington, Louisiana is from Milledgeville, Georgia, but if you and your wife ever drive through Milledgeville stop and see Flannery O'Connor."[69] Gordon was delighted to have received these two novels from the Deep South in this "season where good things come out of Nazareths" and made sure that her new charges were aware of one another; indeed, when she returned the manuscript of *The Charterhouse* to Percy, she sent along an old copy of the *Wise Blood* manuscript in the package, "partly for ballast, and partly because I thought you might like to read her book."[70]

In this second letter to Percy, Gordon also made insightful remarks about the two manuscripts that reveal her ideas on the writing of fiction, ideas now being articulated largely in "Catholic" terms. She had already critiqued *The Charterhouse* for portraying characters who spent too much time thinking and not enough time acting, who tended to become "disembodied voices" rather than people. She urged Percy to keep his characters grounded in the concrete world: "It takes five senses to make a man fully live . . . when we no longer have *any* sensuous apprehension of the universe we are no longer living in this world."[71] Such an understanding, she believed, should come naturally to the Catholic novelist. For precisely this reason Gordon must have preferred *Wise Blood* to *The Charterhouse*, though she diplomatically told Percy that he

68. Gordon to O'Connor, quoted in Fitzgerald, "Master Class," 830.

69. Gordon to Percy, December 11, 1951, Walker Percy Papers, Southern Historical Collection, University of North Carolina at Chapel Hill (henceforth SHC).

70. Gordon to Percy, n.d. [probably early 1952], SHC.

71. Gordon to Percy, December 11, 1951, SHC.

and O'Connor "have the opposite weaknesses. It is hardly possible, I suppose, to 'render' too much, but her story is too bare, too stripped, I think, of all but the essential core of action. . . . As I wrote her, her focus seems to me like the spotlight a burglar plays on the safe he is cracking. You don't see anything else in the room. But she is sure good."[72]

O'Connor was in fact "sure good" by this time, and she was far less in need of instruction than Percy was. As Percy himself said in a 1981 interview, despite Gordon's charitable comparisons, "*Charterhouse* was a very bad novel, and *Wise Blood* was a very good one."[73] Accordingly, O'Connor had found a publisher for her work on her own even before sending her work to Gordon. But, as Gordon and her husband knew (Tate too read and admired Percy's manuscript, specifically praising his observation that "the South is not really Christian" but rather under the sway of "the Roman [Stoic] myth"), Percy would need more help: "He's got a lot to learn that boy, almost everything," Gordon wrote to Brainard Cheney.[74] Both of the Tates would expend a good deal of effort trying to secure a publisher for *The Charterhouse*. Gordon even wrote to her publisher at Scribner's that in Percy's novel he would find "a new attitude towards the South on the part of a Southerner . . . and—Allen and I both think—the most important talent to come out of the South since Faulkner."[75] But they ultimately failed, even as they encouraged Percy to begin a second novel, *The Gramercy Winner*, which was completed in 1954 but also never published, and Percy for a time grew disheartened with writing fiction.

Nonetheless, these established and respected writer-critics had done all they could to give Percy a degree of confidence in his abilities. One can only imagine the pride the novice must have felt in reading Tate's closing comments in his letter regarding *The Charterhouse:* "I congratulate you. You have great intelligence and power, and you're going to be a valuable novelist."[76] They were similarly encouraging when, in 1954, he turned for a time from literature to formal philosophy: his first publication, "Symbol as Need," was in the Catholic journal *Thought,* published at Fordham University and edited

72. Gordon to Percy, n.d. [probably early 1952], SHC.

73. Lawson and Kramer, 232.

74. Tate to Percy, January 1, 1952, SHC; Gordon to Cheney, February 1952, quoted in Samway, 163.

75. Gordon to Jack Wheelock, n.d., quoted in Samway, 167.

76. Tate to Percy, January 1, 1952, SHC.

by the Jesuit William Lynch. Here, as in essays to come, Percy was trying to reconcile contemporary scientific observations about language with existential and neo-Thomist philosophy. When Gordon wrote Percy to congratulate him on "Symbol as Need" and ask for copies of his article, she no doubt emboldened him to send a copy of his next essay, "Symbol as Magic Cognition," directly to Maritain, whom she often mentioned in letters to Percy as a close friend. Maritain graciously read the piece and responded to Percy from Princeton that he was "very pleased by the way in which you make [my own] idea of magic sign as a 'state' of human mentality bear new and remarkable fruit."[77] Such comments must have encouraged Percy—who was constantly being chastised by Shelby Foote for his "existentially ethereal" interest in philosophy and his Catholic commitments generally—at a time when he seemed to be working in obscurity.[78]

O'Connor was a part of the very small audience that was aware of Percy's work in the 1950s. As she noted in the letter to Cecil Dawkins already mentioned above, she admired *Thought* and was a subscriber to the journal (*HB*, 132). There is no direct evidence that she read "Symbol as Need" closely in fall 1954, though it is certain that at least that spring's issue had been extremely important to her, and by 1957 she had read at least one of Percy's essays on southern society and was referring to him as the object of "our mutual admiration" in a letter to her anonymous correspondent "A."[79] O'Connor herself was reaching a much broader audience than Percy by this time; the collection *A Good Man Is Hard to Find* came out in 1955 and demonstrated that the author of *Wise Blood* was even more talented as a short story writer than as a novelist. Again, she did not need the encouragement and support from the Tates that Percy did, but she received it as the Tates praised and interpreted her for fellow critics and the reading public. Beginning with a review of *A Good Man Is Hard to Find* in the *New York Times Book Review* in June 1955,

77. Maritain to Percy, August 21, 1954, SHC. See Quinlan, 63 and following, for a thorough overview of Percy's early work on language with regard to the intellectual milieu of the Revival.

78. See Samway, 178; and Tolson, *Correspondence of Foote and Percy*, 7, 136, for example.

79. "A." has recently been identified as Betty Hester. O'Connor admired William Lynch's article "Theology and the Imagination" in the spring 1954 *Thought*, which she annotated heavily and kept in her personal library; see Kinney, 179–80. After "Symbol as Need" in 1954, Percy published "The Message in the Bottle" in *Thought* in fall 1959. For O'Connor's admiration of Percy in 1957, see *HB*, 238, and note 95 below.

Gordon in particular did her best to make O'Connor's work more readily accessible and understandable; for example, the second edition of *The House of Fiction* (1960) (the critical anthology coedited by the Tates) contains "Good Country People" and favorably contrasts O'Connor with Truman Capote for working from an implicit theological framework that gives her grotesques a depth that his lack.[80]

Gordon stayed in touch with O'Connor until O'Connor's death in 1964 and continued to bolster the reputation of her "pupil" even thereafter; likewise, she encouraged Percy in his remaining philosophical endeavors in the 1950s and exulted in his success at writing fiction in the 1960s. But she gradually drifted out of touch with Percy after the mid-1960s, and ultimately her contribution to the achievement of both writers was of a limited nature. By the end of her life, O'Connor was obviously an accomplished writer, one whose reputation had overshadowed Gordon's, and though she continued to value her mentor's friendship, she had little to learn from Gordon technically. She remained "grateful to her but [sent] her stories more out of a sense of obligation than devotion."[81] In fact, one of the few letters O'Connor sent to Percy, in 1962, concerns an article Gordon had written that contained a confused recollection of *Wise Blood:* Gordon "had things going on that didn't at all happen in the book. Very delicate matter not to set her straight on anything. . . . Also I am afraid old age has something to do with it."[82] Even earlier in their careers, Gordon's rigorously technical comments—which usually pointed to the novels of Henry James as the highest achievement of American fiction— were of limited value to Percy and O'Connor. Asked pointedly whether he followed her often painstakingly specific advice on his early manuscripts, Percy perhaps spoke for both when he replied that what was most valuable to him was "the relationship with her."[83]

80. See Gordon, "A Glitter of Evil," in Friedman and Clark; and Gordon and Tate, eds., *The House of Fiction: An Anthology of the Short Story with Commentary,* 2d ed. (New York: Scribner's, 1960), 382–6.

81. Christenbury, 42; see 49–60 for an overview of Gordon's post-1964 articles on O'Connor.

82. O'Connor to Percy, June 24, 1962, SHC.

83. Walker Percy, 1984 telephone interview with Ann Waldron; see Waldron, 284. Gordon was important in other ways that I have not fully outlined here. For instance, she introduced both Percy and O'Connor to a common correspondent, Jack English (a Trappist monk at Holy Ghost Monastery in Conyers, Georgia), who in turn put Percy in touch with Merton in the midsixties. See Samway, 230, 248–9; and O'Connor, *HB,* 454.

*   *   *

GORDON AND HER HUSBAND were important to O'Connor and Percy, then, not only in conveying their general sense that the Catholic faith could cast light upon the shortcomings of modern southern society but also, and more profoundly, in their enthusiasm for the Catholic literary imagination, which they often described in specifically neo-Thomist terms. They were valuable supporters and sources of inspiration at that crucial juncture in 1951 when all four were immersing themselves in the works of the Catholic Revival and the younger writers were at the beginning of their careers. But at that very moment, when Tate and Gordon had just entered the Church and seemed secure in their literary reputations, their careers would begin a steady decline even as O'Connor and, later, Percy joined the ranks of the foremost southern fiction writers. All four were southerners and Catholics, but unlike their mentors, O'Connor and Percy both remained in the South and formulated a Catholic vision that enabled them to capture the region in its peculiar postwar state.

Even at the early stages of their communication, there were some telling differences with regard to opinions of how the Catholic faith should inform contemporary fiction. In the middle of 1952, Gordon—inspired by Dorothy Day, who had "succeeded in doing what the Agrarians talked about" by building a Catholic community for displaced street people at an upstate New York farm—wrote Percy about establishing a "School of the Holy Ghost" where Catholic writers might gather to work and draw inspiration from the traditional liturgy. Although Gordon claimed that Maritain's ideas implicitly supported her project, Percy forthrightly wrote back that such a project was not appealing to him at all, partly because if a writer "cleaves too close to the liturgy he is liable to breed something quaint and cultish."[84] We might assume that Percy rejected Gordon's vision of what sounded curiously like some sort of medieval artists' guild in favor of remaining isolated in Covington precisely because he knew that to immerse himself in such a religious community would be to remove himself from what he saw as the alienated condition of contemporary humanity in a mass society. In recalling Percy's attraction to Marcel and Guardini, who had a different understanding of the contemporary believer's problematic relationship to the faith than did Maritain, we might likewise understand O'Connor's ambivalent reaction to Gordon's 1956 novel

84. Gordon to Percy, [late summer 1952], [October–November 1952], SHC.

The Malefactors. While O'Connor publicly admired Gordon's roman à clef treating Day and the Tates's own entry into the Church, a novel replete with images of Europe and ending on a Catholic "Agrarian" farm like Day's, she privately wrote that "in the last analysis I don't think *The Malefactors* comes off either—a conversion is an almost impossible subject for fiction."[85] Like Percy, she remained less interested in portraying the richness of an ideal Christian life, medieval or otherwise, than the realities of the immediate society she lived in, one that bred the fundamental displacement she saw in the contemporary soul, which she would deem "Christ-haunted" and he called "Christ-forgetting."

In choosing such a focus, O'Connor and Percy shaped the direction of postwar southern fiction, while their mentors gradually withdrew from any engagement with the contemporary South and even, to a degree, with contemporary literature. Whereas Tate's movement toward Catholicism had occasioned significant poems such as "Seasons of the Soul," after his 1950 conversion he produced very little poetry: only some Latin translations, "The Maimed Man," "The Swimmers," and "The Buried Lake." The traditional Christian imagery and medieval allusions common in these works—and in some cases the terza rima form favored by Dante—indicate Tate's firm new allegiances, as do several significant essays from this period, such as "The Angelic Imagination" and "The Symbolic Imagination." But once again he became less concerned with poetry than with larger cultural issues: as Gordon wrote Percy in 1952, "Allen, . . . you know, can't keep out of politics in one form or another."[86] He invented a new role for himself: "[The years] roughly between 1951 and 1958 marked the high watermark of Tate's Catholic experience. Already well known outside the United States, he fast became a member of the international Catholic lecture scene. . . . [While officially in a tenured position at the University of Minnesota,] he spent much of his time traveling to a variety of foreign countries, acting as something of a self-appointed ambassador of Christian humanism."[87] Tate returned to the South in his final years as a sort of grand old man of southern letters, and he produced a few

85. O'Connor, unpublished letter to Mrs. Rumsey Hayes, May 1956, quoted in Christenbury, 30.

86. Gordon to Percy, n.d. [1952?], SHC.

87. Huff, 84.

more important critical essays, such as "A Southern Mode of the Imagination" (1968), but his productive career came to a comparative standstill after the mid-1950s. Paul Giles suggests that such was the inevitable result of Tate's full-fledged acceptance of neo-Thomism as a system, especially as interpreted in light of his consistent historical concerns; his nostalgia for the medieval order—which was, again, finally not in contrast to but rather in keeping with his earlier concerns as a literary modernist—and his "final acquiescence in church dogma . . . led him further away from the material landscapes of America and into a disembodied realm of the spirit."[88] Given Tate's long-standing hopes that the Catholic faith would provide him a means to overcome just such narcissistic detachment, such an assessment is particularly damning.

Caroline Gordon suffered a similar fate. Productive in the 1950s, publishing not only *The Malefactors* but also critical works such as *How to Read a Novel* (1957) and a study of Ford Madox Ford, she began a steady decline after coediting the second edition of *The House of Fiction* (1960) with Tate (their often tempestuous marriage came to a final end in 1959). She published only *Old Red and Other Stories* (1963), which included many stories that had been published previously, and *The Glory of Hera* (1972) before her death in 1981. Her lapse in productivity might be attributed, like Tate's, in part to the dislocated life she led as a traveling academic and in part to the difficulty she experienced in integrating her religious faith with the world she found herself living in. Andrew Lytle's comments comparing Gordon with O'Connor are suggestive in this regard:

> [I]t could be said that fundamentally their subject was the same: what a society, materialistic and mechanical, does to the human psyche. They were both Roman Catholic, Miss O'Connor by cradle, Miss Gordon by choice. This distinction made the difference in their work. They were both southern to the marrow of their bones. Being set apart by her formal religion gave to Miss O'Connor a perspective on the Protestant world about her. Miss Gordon was born into that world but understood better the range of its hierarchy. She had a peculiar sense of it as it was before its defeat and degeneration. But her view was historic and tragic. The defeat

88. Giles, 209. For a more comprehensive account of Tate's "decline"—one that suggests his disenchantment with the post–Vatican II Church—see Huff, 100–1.

of the Confederacy and the consequent destruction of Southern, that is, the transplanted segment of European, society, and its effect upon the succeeding generations gave her the substance for her earlier fiction. Her later fiction concerns the damage into the third generation of what cracked and broken forms do to human beings. Her actors belong to a different category from Miss O'Connor's. Most of her work was done before she joined the Roman church, and it seems to me that the fiction whose complications derive from her immersion in the new faith is less satisfactory. A universal church that in her known society is not universal cannot find the concrete images or manners to deliver a satisfactory fiction.[89]

Lytle's comparison is particularly trenchant in its description of Gordon's essential vision as "tragic and historic," a statement that has implications beyond this immediate context. Such a vision has, of course, been ascribed to the Southern Renascence itself, to that literary phenomenon that included not only Tate and Gordon but also Faulkner, Toomer, Porter, Warren, and Welty (at least the early Welty), to name just some of its most prominent writers. Tate himself set the terms that Louis D. Rubin Jr. and others would adopt to define the Renascence when, in 1935, he described the contemporary southern writer as being characterized by a "peculiarly historical consciousness" and when, in 1945, he claimed that "with the war of 1914–1918, the South reentered the world—but gave a backward glance as it stepped over the border: that backward glance gave us the Southern renascence, a literature conscious of the past in the present."[90] That such a literature was largely "tragic" is implicit in Tate's definition; such a backward glance would of necessity be a despairing one, and he saw the Renascence itself, along with a distinctive southern culture, coming to an end even as he defined it.

We have seen how Tate and Gordon's entrance into the Catholic Church seems largely to have been occasioned by just such a historical consciousness, at least in part attributable to the ultimate backward glance, one that resulted in "the whole hog of reaction" and left the shores of the New World behind for good. Even in their conversions, Tate and Gordon essentially remained

89. Andrew Lytle, *Southerners and Europeans* (Baton Rouge: Louisiana State University Press, 1988), 186–7.

90. Tate, "The Profession of Letters in the South," in *Essays*, 533; and "The New Provincialism," in *Essays*, 545–6.

literary modernists in both their literary sensibilities and their themes, and they never wrote about the post–World War II South (*The Malefactors*, for example, is set in upstate New York and is only "postwar" in a superficial sense; a large part of the novel is really a look back at turn-of-the-century southern childhood and expatriate life in Europe, a reinterpretation of the Tates' own days as high modernists). And it is in this regard that they differed so fundamentally from their former pupils.

A number of critics have implicitly suggested the radical differences between the "Catholic" fictions of the older writers and those of O'Connor and Percy. Whereas "Tate's religious strictness eventually came to ensure the alienation of his art from the main currents and energies of American life," Giles notes O'Connor's explicit concern with the "'concrete reality' of the twentieth-century American environment."[91] Richard King's *A Southern Renaissance* (1980) closes by considering the future direction of southern culture: while "certainly the retreat of men such as Allen Tate to Catholicism offers no general solution" (neither does "Faulkner's sonorous but empty stoic humanism"), "the value of the work of a contemporary Southern writer such as Walker Percy is that he recognizes that the tradition of the fathers is gone forever, as are the heady days of the Southern Renaissance. The fathers and Faulkner must both be transcended." Percy is so valuable because he realized, unlike the later Tate or even Faulkner, that "the South and the modern world which it has finally, albeit reluctantly, joined, must now deal with a new cultural situation."[92] What King does not make explicit is that the same faith that led Tate (and Gordon) to "retreat" from their world somehow led Percy (and O'Connor) to rigorous engagement with it.

Indeed, their faith led them to a vision that, in comparison with their Southern Renascence predecessors, was virtually ahistorical in its concentration on their contemporary moment. If we recall O'Connor's comment that the fiction writer operates at "a peculiar crossroads where time and place and eternity meet," we might say that O'Connor and Percy's focus lay almost entirely on the axes of not place and time but rather place and eternity at a single—and emergently postmodern—cultural moment.

A simple observation: every piece of fiction written by O'Connor and Percy

91. Giles, 209.

92. King, 292.

alike is set in their contemporary world. That world may be manifested grotesquely, as with O'Connor's fiction generally and in the not-too-distant-future settings of Percy's *Love in the Ruins* and *The Thanatos Syndrome*, but it is their contemporary world and is not characterized by a strong sense of "the past in the present."[93] This latter claim is admittedly more problematic with regard to Percy's work than O'Connor's, which, to adapt Gordon's earlier observation, inevitably focuses a glaring searchlight on a moment in contemporary life. Certainly Percy's novels have a recurring concern with family history, most often with confronting the memory of the father, but I would argue not only that this history is largely obscured but also that in every case Percy's work confronts such a history only to emphasize more radically the final irrelevance of the past in comparison with the present moment, which, properly seen, eternally bears witness to the goodness and radical newness of an ever-ongoing Creation. *The Last Gentleman* is the paradigmatic example of this pattern, as I argue more fully in chapter 3.[94]

In a panel discussion in 1960, O'Connor told Louis Rubin—who was not entirely pleased with the observation—that "Walker Percy wrote somewhere that his generation of Southerners had no more interest in the Civil War than in the Boer War. I think that is probably quite true."[95] Her remark revealed more than the increasing historical distance between southern writers and

93. See Robert Rudnicki, *Percyscapes* (Baton Rouge: Louisiana State University Press, 1999), 67, for the suggestion that the dystopias *Love in the Ruins* and *The Thanatos Syndrome* fit into the category of the southern grotesque.

94. For example: *Absalom, Absalom!* is *entirely* concerned with reconstructing the Sutpen—and southern—past over the course of a century, and with the effects of that past on Rosa Coldfield, Quentin, and indeed all of Yoknapatawpha County; by contrast, *The Last Gentleman* is primarily concerned with the predicament of an individual, Will Barrett, a partial amnesiac adrift in 1960s America. Will's brief recovery of the memory of his father's suicide is literally "pivotal" in the novel, but only in the sense that it is a single, brief step on a longer journey—one that takes place in a dislocated present and ends not with death and doom in Mississippi but rather with baptism and new life in the western desert, the "locus of pure possibility" where "what a man can be the next minute bears no relation to what he is or what he was the minute before" (278).

95. "Recent Southern Fiction: A Panel Discussion" (October 28, 1960), in *Conversations with Flannery O'Connor*, ed. Rosemary Magee (Jackson: University Press of Mississippi, 1987), 75. O'Connor's reference is apparently to Percy's article "The American War" in the March 29, 1957, issue of the Catholic magazine *Commonweal* (reprinted in *SSL*, 71–6; his "Boer War" reference is on 72) and is just one indication of her engagement with his 1950s nonfiction.

the Civil War. While so many of the writers of the Renascence wrote at least some fiction or poetry that not only meditated directly on southern history but was actually set in the past (Tate's *The Fathers,* Gordon's *The Forest of the South* and *None Shall Look Back,* Faulkner's *The Unvanquished* [and other works], Warren's *Night Rider*), O'Connor and Percy did not. They refrained from doing so not because the historical mode had passed out of vogue by their time: in the 1940s Welty wrote *The Robber Bridegroom* and stories such as "A Still Moment" and "First Love" that captured the frontier history of the Natchez Trace, as well as *Delta Wedding,* set at the beginning of the twentieth century; Warren wrote *World Enough and Time* and *Band of Angels* in the 1950s. William Styron not only persisted in the Faulknerian mode of tragic family history in *Lie Down in Darkness* (1951); in the 1960s he returned outright to the historical mode, albeit in an innovative and controversial manner, in *The Confessions of Nat Turner* (1967). In 1952 Shelby Foote, another longtime emulator of Faulkner, published *Shiloh*—a seemingly classic Renascence text in both form and subject matter, recounting a tragic moment in regional history through the voices of multiple narrators—before beginning a twenty-year immersion in the history of the Civil War.

Ironically, *Shiloh* was dedicated to Percy, then struggling in obscurity. The irony was heightened when Foote, the lover of Marcel Proust and Henry James and Percy Bysshe Shelley who endlessly praised the essentially amoral aesthetic vision of the high modernists and longed to be the next Faulkner, became best known as a historian, while the former doctor whom he often chided for his religious and existential interests became one of the foremost novelists of his generation. Percy did so precisely by bringing his own interests to bear on the postwar South he found himself living in.[96]

96. Foote's correspondence with Percy from the 1950s on reveals Foote's belief that no novel focusing on an individual living in a deracinated contemporary society could be very worthwhile. At about the time he published *Shiloh,* he wrote to Percy that what any good novel needs "is a sense of proceeding from generations of knowledge. This may come from my being Southern, I guess it does. . . . There has to be a family and a past, or else the book is like a freeflying balloon being carried whichever way the wind blows." Hence in the big novel he was attempting at the time (*Two Gates to the City*), he wrote, "the time is the present: yes, it must be: but all the past is behind it, you know it's there." December 11, 1951, Tolson, *Correspondence of Foote and Percy,* 71–2. Foote does not state here that preoccupation with religious mysteries necessarily detracts from this historical sense, but he repeatedly makes clear in other letters that he sees faith in general as detrimental to the novelist—not only attacking Graham Greene as "banal and morose"

Before I conclude by arguing precisely how O'Connor and Percy's reading of the Catholic Revival helped to bring about their radical break from Renascence tradition, it is worth noting how many different critics have touched upon that break. Over and over again, both O'Connor and Percy —but not, for example, Welty or Styron, who are roughly of their generation—are cited as radical departures in southern fiction, whether negatively, as sounding the death knell of the Renascence, or positively, as signaling some necessary progression from a potentially moribund tradition. Even early southern critics were puzzled by what to do with O'Connor, who seemed less an epic or domestic historian than a Caldwellian naturalist with certain religious preoccupations, and recognized *The Moviegoer* and *The Last Gentleman* as indebted more to Sartre and Camus than to Tate or Faulkner. But by the 1970s critics were able to survey the history of southern literature more broadly and place the two writers in a larger context.

In 1976 Walter Sullivan first linked the work of O'Connor and Percy as emblematic of the end of the Southern Renascence, claiming that the final disappearance of a healthy southern culture explains their peculiar and—in his reading—finally defective fiction. "The postmodern world with its loss of community and myth" is not their creation, but it prevents them from writing anything other than what they have written.[97] Given "how rapidly the country and her section of it were changing during the fifteen years between 1949 when Flannery O'Connor began to publish and 1964 when she died," Sullivan argues, she in fact "lived and wrote through the very last years of a southern culture that was literarily viable" (61, 59). Some of her early work can be explained as being in the southern tradition and even essentially realistic, in the light of her particular "eye for the cheap and the obscene and the spurious, no matter under what guises they presented themselves." But after 1955— when, Sullivan asserts, the older southern community had collapsed for good—"she attempted to furnish for herself and for her work the consciousness of metaphysical and moral reality that was missing from the society

---

(October 31, 1951, p. 59), but also dismissing O'Connor as "a minor-minor writer" (October 28, 1969, p. 136). The Mississippi Delta he and Percy alike grew up in—its people and the land itself—are, Foote suggests in a manner largely consistent with Renascence tenets, sufficient unto themselves for the generation of great fiction.

97. Walter Sullivan, *A Requiem for the Renascence* (Athens: University of Georgia Press, 1976), 57.

around her" (61–2). The result was bound to be not only grotesque but, to Sullivan, artistically inferior: O'Connor is "not as profound and finished an artist as Faulkner or Miss Welty" precisely because "her resources were strained" by the final "deterioration of myth and community" in the postmodern South: "time had run out on her." And "an even better example of the deleterious effect of modern culture on southern literature can be seen in the work of Walker Percy" (63). As with O'Connor, Sullivan sees Percy's problem as lying not in his Christian vision but rather in the utterly untraditional society he dwells in; when in *The Last Gentleman* Percy moves "not into, but out of his own [southern] culture," he may well accurately portray the "plight of contemporary human beings" detached from the past, but such literature is bound to be deficient (65–6). Hence, the works of O'Connor and Percy alike indicate that it is time to sound a requiem for the Renascence.

Lewis P. Simpson, aware of Sullivan's argument, put the case somewhat differently in 1980. In *The Brazen Face of History,* he clearly outlines the extent to which Faulkner, Welty, Warren, and other writers of the Renascence practiced a "southern aesthetic of memory [which] is imbedded in the European matrix of memory, and so greatly complicated and enlarged the possibilities of the southern novelist."[98] But more recently there have emerged "southern writers who ardently desire to free themselves from the work of memory": "I am thinking expressly of Flannery O'Connor and Walker Percy. As committed Roman Catholic writers, they may be considered eccentrics in a still largely Protestant South; but not only are they the most remarkable southern fictionists of the past twenty-five years, they are pivotal figures in the resolution of the drama of history and memory in southern fiction" (244). Simpson's remarkable discussion of O'Connor and Percy is unlike Sullivan's in that it assigns each writer, rather than their culture, the final responsibility for refocusing the "southern fictional imperative" by "rejecting the mode of remembering" and embracing "the mode of revelation." He is less concerned than Sullivan with arguing the merits of their fictions, but he is more critical of O'Connor than of Percy. Although Simpson senses the power of O'Connor's fiction, he regrets the fact that she sees "the debasement of memory" as a necessity in "preparing the way to assume the vocation to prophecy" (246).

98. Lewis P. Simpson, *The Brazen Face of History* (Baton Rouge: Louisiana State University Press, 1980), 244.

Her suppression of "the motive of the southern literary imagination known to Faulkner, Eudora Welty, and Warren: a tension between memory and history" finally "oversimplifies the modern situation of the self" (247). Although her focus on revelation does not lessen her "detailed portrayal of the manners of her region," it does divest her work "of a tension toward historical reality" (248). In other words: O'Connor's stark focus on eternity does not hinder her perception of place, but it does detract from any concern with time. Likewise, Percy "has followed the prophetic inclination into apocalyptic eschatology" and has portrayed "the self in the loneliest possible state of being . . . [a self] who knows that the modern world either already has ended or soon will" (248). Simpson credits Percy with a greater sense of the "relation among history, memory, and prophecy" than O'Connor possessed, but he ultimately acknowledges that a primary concern of Percy's fiction is to subject "the southern aesthetic of memory" to "the ethos of a profound and severe Christian existentialism" (253).

In *Another Generation: Southern Fiction since World War II*, Lewis Lawson is more forthrightly positive than either Sullivan or Simpson in seeing both O'Connor and Percy as possessing exactly the vision that was *necessary* for a thriving postwar southern fiction. Lawson posits that southern fiction since 1950 is *appropriately* characterized by "the loosening grip of history" and the profound "loneliness" of its characters, whose primary concern is now not the already accomplished "disintegration of society" but rather the "disintegration of self" in a time when they are "almost completely deprived of the help of tradition, custom or community" that were the previous generation's birthright.[99] As Thomas Daniel Young notes in his foreword, Lawson sees the best postwar southern writers as striving to achieve not only a realism appropriate to such a time but even an "extra-realism," primarily through "two different fictional techniques: the grotesque and the existential/phenomenological" (x). Although Lawson treats writers as diverse as Harriette Arnow, Richard Wright, Styron, and Mitchell F. Jayne, these two fictional techniques are obviously best exemplified by the authors he treats first and last: O'Connor and Percy. Furthermore, they best demonstrate Lawson's contention that the superficial bleakness of much contemporary southern fiction actually "sug-

99. Lewis A. Lawson, *Another Generation: Southern Fiction since World War II* (Jackson: University Press of Mississippi, 1984), 16–17.

gests a sense of optimism about the South. For once these writers have made their point that life without some transcendent controlling principle is a shambles, they can begin to suggest, however tentatively, alternatives to such a life" (18).

My own sentiments regarding O'Connor and Percy are finally more akin to Lawson's than to Sullivan's or Simpson's, though I think that Simpson's statement regarding O'Connor's and Percy's essential departure from the southern "aesthetic of memory" is consummately articulated. O'Connor and Percy were the perfect postwar southern realists, and, I would contend, they were able to avoid the potentially moribund Renascence tradition—and to capture their cultural moment so profoundly—precisely because of their religious vision. One can, I think, make this argument without necessarily engaging in what Kieran Quinlan calls "Catholic triumphalism" or going so far as Lawson does in claiming that "Southern fiction must fight its way toward a vision of life made vital by Christianity or die."[100] Regardless of what one believes about the ultimate truth of Christianity, or its appropriate role in the fiction of its adherents, open-minded critics should be prepared to accept that writers as forthrightly Catholic as O'Connor and Percy were profoundly shaped in their perception of the world by that faith. If their fiction in fact expresses any insight into contemporary southern society or the state of postmodern humanity, the source and power of that insight should be credited at least partly to their religious vision.

What I have attempted to suggest thus far is the extent to which O'Connor and Percy's specific vision was shaped by the Catholic Revival in a manner finally distinct from that of Tate and Gordon, quintessential literary modernists who were immersed first in the Southern Renascence and its "peculiarly historical consciousness" and, ironically, encountered the Revival largely in terms of that consciousness. The Catholic vision that the two younger writers finally shared, by contrast, is succinctly captured from a forthrightly theological perspective in Merton's 1965 essay. Again, he here examines O'Connor as the American writer who best exemplifies a Christian use of existential "intuitions" but ends by using language reminiscent of Percy, with whom he was corresponding at the time. Merton's claim that for the Christian existentialist "the authentic person is not born in stoic isolation but in the openness

100. Ibid., 21 n.

and dialogue of love," and that "only between such free persons is true communication possible," reverberates throughout Percy's novels (and is strongly reminiscent of Marcel as well). But what is most relevant to our present concerns is Merton's commendation of both existentialism's insistence on the contemporary individual's isolation in mass society and its virtually ahistorical focus: "[T]he Christian existentialist knows precisely that he cannot evade the present and fly from it into a safe and static past, preserved for him in a realm of ideal essences to which he can withdraw in silent recollection. This recollection will be of no use to him if it merely serves as a pretext for not being open to his brother in the here and now. The existential insistence on grace as event, as an ever-renewed encounter with God and one's fellow man *now,* in present reality, disturbs the idealistic and static outlook. . . ." And if we take into account a letter Merton wrote to Percy in 1964, the Christian existentialist might further be characterized as "hopeful": "you are one of the most hopeful existentialists I know of," he writes, for *The Moviegoer* presents "a merry kind of nausea."[101] Finally, then, the definition of Christian existentialism provided here is antithetical to the Southern Renascence aesthetic—it is not historical and tragic, but rather ahistorical and comic.

Such a vision, then, differentiated O'Connor and Percy from the major writers of the Renascence generally and even from their fellow Catholics Tate and Gordon. They shared with the older couple both an enthusiasm for the Catholic literary imagination's tradition of sacramental realism and an accompanying disdain for romanticism; but Percy and O'Connor were distinctive in their sense of the radical displacement of the individual adrift in the nascent postmodern world, and they were therefore particularly well suited to write about their own South. While O'Connor and Percy may have shared some of Tate and Gordon's aesthetic sympathies, the younger writers each possessed a vision that was essentially planted in the spiritual drama of the here and now.

The source of such differing visions might be seen even in their initial approaches to the Catholic Revival: if, for example, Tate was looking back and longing for a social order, Percy was looking around himself and longing for a life. Ironically, Percy's scientific training might even be said to characterize

101. Merton, "Other Side," 18, 22; Merton, *The Courage for Truth: The Letters of Thomas Merton to Writers,* ed. Christine M. Bochen (New York: Farrar, Straus and Giroux, 1993), 282.

his approach to the Church, particularly if we recall the subtitle of his essay "Physician as Novelist": "Or, Why the Best Training for a Novelist in These Last Years of the Twentieth Century Is an Internship at Bellevue or Cook County Hospital, and How This Training Best Prepares Him for Diagnosing T. S. Eliot's *The Waste Land*" (*SSL* 191). Such a self-description both clearly distinguishes Percy from the literary modernists and seems to place him in the latter of two categories of Catholic writers defined by Paul Giles. Many "twentieth-century European Catholic writers—Evelyn Waugh, George Bernanos"—and, I would suggest, Tate and Gordon—exhibit "a sense of exile and nostalgia for the lost enchanted garden," "the social order and ecclesiastical authority of an Age of Faith," "the medieval ideal." But there is a different tradition of "Catholic skepticism" within which I would finally place O'Connor and Percy, one that searches for elements of the spiritual "within the debris of contemporary civilization" and, like Montaigne and Pascal, glimpses "the possibilities of faith not within the archaic structures of feudalism but amid those lacunae and absences lurking within the brave new world of humanist reason."[102]

102. Giles, 525.

CHAPTER 3

Toward a Catholic Theory of Fiction

A Christian Realism of the "Here-and-Now"

Like Flannery O'Connor, I would defend the Christian culture of the South as, on the whole, a literary asset. From a Catholic perspective at least, Christianity . . . underwrites those very properties of the novel without which there is no novel: I am speaking of the mystery of human life, its sense of predicament, of something having gone wrong, of life as a wayfaring and pilgrimage, of the density and linearity of time and the sacramental reality of things. . . . Another way of saying this is that I don't recall reading a good novel which was informed by a belief in [Marxism, Freudianism, behaviorism,] . . . or the illusoriness of this here-and-now life in this here-and-now world. If the world is not real, why bother to write a novel about it or read a novel about it?

—WALKER PERCY, "How to Be an American Novelist in Spite of Being Southern and Catholic"

Well, if it's a symbol, to hell with it.

—FLANNERY O'CONNOR, regarding the Eucharist

AT THE END of O'Connor's final story, "Parker's Back," the rakish sensualist O. E. Parker confronts his stern fundamentalist wife with the image now tattooed on what was previously the sole unmarked spot on his body. Sarah Ruth Parker, staring at "the haloed head of a flat stern Byzantine Christ with all-demanding eyes," states flatly that this figure "ain't anybody I know"; even when told by her husband that she is looking at God, she responds, "He's a spirit. No man shall see his face." Parker retreats into claiming, "this is just a picture of him," but even so is met with outrage. "Idolatry!" she screams, and begins to beat him across the back until "large welts had formed on the face of the tattooed Christ" (CS, 522, 529).

Here the worldly Parker experiences the divine in a manner that the rigid "Straight Gospel" believer, who cannot see the presence of God in the flesh of her own husband, fails to perceive. O'Connor would doubtlessly have been pleased with Caroline Gordon's interpretation of this story as "the dramatization of that heresy which denies Our Lord corporeal substance," one particularly offensive to the Catholic tradition.[1] For while O'Connor may have struggled with flesh-denying Manichean tendencies of her own and tended to view the world as radically fallen and humanity as accordingly depraved (as Allen Tate once remarked, "she was not doctrinally but temperamentally a Jansenist," referring to the most "Calvinistic" of Catholic sects), she was compelled to understand the created world as essentially good precisely because of her belief in Catholic dogma.[2] This understanding, of course, has particular relevance to the imagination of the Catholic artist, as the transubstantiation theme in this particular story suggests (Parker is initially described as being "as ordinary as a loaf of bread"). Yet Parker's transformation is accomplished not by a priest but rather, O'Connor would say, by both the grace of God and the handiwork of a quite irreverent, matter-of-fact "artist"—the tattooist, of whom Parker thinks, "artists were all right in their own place but he didn't like them poking their noses into the affairs of regular people" (CS, 525). As Gordon would likely have agreed, "Parker's Back" is finally a story as much about art as about religion, and it dramatizes not only theology but also a "theory of fiction" that appealed greatly to O'Connor and Percy alike.

That theory is essentially continuous with "the Catholic imagination in American literature" as it has been described by Ross Labrie. Taking his cue from Thomas Merton's claim that to the Christian poet "the whole world and all the incidents of life tend to be sacraments—signs of God, signs of His love working in the world," Labrie further argues that such a theological understanding is manifested particularly in the Catholic imagination because of the Church's emphasis on the sacraments. For the Catholic writer the divine is

---

1. Caroline Gordon, quoted by Robert Giroux in the introduction to *The Complete Stories of Flannery O'Connor*, ed. Robert Giroux (New York: Farrar, Straus and Giroux, 1971), xv. For the O'Connor epigraph that opens the chapter: O'Connor made this remark to the novelist Mary McCarthy. O'Connor held that "the Host is actually the body and blood of Christ"; McCarthy, a lapsed Catholic, that it was merely a "pretty good . . . symbol" (HB, 124–5).

2. Allen Tate, untitled memorial, in *Flannery O'Connor: A Tribute*, ed. John J. Quinn, S.J. (Scranton, PA: University of Scranton Press, 1995), 90.

found not only in sacred Scripture but also in the world, which begins in the Word: "Thus, Catholics, without being pantheistic, regard the sacred as continuous with the secular and somehow involved in the secular, though this involvement is always seen as subject to the final interpretation of the church." Accordingly, Catholicism finally affirms a "relatively positive view of nature," one that has traditionally "made Catholic writers open to some parts of nature that other Christian writers have eschewed"; though, Labrie notes, in the twentieth century "the Catholic view of nature . . . has been more rational than romantic" and in the United States has sometimes been marred by strong tendencies toward Jansenism (tendencies that, I would claim, are reflected more in O'Connor's fiction than in Percy's).[3]

Given such an understanding of God's ongoing presence in creation, the orthodox Catholic writer should therefore understand that to *be* a "Catholic" writer is essentially to be a realist. He or she should not feel constrained by a duty to promulgate Church teachings—for to the believer these are continuous with the real—but rather should be concerned with seeing the world as it is and telling the truth about it. Labrie writes:

> The best [religious] writers will be those who test their ideologies against experience, something that Catholic writers, with their incarnational theology and consequent dedication to the world, ought to, in theory at least, be prepared to do. In these writers, the fiction and poetry will often end with a lingering, unresolved air of complexity—even if the moral foundations of the universe have been made adequately clear to the reader. In adhering to the world as sacrament, Catholic writers have, whether deliberately or not, committed themselves to reality in whatever unwelcome and inconsistent form it might appear, in the expectation that God, the epitome and ultimate author of all reality, will thereby somehow be present.[4]

Paul Giles has also speculated on the role of the Catholic imagination in American literature, but he is more coolly detached from his subject than Labrie. Conversant with the claims of Michel Foucault, Jacques Derrida, and Roland

3. Ross Labrie, *The Catholic Imagination in American Literature* (Columbia: University of Missouri Press, 1997), 4–5.
4. Ibid., 18–19.

Barthes, he is careful to "demythologize" his treatment of Catholicism but holds that, even "deprived of their idealist and universalist inclinations, Catholic fictions will nevertheless be granted a particular and historical existence as one form of discourse as valid, within its own terms, as any other." With such a qualification in place, he goes on to describe the Catholic imagination in terms similar to Labrie's and finally goes a step further. He asserts that a full understanding of American Catholic literature will "problematize that rigid affiliation between American literature and an ideology of romanticism, an affiliation institutionalized by critics from F. O. Matthiessen to Douglas Robinson." Giles argues that the romantic "mainstream" of American literature is essentially Protestant and that there exists alongside it "a competing antiromantic 'Catholic' tradition" consisting of writers who have sometimes received less than their critical due because of their alien role in that mainstream.[5]

Giles's corollary remark that "without at all waging war on Emerson, it is important to recognize that not all American literature conforms to the premises of the Emersonian tradition" calls to mind O'Connor's own clearly stated reservations about transcendentalist spirituality: "When Emerson decided, in 1832, that he could no longer celebrate the Lord's Supper unless the bread and wine were removed, an important step in the vaporization of religion in America was taken. . . . When the physical fact is separated from the spiritual reality, the dissolution of belief is eventually inevitable" (*MM*, 162). The final unity of the physical and spiritual worlds that she affirms here—a unity that, given the context of her remarks, obviously has implications for literature—is according to Giles one of the hallmarks of the Catholic imagination. His straightforward claim that "Protestant romance dissolves the mundane world into a more lucid spiritual allegory; Catholic realism invests the mundane world itself with sacramental significance" is all the more interesting in that it is presented in the context of two lapsed Catholics who became naturalists: Theodore Dreiser and James Farrell.[6] O'Connor herself preferred not the narcissistic romantic who divorces himself from the world but rather the writer who produces "a great tragic naturalism" precisely because "by his responsibil-

5. Paul Giles, *American Catholic Arts and Fictions: Culture, Ideology, Aesthetics* (New York: Cambridge University Press, 1992), 4–5, 25.
6. Ibid., 168.

ity to the things he sees, [the naturalist] may transcend the limitations of his narrow vision" (*MM*, 42).

Certainly neither she nor Percy could by any means be categorized as a naturalist (though, significantly, some early critics did place O'Connor in this category), but they do share an essential commitment to a broadly conceived realism, one often articulated in theological terms in the wealth of discursive writing they have left commenting on their approaches to fiction. Over and over again in her essays, O'Connor emphasizes the artist's responsibility to capture the concrete, physical world she lives in, claiming that such is the only legitimate way to approach the fundamental mystery at the center of reality. In her eyes, doing such properly involves a great deal of craft, that careful attention to form that marked the best writers of the Southern Renascence, including her mentor Caroline Gordon. The inherent connection she saw between realism, form, and the artist's vocation as truth-teller is strongly declared in her letters: "The artist dreams no dreams. That is precisely what he does not do. . . . You don't dream up a form and put the truth in it. The truth creates its own form . . . [which] is necessity in the work of art" (*HB*, 216–8).

Percy's approach, as the epigraph to this chapter indicates, is occasionally couched in language similar to O'Connor's, though in both theory and practice it is in many ways quite different.[7] His ideas about fiction in some sense owe as much to his scientific training as to his faith, for he not only sees the novelist as performing a peculiar "diagnostic function" in the twentieth century but also understands literature as fundamentally "cognitive": the poet and the scientist are "co-celebrants of being," and good literature is accordingly not an exercise in subjectivity but an engagement with reality, just as science is (*SSL*, 137). This claim is particularly consistent with much in Catholic Revival thought, and Percy's own interest in a sort of existential Thomism led him to write about the individual whose very real experience is left out in the abstract schemes of modern science. Hence in *The Moviegoer* he began neither with psychological theories nor with "the conventional notions of a

7. In "How to Be an American Novelist in Spite of Being Southern and Catholic," Percy also explicitly foregrounded his incarnational theology in his claim that "the intervention of God in history through the Incarnation bestows a weight and a value to the individual human narrative which is like money in the bank to the novelist" (SSL, 178).

plot and a set of characters": "rather would I begin with a *man* who finds himself in a *world*, a very concrete man who is located in a very concrete place and time." When such a man turns his eyes to the created world in which he lives—as Binx Bolling does when he abandons the essentially abstracted and inward "vertical search" for the outward "horizontal search"—he discovers not the often terrifying experience of mystery that O'Connor's characters are confronted with, but a more understated form of that same mystery that is nonetheless just as compelling. The character who begins to perceive the depths of the world around him, Percy says, "might be represented as *coming to himself* in somewhat the same sense as Robinson Crusoe came to himself on the island after his shipwreck, with the same wonder and curiosity" (*SSL*, 190). Such an understanding also partly accounts for Percy's comparative disregard for the rigorous formal structure favored by the literary modernists and his embrace of a looser, exploratory narrative usually focused on the experience of a single consciousness.

Even in the bare bones, as it were, of the theories of fiction outlined by O'Connor and Percy, we can see behind the obvious differences a fundamental similarity that is consistent with Labrie's and Giles's descriptions of the Catholic literary imagination: a common emphasis on the concrete and a faith that the immediate world itself holds a mystery and a meaning that does not have to be imposed by the artist but is already present, if only recognized. It is, of course, ironic that any writer would have to formulate a theory of the concrete, but it is perhaps precisely due to the potential tension between their faith and their capacities as fiction writers that O'Connor and Percy have left us with such extensive discursive reflection. Certainly religious concerns have the potential to become abstract, and O'Connor and Percy apparently felt the need to work through for themselves the extent to which their own religious tradition countered this tendency precisely because it valued the concrete. Yet in considering the essays that put forth their theories of fiction, we should keep in mind both O'Connor's final caveat that "the virtues of art, like the virtues of faith, are such that they reach beyond the limitations of the intellect, beyond any mere theory that a writer may entertain" and Percy's wry acknowledgment that writing is finally "a peculiar activity, as little understood as chicken fighting or entrail reading" (*MM*, 158; *SSL*, 403). The very fact that their fictions are so different bears witness to this observation—accord on certain points of theory does not necessarily mean similarity in practice—but in principle they very much agreed on a Catholic vision that committed them to a realism of the here and now, the created world they found themselves in. Both would finally agree with O'Connor's description of serious novelists as "fundamentally seekers and describers of the real," but their own "view of the ultimate reaches of reality" went beyond that of many so-called realists of the modern era (*MM*, 42).

The fundamental similarities and differences in O'Connor and Percy's literary imaginations are best understood in relation to their development during the Catholic Revival and under the particular influence of Tate and Gordon. In this milieu we will find the roots of not only the fundamental theoretical similarity in their approaches but also a partial understanding of the differences between O'Connor's and Percy's fictions in both theory and practice. The realism that each embraced in this milieu, I will argue, further accounts for the antiromantic bias that both show in the satire of certain artist "types" in their own fiction—romantics who, ironically, often perceive themselves as politically topical realists. Finally, I will suggest how the sacramental sense of the real subscribed to by each not only bolstered their convictions as realists but also contributed to the ahistorical perspective that enabled them to write of their contemporary South in a manner alien to their great predecessors in the Renascence—and as a legacy to contemporary Southern writers, even those of secular sentiment, who believe that their postmodern world is worth writing about as it is.

THE NOTIONS of the Catholic literary imagination outlined by Labrie and Giles are admittedly broad, and one might well be skeptical about the usefulness of lumping together figures as diverse as, say, Orestes Brownson and Louise Erdrich in terms of that imagination. But with O'Connor and Percy we can more specifically examine the working out of their Catholic theories of fiction in light of their common intellectual milieu and mentors. Each one's understanding of the Catholic imagination owed a debt to Maritain's writing on aesthetics and to the work of lesser-known figures such as William Lynch, S.J., as well as to Tate and Gordon.

O'Connor called Maritain's *Art and Scholasticism* "the book I cut my aesthetic teeth on," and Jay Tolson and Patrick Samway alike cite the slim volume as central to Percy's thought by at least the early 1950s; it is the essential starting point in any discussion of O'Connor's and Percy's commitment to realism and an important source for their understanding of art's moral function.[8] First published in France in 1930, this seminal Catholic Revival work provides a new formulation of a Thomist aesthetic. Or, to be more accurate, it articulates the aesthetic that Maritain sees as implicit in scholastic treatises that touched on art only indirectly and in which the fine arts were not distinguished as such. For Aquinas as for Aristotle, the painter, sculptor, musician, or poet was essentially an "artisan" and not granted the exalted place he later claimed in the Western mind (though the "liberal arts" that had no immediate utilitarian end were carefully distinguished from the "servile arts"). Maritain defines the maker of what the modern mind calls the fine arts as concerned with "intelligible arrangement"—with form—but also as profoundly grounded in the concrete: "this brilliance of the form, no matter how purely intelligible it may be in itself, is seized *in the sensible and through the sensible,* and not separately from it. The intuition of artistic beauty thus stands at the opposite extreme from the abstraction of scientific truth. For with the former it is through the very apprehension of the sense that the light of being penetrates the intelligence."[9] O'Connor herself might question the use of the term *intuition* here; she wrote that "even some of the things he [Maritain] says get soft at times. He is a philosopher and not an artist," but "he does have great understanding of the nature of art, which he gets from St. Thomas" (*HB*, 216). Both she and Percy (as well as Tate and Gordon) finally agreed with all the claims put forth in this brief but dense passage: that art, including literature, is a form of knowledge; that it approaches the real ("being") by a means entirely different from that of science; and that that means finally depends upon sense experience of the concrete rather than an abstract knowledge of general truths. As noted in the previous chapter, neo-Thomism generally posited that human knowledge began in sense experience. Here we can see even more specifically the theoretical grounding for O'Connor's repeated claims regarding the writer's responsibility to the world of matter, as well as Percy's claim that the novel is essentially cognitive but approaches the empirical from a direction altogether different from that of modern science.

8. O'Connor, *HB*, 167; Jay Tolson, *Pilgrim in the Ruins: A Life of Walker Percy* (New York: Simon and Schuster, 1992), 216, 237; Patrick Samway, S.J., *Walker Percy: A Life* (New York: Farrar, Straus and Giroux, 1997), 175.

9. Jacques Maritain, *Art and Scholasticism and The Frontiers of Poetry*, trans. Joseph W. Evans (New York: Scribner's, 1962), 25.

Maritain further defines art as essentially imitative of the real, but he notes that such imitation is a means rather than an end; the end is to present a semblance of real things "as making known something other than themselves, that is to say, as *signs*." Doing so involves a proper understanding of form, which, again, is not drawn from the isolated sensibility of the artist but rather is discovered in reality itself: "The human artist or poet, whose intellect is not the cause of things, as is the Divine Intellect, cannot draw this form entirely from his creative spirit: he goes and imbibes it first and above all in the immense treasure-house of created things, of sensible nature as also of the world of souls, and of the interior world of his own soul." He does not create ex nihilo, but rather from what has already been given to him; his own sensibility is included among such gifts and is properly understood only in relation to the rest of the created world in which he finds himself. Granted this understanding, according to Maritain, the Christian artist should properly consider all the world to be his subject: "everything belongs to [Christian art], the sacred as well as the profane." And rather than worry about spreading the Good News, the artist should concern himself with the internal integrity of his work, or, as O'Connor paraphrased it, "the good of that which is made." Art as discussed by Maritain, she notes, "has no utilitarian end. If you do manage to use it successfully for social, religious, or other purposes, it is because you make it art first . . ." (*HB*, 157). Percy agreed with this understanding in his oft-repeated observation that the novelist should never attempt to "edify" the reader, a direct echo of Maritain's claim that "if you were to turn desire to edify into a method of your art, you would spoil your art."[10] It was precisely Percy's engagement with Catholic philosophy that countered the tendency toward heavy-handed moralizing with which he, to a greater degree than O'Connor, always struggled.

The goal of avoiding didacticism should not, however, prevent the artist from presenting his characters as ethical agents; to fail to do so would be to fail to engage with reality. Maritain's claim that the artist must not moralize is balanced by the claim that the world itself in fact possesses a moral dimension that the artist has an obligation to recognize: "For morality is not, as Kant would have it, a world of imperatives descended from the heaven of liberty and alien to the world of being: it is rooted in reality as a whole, of

10. Ibid., 55, 59, 65–6.

which it manifests a certain category of laws; to ignore morality is to narrow the real and consequently to impoverish the materials of art. An integral *realism* is possible only for an art responsive to the whole truth of the universe of good and evil—an art pervaded by the consciousness of grace and sin and the importance of the *moment*."[11] The fruits of such an understanding are readily found in the best work of O'Connor and Percy, which may—to recall Labrie—end with an air of complexity and ambiguity but nonetheless reveal the "moral foundations of the universe" underlying the lives of contemporary characters.

Another important but less often remarked mutual influence on O'Connor and Percy, one deeply entrenched in the Catholic Revival milieu, was William Lynch, S.J., the editor of the Fordham philosophical and literary quarterly *Thought*, which O'Connor subscribed to and Percy published in during the 1950s and 1960s.[12] In articles and books such as "Theology and the Imagination" (1954) and *Christ and Apollo* (1960), owned and annotated by both O'Connor and Percy, Lynch outlined a vision of the Catholic literary imagination that was clearly important to both authors. His notion of the concrete literary imagination as particularly Christian was essentially continuous with Maritain's, but his emphasis on the role of limitation and form in shaping such a "Hebraic" imagination, which he defined in contrast to an "Appollonian" one, was largely his own. In O'Connor's essays particularly, there are further extensions of Lynch's ideas that help to distinguish her vision from that of Percy.

Lynch begins "Theology and the Imagination" with the forthright claim that "only a correct and bold Christian theology can lead us to healthy theory and practice in the life of the imagination" (the highlights of the piece, con-

11. Ibid., 147 (Maritain's emphasis). Another remark by Maritain is particularly relevant to O'Connor: "to be truly docile and faithful to the invisible spirit that plays in things, [the artist] can, and he even must, distort in some measure, reconstruct, transfigure the material appearances of nature" (60). Certainly O'Connor's use of the grotesque and her occasional ventures into the surreal—as in the visions of Mrs. Shortley in "The Displaced Person" and Ruby Turpin in "Revelation"—might be examined in light of this statement.

12. O'Connor, *HB*, 132. Percy published his first essay, "Symbol as Need," in *Thought* in autumn 1954, then "The Message in the Bottle" in autumn 1959. Samway acknowledges Percy's personal admiration for Lynch as well (174).

densed below, were all marked by O'Connor). His essential claim here is that "Christianity has from the beginning demanded that the search for redemption and the infinite be through the finite, through the limited, through the human" and that such an understanding is a clear asset to the literary imagination. Modernity, through its "overzealous dichotomizing of the body and the spirit," has lost this understanding and accordingly has "produced vast waves of new and pure sensibility and sheer experience" in literature. Such subjectivity tends toward "a non-human, non-evidential, and purely mystical thrust into a vague infinite." Thus, modernity's lost sense of "the finite, the limited, and the human levels of reality" results not only in heresy but also in bad literature, which is Lynch's final concern here: "No one will understand that we are pleading in these pages for a poetry that is formally Christic or religious. All we are saying is that something must reorientate our relation to the limited image, to the finite and the human."[13] Implicit in these words, as O'Connor surely recognized, is a sense of the special value of a sacramental imagination.

Lynch further developed such ideas in his *Christ and Apollo* (1960). Percy owned and annotated this study, probably reading it as he finished work on *The Moviegoer*, and O'Connor praised it highly in a review she wrote for her diocesan newspaper. Her comments reveal both the extent to which the book grew from seeds planted in "Theology and the Imagination" and her own essential agreement with its argument:

> Fr. Lynch describes the true nature of the literary imagination as founded on a penetration of the finite and the limited. The opposition here is between Christ, Who stands for reality in all its definiteness, and Apollo, who stands for the indefinite, the romantic, the endless. It is again the opposition between the Hebraic imagination, always concrete, and the agnostic imagination, which is dream-like. In genuine tragedy and comedy, the definite is explored to its extremity and man is shown to be the limited and finite creature he is, and it is at this point of greatest penetration of the limited that the artist finds insight. Much modern so-called

13. William Lynch, "Theology and the Imagination," *Thought* (Spring 1954): 64, 66, 70–1, 81. For O'Connor's admiration of this piece, see *HB*, 132. Her annotated copy is held at the Flannery O'Connor Collection, Georgia College and State University, Milledgeville, Georgia.

tragedy avoids this penetration and makes a leap toward transcendence, resulting in an unearned and spacious resolution of the work. . . .[14]

Lynch's work—which is not, of course, inconsistent with Maritain's—finally not only posits the value of the concrete Christian-Hebraic imagination, but also by comparison disparages the abstracted Apollonian-agnostic imagination, which left unchecked culminates in what he calls "angelism."[15] The term is an important one in this milieu, coined by Maritain but used frequently by Tate, whose essay "The Angelic Imagination" is cited approvingly throughout "Theology and the Imagination" and also by Percy. For this reason we shall examine it in the context of the Tates' influence.

Before doing so, however, it seems appropriate to consider issues raised by Lynch's work that point to a significant distinction between Percy and O'Connor. While Percy would have agreed in theory with Lynch's observations above (as his epigraph to this chapter indicates), O'Connor by and large was more gifted at putting that theory into practice, in large part because she valued the concrete language of the backwoods southern Protestants she lived among in a way that Percy did not. In fact, she saw their devotion to their own sort of "Hebraic" language as offsetting Catholicism's tendency toward theological abstraction. Such an understanding is clearly outlined in her essay "The Catholic Novelist in the Protestant South":

> To be great storytellers, we need something to measure ourselves against, and this is what we conspicuously lack in this age. . . . The Catholic has the natural law and the teachings of the Church to guide him, but for the writing of fiction, something more is necessary.
>
> For the purposes of fiction, these guides have to exist in a concrete form, known and held sacred by the whole community. They have to exist in the form of stories which affect our image and our judgment of ourselves. Abstractions, formulas, laws will not serve here. We have to have stories in our background. It takes a story to make a story. It takes a story of mythic dimensions, one which belongs to everybody, one in which

14. Flannery O'Connor, *The Presence of Grace and Other Book Reviews*, comp. Leo J. Zuber, ed. Carter W. Martin (Athens: University of Georgia Press, 1983), 94.

15. William Lynch, *Christ and Apollo: The Dimensions of the Literary Imagination* (New York: Sheed and Ward, 1960), 68.

everybody is able to recognize the hand of God and its descent. In the Protestant South, the Scriptures fill this role.

The Hebrew genius for making the absolute concrete has conditioned the Southerner's way of looking at things. That is one of the reasons why the South is a storytelling section. Our response to life is different if we have been taught only a definition of faith than if we have trembled with Abraham as he held the knife over Isaac. Both of these kinds of knowledge are necessary, but in the last four or five centuries, Catholics have overemphasized the abstract and consequently impoverished their imaginations and their capacity for prophetic insight. (*MM*, 203–4)

Such comments—which reveal, among other things, a specific way of reading Lynch—give a good deal of insight into what lies behind the radical difference between the experience of reading an O'Connor story and a Percy novel. Whatever the thematic similarities of their work, Percy's interest in the novel as a "scientific" tool and his explicit postmodern concern with language as such are worlds removed from O'Connor's implicit faith in the power of the word. He sensed as much. Reflecting once on American Catholic novelists in an interview, he described O'Connor in terms that suggest the vast stylistic, and perhaps temperamental, difference between him and the woman he so greatly admired: "then there's Flannery—although she's a Georgia fundamentalist."[16]

Nonetheless, they shared not only similar reading material but also similar mentors. For, having established the essential debt O'Connor and Percy owed to Maritain and Lynch with regard to their understanding of the Catholic literary imagination, we must recognize that such ideas were reinforced and to some extent interpreted for them by the Tates. While their approaches to the Catholic Revival finally differed radically in thematic terms, the older writers and the younger were in closer agreement on aesthetic theory: Percy and O'Connor alike often drew on the experience and intellectual legacy of the Tates, in both the specific close-reading advice of Caroline Gordon and the broader theoretical essays of her husband. In fact, the Tates finally influenced—or at least encouraged—O'Connor and Percy in three distinct but

16. *Conversations with Walker Percy*, ed. Lewis A. Lawson and Victor A. Kramer (Jackson: University Press of Mississippi, 1985), 47.

interrelated areas: in the explicit understanding of literature as a form of knowledge (a particular concern for Tate and Percy); in the concomitant embrace of a modified classical aesthetic that emphasized limitation and form in the service of a broadly conceived realism (an understanding O'Connor paid more heed to than did Percy); and an accompanying distrust of abstraction, intuitive subjectivity, and romanticism, all three of which were occasionally lumped together under the Thomistic rubric of "angelism."

So far we have discussed the Catholic literary imagination as being committed to a kind of realism. But implicit in any discussion of literary realism is the question of the extent to which literature can in fact engage with reality, which is inherently bound up with the question, as Tate would put it, of whether literature is a form of knowledge. Percy in particular directly concerned himself with this question as well as with the nature and ability to engage reality of language itself, an ability that Gordon and O'Connor seemingly held more implicit faith in. Although Tate's interest was passing and subservient to his interests as literary critic proper, whereas Percy was more interested in the subject for its own sake, the latter's essays on literature and language may owe a greater debt to Tate than has been heretofore realized in their common quarrel with the positivists.

The stakes of their engagement are perhaps more clearly seen from the perspective of our present age of literary uncertainty and self-doubt, an age that has not, however, reconstructed the traditional southern literary imagination. As Fred Hobson, building on the work of Julius Rowan Raper, has noted:

> [T]he contemporary southern writer, like the contemporary American writer, lives in a postmodern world, a world in which order, structure, and meaning—including narrative order, structure, and meaning—are constantly called into question. [But] . . . the southern writer in a postmodern world is not necessarily, is not usually, a postmodern *writer*. That is to say, the contemporary southern writer [with a few exceptions, mainly John Barth] essentially *accepts*, rather than invents, his world, is not given to fantasy, does not *in his fiction* question the whole assumed relationship between narrator and narrative, does not question the nature of fiction itself. The contemporary southern fiction writer, although he or she may experiment with time sequence and point of view (as the great southern

modernist Faulkner did, after all), in more basic respects usually plays by the old rules of the game.[17]

While most contemporary southern writers likely feel no need for a theoretical underpinning to justify such literary conservatism, insofar as such a framework exists in southern letters, it has been articulated not only by the New Critics (Ransom, Cleanth Brooks, Warren) but also by Tate and Percy, who have done so in terms that draw specifically upon the Catholic intellectual tradition. That the underlying foundations of our age's linguistic skepticism are ultimately religious is clearly suggested in Roland Barthes's "The Death of the Author," wherein he triumphantly claims that postmodernism "liberates what may be called an anti-theological activity." In one apt paraphrase of Barthes's legacy, such postmodernism has happily "deconstructed the notion of the transcendental signified. It is that mode of consciousness which has turned the universe from . . . a work [of the Author-God] into a text" that has "a multiplicity of meanings."[18]

But even apart from such overtly antitheological sentiments, much of the most prominent postmodern thought regarding language and literature is fundamentally opposed to the tradition Tate and Percy subscribed to on purely philosophical grounds. In his consideration of the Catholic imagination and the contemporary literary scene, Ross Labrie notes that "the realistic epistemology that characterized Thomist thought and thereby the Catholic sensibility has led to a distaste among Catholic writers [even those often disenchanted with the institutional Church] for the nominalism in some contemporary literary theory."[19] In citing the essential sympathy of Catholic writers with "critics

17. Fred Hobson, *The Southern Writer in the Postmodern World* (Athens: University of Georgia Press, 1991), 9. Hobson cites Raper's "Inventing Modern Southern Fiction: A Postmodern View," *Southern Literary Journal* (Spring 1990): 3–18.

18. Roland Barthes, "The Death of the Author," in *Image-Music-Text,* trans. Stephen Heath (New York: Hill and Wang, 1977), 147; Lance Olsen, "Neorealism, Postmodern Fantasy, and the American Short Story," in *Since Flannery O'Connor: Essays on the Contemporary American Short Story,* ed. Loren Logsdon and Charles W. Mayer (Macomb: Western Illinois University Press, 1987), 125.

19. Labrie, 7. Several recent Christian responses to late-twentieth-century linguistic skepticism would doubtlessly have fascinated O'Connor and especially Percy. John Deely, a Catholic philosopher and expert on semiotics who corresponded with Percy, has recently argued that a truly

like George Steiner, who in his book *Real Presences* affirmed the writer's ability to communicate experience, thought, and feeling," Labrie agrees with John F. Desmond's assessment of contemporary Catholic fiction. Desmond writes: "Any nominalistic view of language as the 'play' of signifiers, or of words as merely arbitrary tokens of meaning, is fundamentally antithetical to a Catholic vision. [But] our age of linguistic skepticism presents a bracing challenge to the Catholic writer. Such a writer is forced to probe the most extreme human experiences, pressuring language's revelatory powers, to articulate the movements of the spirit. . . . Today, Catholic writers still affirm the power of language to reveal the truth of the invisible world; and those who write it are searchers and discoverers of the real."[20] One such writer, Richard Bausch, whom Percy knew and admired and whose first novel of rural Virginia James Dickey judged to be set in "Flannery O'Connor country," seems to validate such an analysis in his account of how nightly recitation of the rosary while growing up affected his view of language: "I believe we learned from that experience that words counted for everything: one could address them to the dark, to the night stars in faith that they could be heard and that they mattered."[21] In such a view of language, we see the experiential foundations of the Catholic writer's commitment to realism—as opposed to nominalism—in

---

postmodern philosophy might come to embrace the Thomistic view of language by way of Charles Sanders Peirce. See "Quid Sit Postmodernismus?" in *Postmodernism and Christian Philosophy*, ed. Roman T. Ciapolo (Washington, DC: Catholic University of America, 1997), 68–96. Catherine Pickstock's *After Writing: On the Liturgical Consummation of Philosophy* (Oxford: Blackwell, 1998) poses a differently nuanced argument, one perhaps more in the spirit of Marcel and Kierkegaard than Aquinas. Pickstock describes her project as falling within the "new theological imperative of 'radical orthodoxy'" recently associated with the University of Cambridge: "while conceding, with postmodernism, the indeterminacy of all our knowledge and experience of selfhood, [radical orthodoxy] construes this shifting flux as a sign of our dependency on a transcendent source which 'gives' all reality as a mystery, rather than as adducing our suspension over the void" (xii). Taking to task the assumptions behind and implications of Derrida's theory of the sign, Pickstock presents a reading of Plato's *Phaedrus* as preparatory to her final assertion that "the event of transubstantiation in the Eucharist is the condition of possibility for all human meaning" (xv).

20. John Desmond, "Catholicism in Contemporary American Fiction," *America*, May 14, 1994, 7–8.

21. Richard Bausch, quoted in introduction to *Selected Stories of Richard Bausch* (New York: Modern Library, 1996), v. Dickey quoted, vi.

a more thoroughgoing philosophical sense, one familiar to Tate and Percy explicitly, if only implicitly to many southern and Catholic writers.

Our present linguistic skepticism, Percy might well argue, is the necessary fallout of the positivistic conception of language—and devaluing of literature—that he began battling in the 1950s. He did so partly by drawing on Tate's work, though Tate, unlike Percy, engaged such questions largely in the context of his interests as a practicing literary critic. As Peter Huff has described, in the 1940s and beyond, Tate "endorsed New Criticism's call for an 'ontological' criticism" in crypto-Catholic terms: "Affirming a form of real knowledge by means of the concrete literary image, distinct from that obtained through rational, scientific cognition, this type of criticism echoed traditional points of Aristotelian literary theory. . . . Though other New Critics turned for metaphysical support to the aesthetic theory of Immanuel Kant or the Protestant Neo-Orthodoxy of Reinhold Niebuhr, Tate capitalized on New Criticism's apparent similarities to Catholic thought."[22]

Tate laid the foundations for such a criticism in essays such as "The Present Function of Criticism" (1940), where he claimed that "[l]iterature is the complete knowledge of man's experience, and by knowledge I mean that unique and formed intelligence of the world of which man alone is capable." He expanded on this statement in "Literature as Knowledge" (1941). Beginning with a reflection on the possibilities and shortcomings of semiotic theory of the time, a relatively young field "of great interest from the point of view of literary criticism," Tate devotes the bulk of the essay to exploring the modern conviction that "truth is only the second consideration of the poet, and from the point of view of positivism the knowledge, or truth, that poetry gives us is immature and inadequate." Here Tate cites I. A. Richards's "two doctrines" of poetry in order to note the discrediting of the first and the prevalence of the latter in the modern world: "1. The mind of the poet at moments . . . gains an insight into reality, reads Nature as a symbol of something behind or within Nature yet not ordinarily perceived[;] 2. The mind of the poet creates a Nature into which his own feelings, his aspirations and apprehensions, are projected." The essential affinity of the first doctrine, particularly if we empha-

22. Peter Huff, *Allen Tate and the Catholic Revival: Trace of the Fugitive Gods* (Paulist Press, 1996), 81–2.

size the word *within*, with the Catholic literary imagination is clear. But positivism, Tate claims, has undermined this doctrine by claiming "Nature" as its own; "the language of poetry" has thereby "ceased to represent [Nature,] . . . ceased, in fact, to have any validity, or to set forth anything real." The second doctrine, "the standard poetics of our time: projection of feeling" by a narcissistic intellect, is inadequate.[23]

"Literature as Knowledge" does not so much propose a solution to this problem as explore its deep roots in the modern mind. In "The Hovering Fly: A Causerie on the Imagination and the Actual World" (1943), however, Tate is more polemical. Although he acknowledges the authority of the positivists "in a single field of discourse which may be briefly labeled as physicalism," he argues that they are fundamentally mistaken and even corruptive in their claim "that [theirs] is the sole field of discourse, all others being illusion, priestcraft, superstition. . . ." Positivism finally performs upon literature and religion alike "an act of occultation," "a hiding away, an ascription of dark motives, even an imputation of black art."[24] In doing so, it impoverishes our sense of the real. To lose our faith that language—especially rigorously crafted language—engages with reality, Tate says, is to lose our sense of the fullness of reality itself.

Tate continued to probe similar themes in essays such as "The Man of Letters in Modern World" (1952), in which he derides the contemporary conception of language not as facilitating "communion" among persons and the world, but rather as an essentially manipulative means of "communication" conceived in terms of "stimulus" and "response."[25] Because of his own scientific training, Percy was better equipped than Tate to confront such crudely behavioristic models of language, and they were among his own primary targets when he began writing essays on language in the early 1950s. His first published essay, "Symbol as Need," drew clearly on Maritain, as well as other Catholic Revival thinkers, in describing language as our most fundamental means of engaging the real: for example, in two people's agreement upon a name for some part of the created world, Percy claims, "our common existence is validated. It is the foundation for what Marcel calls the metaphysics

23. Allen Tate, *Essays of Four Decades* (Chicago: Swallow, 1968), 210, 78, 97, 102–3.
24. Ibid., 115–6.
25. Ibid., 12.

of *we are* instead of *I think*" (*MB*, 295). What is less explicit is the extent to which Percy is indebted to Tate's work in this essay: as Kieran Quinlan has noted, the example that Percy uses here (and elsewhere) to refute positivist semioticians by distinguishing between "sign" and "symbol" owes something to "Literature as Knowledge."[26]

Percy's 1958 essay "Metaphor as Mistake" continued in the same vein, both relying on Tate as an authority in speaking of literary concerns per se and paralleling his thought again with regard to the nature of language itself. In citing Tate's reading of Dante, Percy conveys his particular appreciation of what he sees as the essential realism of the Catholic literary imagination: "Dante, as Allen Tate reminds us, uses very few linguistic metaphors. The 'greatest thing by far' which Aristotle had in mind when he spoke of the mastery of the metaphor as a sign of genius may very well have been the sort of prolonged analogy which Dante did use, in which the action takes place among the common things of concrete experience and yet yields an analogy—by nothing so crude as an allegorization wherein one thing is designated as standing for another but by the very density and thingness of the action" (*MB*, 66). Percy goes on to affirm that metaphor has "a cognitive dimension" all its own and to affirm "the discovering power" not only of "analogy" but also of language itself, for humans know "not as the angels know and not as dogs know but as men, who must know one thing through the mirror of another" (77, 82). Words are our most basic "mirrors," and Percy would explain them neither as do the "semanticists"—who somehow maintain both that we know things directly rather than through words and that, nonetheless, "we have no true knowledge of reality"—nor as do the behaviorists, who crudely explain language in terms of "sign-response" (82). Words are, according to Percy, our most fundamental means of knowing the real, and yet they cannot be explained in "empirical" terms. Finally, idealism and positivism alike fail to grasp what language is.

The same line of thought is seen in Percy's "Naming and Being" (1960): "As Allen Tate has pointed out, it was a general belief in the West until the seventeenth century that human beings do not know things directly, as do the angels, but only through the medium of something else: the symbol."

26. Kieran Quinlan, *Walker Percy: The Last Catholic Novelist* (Baton Rouge: Louisiana State University Press, 1996), 65. See also Percy, *MB*, 292–3.

Yet Percy goes further than Tate in the philosophical, and even the broadly "scientific," implications of the views they share. The act of "naming" a "*thing*" by "*pairing*" it with a "*symbol*," he claims, causes in humans "a new orientation toward the world. Prior to naming things, the individual is an organism responding to an environment," but afterward "he no longer coincides with what he is biologically. Henceforth, he must exist either authentically or inauthentically," and he does so in the act of naming. For Percy, therefore, language—and, by extension, literature—is the most fundamentally human of phenomena; in our struggle to tell and respond to the truth, we succeed or fail as human beings. And Percy is finally perhaps more accepting than Tate of the role of a properly conceived science in this quintessentially human endeavor: "No matter whether I give a name to, or hear the name of, a strange bird; no matter whether I write or read a line of great poetry, form or understand a scientific hypothesis, I thereby exist authentically as a namer or a hearer, as an 'I' or a 'thou'—and in either case as a co-celebrant of what is" (*SSL*, 134–5). To recall Huff's phrasing regarding the New Criticism, Percy shared with Tate a belief in the "concrete literary image" as providing "real knowledge"; but Percy was, at least in essays such as "Naming and Being," comparatively less insistent about the extent to which such knowledge *differed* from scientific knowledge, and his phrasing here also shows a debt to existential philosophy (Heidegger and Marcel in particular) that Tate did not share.[27]

Percy and Tate alike remained essentially within the Thomist tradition, of course, and this allegiance explains their affinity not only with one another but also with Gordon and O'Connor insofar as their views regarding the nature of language were concerned. Again, the two women were not explicitly interested in semiotic theory as the men were but shared with them an inherent conviction that the power of language engages a reality of mysterious depths. Drawing on both the importance of acts of naming by characters in O'Connor's stories and her comments in essays and letters (e.g., her claim that "the moral basis of Poetry is the accurate naming of the things of God" and that its accuracy depends upon one's "seeing straight" in a visible universe with invisible dimensions [*HB*, 128, 131]), Emily Archer has argued convincingly

27. Percy also referred to Tate's vision of the "man of letters in the modern world" in "The State of the Novel: Dying Art or New Science?" *SSL*, 143; and in "Novel-Writing in an Apocalyptic Time," *SSL*, 157.

that O'Connor and Percy in particular share such a view. Their conception of language is, again, fundamentally at odds with that prevalent in many contemporary intellectual circles: "O'Connor and Percy provide a dialectic, she implicitly and he explicitly, with those who hold that language is merely a sophisticated reward system or a prison-house of reality (to use Jameson's compelling metaphor) beyond which no Word external to ourselves exists."[28] Archer expands upon this claim elsewhere. She argues that "both writers share a vision of the third-dimensional nature of a reality that holds the secret of new meanings and restored connections" (Percy's "Delta Factor" and O'Connor's "anagogical vision") and that each views proper naming as being concerned with a vision of the depths of the real, with "penetration of the thing itself." Such concerns are not merely peripheral to their fiction, because both believe that a proper understanding of "language is essential to a diagnosis of the twentieth century and a vision of its healing."[29] Hence the nature of language becomes not only a theoretical concern for O'Connor and Percy as writers, but a thematic concern of the utmost importance to their characters.

Finally, then, the vision of language affirmed by both Percy and O'Connor is continuous with the broadly conceived Catholic *realism* discussed thus far, which, at least in this specific regard, has some significant affinities with the ongoing southern literary traditionalism described by Hobson. While such considerations may well have seemed arcane to many writers and critics alike during Tate's lifetime and even for much of Percy's, they have become increasingly prominent in contemporary literary discussion and necessarily underlie any discussion of literary realism.[30] Interestingly enough, even many writers

28. Emily Archer, " 'Stalking Joy': Flannery O'Connor's Accurate Naming," *Religion and Literature* 18:2 (Summer 1986): 21.

29. Emily Archer, "Naming in the Neighborhood of Being: O'Connor and Percy on Language," *Studies in the Literary Imagination* 20:2 (Fall 1987): 97, 99, 101. For another examination of O'Connor and Percy's relationship in this regard—one holding that for both, "language itself can be a key to a sacramental vision"—see Dixie Lee Highsmith, "Flannery O'Connor's Polite Conversation," in *Flannery O'Connor Bulletin* (1982): 94–107. Highsmith is particularly concerned with the role of clichés, and their unexpected transformation into newly meaningful language, in O'Connor's work.

30. As Quinlan has noted, "Percy contemplated a refutation of the philosophical and literary deconstructionists, whose enterprise he saw as 'little more than rehashed Nietzscheanism, an attempt to get rid of God by first disposing of grammar,' but he never got around to writing it" (196).

who might otherwise find fault with Tate, O'Connor, and Percy's broadly "traditional" sentiments rely upon an implicit linguistic conservatism—a faith in the power of the word—that this small group of Catholic thinkers shared and eloquently defended.

Whereas Tate's contributions to Percy's and O'Connor's notions of the Catholic literary imagination remained largely theoretical (and we will see presently how his critique of romanticism interested O'Connor), Gordon's contributions had more to do with practice than theory. Gordon produced a substantial amount of critical writing—including works such as *How to Read a Novel* (1958)—which reveal her essential commitment to form and rigorously practiced fictional technique in the service of symbolic realism, and she also provided more personally tailored advice to her two charges. Gordon's long letter to Percy in reaction to his first draft of *The Charterhouse* bears particularly close examination, for in it we see how that advice specifically endorsed the Catholic literary imagination as we have defined it thus far, though in an engagingly personal, idiosyncratic, and often intentionally humorous manner.

Gordon begins by congratulating Percy for having chosen the faith proper to a serious writer, because the Catholic writer—a category she conceives quite broadly—is one who knows to ground his fiction in the created world: "When one is writing out of the Protestant *mystique*, which is what everyone who isn't a Catholic is doing—even the Communists, I think—one has the responsibility of setting up a new heaven and a new earth as one goes. But a Catholic knows that God has created the universe and that his job is to find his proper place in it."[31] She then proceeds to draft an Orthodox Russian in support of her argument: Dostoyevsky was able to create with such "amazing variety and spontaneity" precisely because "very little of his energy was spent in figuring out the things that our contemporaries feel it is their duty to figure out" (i.e., the nature and moral order of the universe).

In this spirited and often lighthearted letter, we see how wide-ranging Gordon's notion of the "Catholic" writer is. Here Percy receives a basic introduction to techniques of fiction writing based on the examples and/or principles of Aristotle, Aquinas, Homer, Henry James, T. S. Eliot, Saint Ignatius of Loyola, unspecified "medieval schoolmen," Ford Madox Ford, Gustave Flau-

31. Gordon to Percy, December 11, 1951, Walker Percy Papers, Southern Historical Collection, University of North Carolina at Chapel Hill (henceforth SHC).

bert, Sophocles, Shakespeare, an unnamed "old Negro preacher" from Kentucky, Hemingway, Leo Tolstoy, Joyce, and Maritain. Names introduced solely for purposes of disparagement include that of Thomas Wolfe (for failing to limit his novels to Aristotle's definition of a play, "an action of a certain magnitude"), Descartes, Elinor Wylie (for developing "a prose style based on the use of the semicolon"), and—surprisingly—three "Catholic" writers: Graham Greene, François Mauriac, and Evelyn Waugh. It is in her criticism of such novelists that Gordon reveals most clearly that her idea of Catholic fiction derives from a curious blend of neo-Thomist aesthetic theory and reverence for high modernist technique. According to Gordon, the shortcomings of most professing Catholic fiction writers stem not from their piety but rather from formal sloppiness and a failure to stay grounded in the sensible world. The former concern is most emphasized in this letter: "Catholic fiction has not been much good up till now" precisely because "most Catholic writers are poor technicians." Mauriac, for example, is thematically powerful but has "bad technique"; Greene is "fuzzy-minded"; Waugh, she claims, has deteriorated since his conversion. And a later letter to Percy emphasized her related concern with Catholic realism: Gordon claimed that Joyce and even Yeats were not only better writers but also "better Christians . . . than Mauriac, Bernanos, and Greene, partly because their work is based on the natural order, while [the latter writers] reject the natural order and thereby land in Manichean despair. . . . Maritain says that the first thing a novelist must have is honest, authentic, universal realism."[32]

Her main advice to Percy himself regarding *The Charterhouse* conveys such an understanding: his characters must, she says, stay grounded in the sensible world. As it is, they tend to become "disembodied voices," which makes for bad fiction precisely because it proceeds from a flawed conception of the real: "Nobody exists in a vacuum. He is always related to something and somebody else. (Was this not the medieval schoolmen's demonstration of the existence

---

32. Gordon to Percy, n.d. [October–November 1952], SHC. Of course, such a broad definition of "Catholic" fiction risks becoming meaningless. As Thomas Haddox notes, Gordon's (and Maritain's) definition conveniently "provides a means of placing non-Catholic literary works of merit under a Catholic, or at least Christian, rubric"—but "if even Yeats can pass for a Christian writer, then what does a non-Christian writer look like?" Haddox, "Contextualizing Flannery O'Connor: Allen Tate, Caroline Gordon, and the Catholic Turn in Southern Literature," *Southern Quarterly* 38:1 (Fall 1999): 179.

of God? At any rate, it is a most un-Cartesian practice.)" Her most detailed instructions to Percy concern the necessity of helping the reader to *sense* everything that happens, which is far more important than merely conveying theological *ideas*: "I am convinced that the writing of fiction is a religious impulse, which is one reason so many people who would be better employed praying 'want to write.' But if one does write one's task is to imitate the Almighty, to make one's word flesh and dwell among men. If you can't do that you'd better not try to write fiction. It takes five senses to make a man fully live . . . when we no longer have *any* sensuous apprehension of the universe we are no longer living in this world." The master Percy should imitate in this regard, she makes clear, is Flaubert: "where a lesser writer would content himself with invoking sight, Flaubert invokes sound also and touch and sometimes smell."[33]

As suggested in chapter 2, Gordon was more pleased with O'Connor's practice than Percy's in this regard. O'Connor seems to have been more temperamentally inclined than Percy to keep her fiction grounded in the sensible world, but her many remarks about the value of the concrete in the essays and lectures collected in *Mystery and Manners* also show a debt to Gordon. For example, given Gordon's advice to Percy above, there can be no doubt about the identity of the "lady" O'Connor refers to in "The Nature and Aim of Fiction": "A lady who writes, and whom I admire very much, wrote me that she had learned from Flaubert that it takes at least three activated sensuous strokes to make an object real; and she believes that this is connected with our having five senses. If you're deprived of any of them, you're in a bad way, but if you're deprived of more than two at once, you almost aren't present." And, like Gordon, O'Connor attributes the difficulty of writing good fiction in the modern world to the difficulty of mastering an "incarnational art" in an age infected with a spirit much like that of the Manicheans, who thought "all material things were evil" and therefore "sought pure spirit and tried to approach the infinite directly without any mediation of matter" (*MM*, 68–9).

To approach the infinite by way of matter, however, is no easy task. Insofar as the artist attempts it, O'Connor would say, she must do so with a proper understanding of the very finiteness of her materials, of their necessary limita-

33. Gordon to Percy, December 11, 1951.

tion and her concordantly necessary commitment to form. The abstract ideas that undergird stories such as "Greenleaf" and "The Displaced Person" should not be her concern except as they are manifested in the stories themselves. As she once noted, "a story really isn't any good unless it successfully resists paraphrase"; accordingly, the fact that one story both begins and ends with a very concrete bull, and the other with a peacock, is not merely incidental to their meaning (*MM*, 108). The waiting bull with the torn hedge like a wreath across his horns, the peacock with its shimmering tail—"tiers of small pregnant suns floated in a green-gold haze over his head"—embody rather than convey that meaning. And while the formal tautness of, say, "Greenleaf"—its beginning and ending with the figure of the bull—is precisely what makes the story meaningful and therefore susceptible to analysis, it does not, in O'Connor's view, hinder the story's contact with infinite mystery but rather provides the occasion for such contact. A story that appropriately embodies concrete imagery through its formal completeness is never explained away but rather "hangs on and expands in the mind" (*MM*, 108). O'Connor's understanding of form thereby calls to mind Tate's description of poetry as "the art of apprehending and concentrating our experience in the mysterious limitations of form"; again, Paul Giles has argued that such an understanding, with its emphasis on *mystery*, stands "in sharp contrast to that of traditional classical humanism, which associates formal control with what is eminently knowable and so susceptible to human reason."[34]

The Catholic literary imagination as perceived by both the Tates combined this consistently antiromantic concern with form with a seemingly antithetical respect for the essentially mysterious depths of reality. While O'Connor and Percy alike agreed with their mentors in theory, they eventually went their own way in practice. Gordon, in her relentless communication of the necessity of formal and technical rigor, posited the novels of Henry James as the pinnacle of American fiction in both regards and a fit model for aspiring young novelists; O'Connor's and Percy's attitudes toward James thereby become an apt barometer for measuring their commitment to Gordon's notions of form and technique. O'Connor professed a liking for James, though she damned him with faint praise in her comment that she reads him mainly "from a sense of High Duty and because when I read James I feel something

34. Tate, *Essays*, 613; Giles, 195.

is happening to me, in slow motion but happening nonetheless" (*HB*, 99) (similarly, it is difficult to imagine what the author of *Portrait of a Lady* would have made of *Wise Blood*). Nonetheless, O'Connor was more likely than Percy to take Gordon's close-reading advice, and hence she fell more nearly than he did into the established camp of southern modernists, aesthetically speaking; Gordon's commentary on the technical as well as the thematic merits of "Good Country People" in her second edition of *The House of Fiction* suggests the extent to which she saw her "pupil" in this light.[35]

Percy was more of a disappointment to Gordon in this respect. Although he made efforts at reading James, beginning in the mid-1950s (as Shelby Foote had been urging him to do for years), he balked. His negative reaction to the master is suggested by a crack he made decades later: "I once had a student who discovered James. Never heard from her again."[36] To a great extent Percy remained the novelist of ideas that Gordon initially feared he was, one less concerned with form and more openly committed to "intentionality" than either she or O'Connor. As he wrote to his old mentor in a candid moment after winning the National Book Award for *The Moviegoer*: "Actually I do not consider myself a novelist but a moralist or propagandist. My spiritual father is Pascal (and/or Kierkegaard). And if I also kneel before the altar of Lawrence and Joyce and Flaubert, it is not because I wish to do what they did, even if I could. What I really want to do is to tell people *what they must do and what they must believe if they want to live.*"[37] Percy kept such potentially disastrous intentions from spoiling his art by remembering Maritain's injunctions against didacticism and by his own virtually "scientific" commitment to "putting a man in a concrete situation"; yet insofar as he was a writer committed to the concrete, he worked from a far different model than Gordon had proposed. When he read French fiction, he learned from not Flaubert but Camus, and—unlike O'Connor—he did not shine a glaring spotlight on his characters from a detached third-person point of view; rather he set out with them to explore the world of being. His own experience of writing paralleled the searches of

35. Gordon and Tate, eds., *The House of Fiction*, 2d ed. (New York: Scribner's, 1960), 382–6. Haddox argues convincingly that Gordon, in at least some respects, actually underwent a postconversion break with the ideals of the New Criticism (180–1).

36. Tolson, 442.

37. Percy to Gordon, April 6, 1962, in private papers of Ashley Brown (Percy's emphasis). Quoted in Tolson, 300.

his characters, gaining in experiential authenticity what it may have lacked in formal rigor. As Jay Tolson has suggested, Percy wrote less like Gordon or his friend Foote—a true worshipper at the altar of High Modernism who worked from elaborate "architectonic" outlines—than like D. H. Lawrence, "finding his way forward in the act of writing and never quite knowing where he was heading."[38] Such an approach added to Percy's own sense that the openness of his search made it—ironically—akin to that of the empirical scientist, even if his method was fundamentally different.

WHILE, THEN, there are certainly obvious differences in their fictions—O'Connor reveals mystery by shining her glaring spotlight upon grotesque characters or simple natural objects for a glimpse of the invisible universe, whereas Percy's characters (like detectives or scientists) stumble onto more understated clues about the depths of the real—we nonetheless see in their shared faith about the world and our ability to know and represent that world in literature a common "Christian realism" of substantial philosophical depth. Precisely because of their religious commitment, O'Connor and Percy—more self-consciously than any of their fellow southern writers—thought through and articulated their convictions as realists in an emerging postmodern world.

The Catholic intellectual tradition that fostered their imaginations, however, often most articulately conveyed what it was by pointing to what it was *not*. In the milieu of the Catholic Revival, O'Connor and Percy found not only positive support for their own sort of realism but also injunctions against certain forms of the post-Enlightenment literary imagination. Because Allen Tate had for so long been troubled by his own relationship to that imagination, he was one of the most powerful spokesmen on its shortcomings, particularly when it manifested itself in the form of romanticism; O'Connor and especially Percy followed his lead in linking romanticism with the modern tendency toward abstraction under Maritain's general rubric of "angelism." Furthermore, they not only made clear their commitment to realism in their essays but also relentlessly satirized flawed artists, almost inevitably types of the romantic, in their own fiction.

38. Tolson, 225. See also Percy to Foote, February 3, 1971, in *The Correspondence of Shelby Foote and Walker Percy*, ed. Jay Tolson (New York: Doubletake/Norton, 1997), 153, for Percy's description of the "proper planned-out Footean architectonic novel."

Tate's essays are a fitting starting point for understanding what he, Gordon, and ultimately O'Connor and Percy saw as the limitations of the romantic imagination. In "Yeats's Romanticism," Tate (who finally refuses to call Yeats a romantic) echoes Eliot in succinctly phrasing the "historic" problem of romanticism as "the division between sensibility and intellect"; in the twentieth century the term further suggests outright escapism "from problems, forces, and theories 'relevant' to the modern world."[39] Tate wrote a number of pieces on this theme (e.g., the companion essays "The Angelic Imagination" and "The Symbolic Imagination"), but "Hart Crane" (1932–7) best encapsulates his attitudes toward what he would later call the role of "the man of letters in the modern world." This essay reflects the essence of Tate's larger thinking about art, culture, and religion not in a southern context but in the larger context of modernism; furthermore, it was not only admired in itself by O'Connor, but it also contains the seeds of much of Tate's later thought on the literary imagination.[40]

Crane had been a close friend of Tate's, and the essay conveys a strong sense of Tate's own involvement in what he saw as the artistic dilemma of Crane, whom he elsewhere called "our twentieth-century poet as hero."[41] While largely affectionate toward Crane in calling him "one of the great masters of the romantic movement," Tate in this piece articulates what he sees as the profound limitations of that movement. Crane's "aesthetic problem" was the "historic problem of romanticism," first hinted at in Tate's statement that Crane was probably "incapable of the formal discipline of a classical education." Crane's poetry reveals the limitations of romanticism in that it has not only "defects of the surface[;] it has a defect of vision": it fails to engage with the world as it is (310–1). "The locked-in sensibility, the insulated egoism, of his poetry" conflicts with "the ordinary forms of experience," and his portrayal of a reality where objects are not distinguished from one another reveals his "implicit pantheism" (313). While "the impulse in The Bridge is religious, . . . the soundness of an impulse is no warrant that it will create a

39. Tate, Essays, 300.

40. O'Connor, HB, 149. Percy probably read the Crane essay also, at least in its truncated form, as it appeared in his copy of Tate's The Forlorn Demon: Didactic and Critical Essays, now held in the Rare Books Collection, Wilson Library, University of North Carolina at Chapel Hill.

41. Tate, Essays, 328.

sound art form" (317). In all of these statements we see Tate's proclivity for a rigorous and demanding formal aesthetic that communicates the realities of the concrete world.

And, Tate continues, Crane as romantic was completely unaware of the split between his own consciousness and that world. *The Bridge* is an ill-conceived attack upon what Crane perceived as Eliot's "pessimism," which in Tate's estimation is founded on real insight into "the decay of individual consciousness and its fixed relations to the world," but which Crane mistakenly sees as "pure orneryness [*sic*]" in the face of the wonders of the mechanical age. Crane's "vagueness of purpose, in spite of the apparently concrete character of the Brooklyn Bridge, which became the symbol of his epic, he never succeeded in correcting." Such vagueness is characteristic of the undisciplined romantic imagination, which has no sense of limitation and therefore none of form: "the fifteen parts of *The Bridge* taken as one poem suffer from the lack of a coherent structure, whether symbolic or narrative. . . . The single symbolic image, in which the whole poem centers, is at one moment the actual Brooklyn Bridge; at another, it is any bridge or 'connection'; at still another, it is a philosophical pun and becomes the basis of a series of analogies."[42]

Tate's ideas about language come to the foreground in this analysis, and he finally draws a clear connection—one consistent with his work in "Literature as Knowledge" and elsewhere—between a properly grounded sensibility, skillfully employed language, and realistic engagement with the world. He finally assesses *The Bridge* as a cautionary example of the product of a romantic imagination that is very much akin to Lynch's dreamlike Apollonian-agnostic imagination. As such it is fundamentally opposed to the sacramental imagination best represented for Tate by—of course—Dante:

> In the great epic and philosophical works of the past, notably *The Divine Comedy*, the intellectual groundwork is not only simple philosophically; we not only know that the subject is personal salvation, just as we know that Crane's is the greatness of America: we are given also the complete articulation of the idea down to the slightest detail, and we are given it *objectively* apart from anything that the poet is going to say about it. When

42. Ibid., 314.

the poet extends his perception, there is a further extension of the *ground-work* ready to meet it and discipline it, and to compel the sensibility of the poet to stick to the subject. Crane's difficulty is that of modern poets generally: they play the game with half of the men, the men of sensibility, and because sensibility can make any move, the significance of all moves is obscure.[43]

While such a criticism may itself seem obscure and to offer little hope to the postmedieval artist, O'Connor seems to have been in full agreement with Tate. In "Writing Short Stories" she seems to apply his observations on poetry to short fiction: "The fiction writer has to realize that he can't create compassion with compassion, or emotion with emotion, or thought with thought. He has to provide all these things with a body; he has to create a world with weight and extension" (*MM*, 92).

Tate also expands on the shortcomings of romanticism in a manner that has clearer implications in an American context, and he does so in a statement that implicitly recalls his southern Agrarianism. Crane, he says,

> . . . knew little of the history of his country. It was not merely a defect of education, but a defect, in the spiritual sense, of the modern mind. Crane lacked the sort of indispensable understanding of his country that a New England farmer has who has never been out of his township. *The Bridge* attempts to include all American life, but it covers the ground with seven-league boots and, like a sightseer, sees nothing. With reference to its leading symbol, it has no subject matter. The poem is the effort of a solipsistic sensibility to locate itself in the external world, to establish points of reference.[44]

Despite his diplomatic attempt to include the Yankees here, Tate knew that at the time he was writing, the part of America that would bear strongest evidence of the fruits of a regional realism was not New England but the South. Maritain would have agreed with his principle here: *Art and Scholasticism* stated that precisely because "art does not reside in an angelic mind," it is "basically dependent upon everything which the human community, spiritual

43. Ibid., 316 (my emphasis).
44. Ibid., 320.

tradition and history transmit to the body and mind of man. By its human subject and its human roots, art belongs to a time and a country," which is precisely "why the most universal and the most human works are those which bear most openly the mark of their country."[45] And O'Connor likely drew from both Tate and Maritain in formulating her own oft-repeated comments regarding the value to the writer of being rooted in a place. In America, she tells us, the regional writer has been, like Tate's "New England farmer," apt to know his country best: "The best American fiction has always been regional. The ascendancy passed roughly from New England to the Midwest to the South; it has passed to and stayed longest wherever there has been a shared past, a sense of alikeness, and the possibility of reading a small history in a universal light" (MM, 58).

In its sense of being a distinct place, O'Connor wrote, "the South still has a degree of advantage," but one already passing in her own time: northerners moving to Atlanta suburbs were being told, "You'll like this place. There's not a Southerner for two miles." Percy wrote of a South even further gone in becoming a "non-place," of course (to borrow his term from "Why I Live Where I Live"), but his ambivalence about his own status as a regional writer had more to do with his perception of his region's actual disappearance than with any rejection of the inherent value of one's local reality. For, to an even greater degree than O'Connor, he explicitly agreed with Tate's diagnosis of the ills attendant upon the modern mind's disengagement from the real. And for Percy this disengagement was not limited to the sphere of literary romanticism; the broader phenomenon of angelism, as Maritain dubbed it, was manifest in the modern mind generally.

In The Dream of Descartes (1944), a study in intellectual and cultural history, Maritain laid out most succinctly his analysis of the post-Cartesian split of the human self into "beast-machine" body and "angelic" mind. While on the one hand positing a purely physical and mechanistic conception of the world, Descartes claimed for himself and like-minded thinkers a privileged theoretical—even in some sense a "spiritual"—standpoint, on the other hand, from which pure knowledge was attained. Western culture ever since has been characterized by "a theoretical contempt of the body and the senses; nothing worthwhile but pure thought. This means, in fact, the triumph of artificial

---

45. Maritain, Art and Scholasticism, 74.

thought and of false intellectualism; for human intellection is living and fresh only when it is centered upon the vigilance of sense perception. The natural roots of our knowledge being cut, a general drying-up in philosophy and culture resulted, a drought for which romantic tears were later to provide only an insufficient remedy." Maritain went on to develop the connection between Cartesianism and romanticism at some length. Descartes himself, Maritain implied, was a protoromantic in the narcissistic withdrawal from society and tradition that his famous philosophical "method" required, as well as in his "optimism of Reason, forerunner of the sentimental optimism of the eighteenth century, . . . which is even like a very distant, hardly perceptible prelude to the irrational optimism which Jean-Jacques Rousseau was to promote on a far greater plane and with a far greater amplitude." Finally, Cartesian man becomes "the man of Rousseau, naturally good in so far as he is sentiment and instinct." As such, Maritain suggests, he is radically disconnected from reality, and his exuberant optimism easily degenerates to darkest depair.[46]

Unwilling to leave the debate to the French, Tate followed Maritain's lead and joined in a tradition of Descartes-bashing in English letters that dates to *Gulliver's Travels*.[47] He did so by attending to the work not of Crane but of an earlier southern writer who had long fascinated him, one whose own dark romanticism—the flip side of Emerson's exuberance—Tate saw as inexorably bound to Cartesian thought. "The Angelic Imagination: Poe as God" (1951) draws explicitly on Maritain in its lengthy examination of Poe in terms of angelism. It explores, for example, the proclivity of his male heroes for professing "an impossibly high love of the heroine that circumvents the body and moves in upon her spiritual essence."[48] Tate points to *Eureka* as the culmina-

46. Jacques Maritain, *The Dream of Descartes*, trans. Mabelle L. Andison (New York: Philosophical Library, 1944), 180, 100, 183.

47. Swift parodies an entire nation of angelic Cartesians who inhabit the Flying Island of Laputa, whose minds "are so taken up with intense speculations, that they neither can speak, nor attend to the discourses of others, without being roused by some external taction upon the organs of speech and hearing." Jonathan Swift, *Gulliver's Travels and Other Writings*, ed. Louis A. Landa (Boston: Houghton Mifflin, 1960), 128.

48. Tate, *Essays*, 404. Tate's project here recalls Giles's claim that American Catholic literature is generally outside the "mythical 'mainstream' of Protestant romanticism," "the Emersonian tradition" (25). For more on Tate and Percy's reaction to *southern* romanticism, see Samway, 228, on Percy's positive reaction to Tate's mid-1960s essay "Narcissus as Narcissus" explicating "Ode to the Confederate Dead." Percy here says that the essay has helped him to understand the

tion of Poe's project, for in it "he circumvented the natural world and tried to put himself not in the presence of God but in the seat of God." Such an act is bound to fail because "the human intellect cannot reach God as essence; only God as analogy. Analogy to what? Plainly analogy to the natural world; for there is nothing in the intellect that has not previously reached it through the senses" (420). Herein also lies a critique of Poe's notion of the apparently self-sufficient nature of language, one that is countered, as are the presumptions of the Cartesian "romantic" intellect itself, in the companion essay, "The Symbolic Imagination: The Mirrors of Dante" (1951), which largely expands upon Tate's explication of Dante in the Crane essay. Dante succeeds where Poe fails precisely because he does not approach God directly but sees him in the "mirror" of the sensible world and conveys that vision through analogical language.

O'Connor was certainly familiar with the concept of angelism from Lynch's work (in "Theology and the Imagination" he drew on Tate's explication of the term) and probably from Tate and Maritain directly, but it was Percy who most consistently concerned himself with it. Perhaps he did so because Gordon—disheartened by his habit of creating characters who simply "think" without being located in "time and space"—had accused *him* of it in one of her early letters: "I think you are in danger of falling, as a writer, for what Jacques Maritain calls the sin of the age: angelism."[49] In any case, it is certain that Percy read and annotated *The Dream of Descartes* and drew from it throughout his career. It is possible to read Binx Bolling's shift from the "vertical" search to the "horizontal" search in *The Moviegoer* as an escape from the Cartesian mode, but even much later Percy indicated his fascination with angelism-bestialism. In *Love in the Ruins* (1971) Dr. Thomas More at one point prays, "Dear God, I can see it now, why can't I see it other times, that it is you I love in the beauty of the world . . . , and it is pilgrims we are, wayfarers on a journey, and not pigs, nor angels" (104). *Lost in the Cosmos* (1983), perhaps Percy's lengthiest meditation on this theme, posited that "the Self since the time of Descartes has been stranded, split off from everything else in the Cosmos, a mind which professes to understand bodies and galaxies but is by

romanticism of the Confederacy in connection with solipsism, which he previously sensed but had not fully grasped.

49. Gordon to Percy, [1952?], SHC.

the very act of understanding marooned in the Cosmos, with which it has no connection" (47). The angelic self here is a theorizing "ghost" that generally conceives of its own body as a beast-machine the needs of which are essentially those of the consumer—an organism, albeit a complex one, in an environment.

Those selves most given to angelism—in *Lost in the Cosmos* but also in Percy's work generally—include both scientists and artists, and in the twentieth century the latter often have the more difficult time reconciling the transcending angelic mode of artistic creation to the immanent mode of everyday life: much of the latter half of *Lost in the Cosmos* is devoted to tragicomic descriptions of the failures of writers to "reenter" the world they have successfully written about. "What did Faulkner do after writing the last sentence of *Light in August*? Get drunk for a week. What did Dostoevsky do after finishing *The Idiot*? Spend three days and nights at the roulette table" (142). But in rare cases, Percy claims (drawing on Kierkegaard), a writer can in fact achieve "reentry under the direct sponsorship of God" and thereby maintain a proper balance between the transcendent and the immanent:

> In any case, reentry into ordinary life, into concrete place and time, from the strange abstractions of the twentieth century, the reentry undertaken under the direct sponsorship of God, is a difficult if not nigh-impossible task. Yet there have existed, so I have heard, a few writers even in this day and age who have become themselves transparently before God and managed to live intact through difficult lives, e.g., Simone Weil, Martin Buber, Dietrich Bonhoeffer. Some have even outdone Kierkegaard and seen both creation and art as the Chartres sculptor did, as both dense and mysterious, gratuitous, anagogic, and sacramental, e.g. Flannery O'Connor. (157)

It would be a mistake to read Percy's comments as a critique of the work of Faulkner or Dostoyevsky, for whose novels he had the greatest admiration; here he is primarily concerned with not art, but life. But in his admiration of O'Connor's conception of life and art alike, we see presented most strongly the vision of the real—and sense of artistic vocation—that Percy himself strove to attain.[50]

50. Percy saw Eudora Welty as another example of a "grounded" artist who escaped angelism and was actually able to live in "a body . . . in a place, at a street address." See "Eudora Welty in Jackson," *SSL*, 223.

And we can likewise see here the roots of the satire O'Connor and Percy both leveled upon "artists" with no sense of the real whatsoever, in life or in art. For both shared not only a positive commitment to realism but also a strong bias against romanticism that manifests itself in the presentation of flawed writers in their fiction. These are typically solipsistic, romantic dreamers who have no connection with reality whatsoever, and (often simultaneously) self-described topical "realists" whose angelically conceived political theories become mere clichés that isolate them from the real. Such figures populate the pages of O'Connor's and Percy's fictions. While O'Connor has a few stories that focus relentlessly on the "bad artist," Percy has a minor character in almost every one of his novels who falls into this category.

O'Connor is well known for her satire of abstracted intellectuals generally, but three stories focus particularly on the self-absorbed artist: "The Crop," "The Enduring Chill," and "The Partridge Festival." "The Crop" formed part of O'Connor's M.A. thesis at Iowa, at a time when she was first struggling to understand the nature and practice of fiction herself. While this early story is often overlooked, it sets the pattern of the aspiring creative writer who looks inside herself rather than around her for the source of her fiction. Miss Willerton lives in a small southern town in which she must spend a considerable amount of time doing domestic chores and listening to the banal conversation of the women she lives with. In the narrative, O'Connor carefully describes this world with an amused eye for the often absurd details that would color her own mature fiction: during the morning meal, "Lucia said a regular breakfast made for other regular habits, and with Garner's tendency to upsets, it was imperative that they establish some system in their eating" (CS, 33). But Miss Willerton ignores this world, instead turning within herself and daydreaming about a catchy "subject" for her fiction.

Unfortunately, "[t]here were so many subjects to write stories about that Miss Willerton never could think of one" (33). In the act of crumbing the table, she briefly wonders if baking might make a good subject and decides it might, but only if she wrote of "foreign bakers," who are very "picturesque" in photos she has seen. She finally decides that a "social problem" would be a better subject: "Sharecroppers! Miss Willerton had never been intimately connected with sharecroppers, but, she reflected, they would make as arty a subject as any, and they would give her an air of social concern which was so valuable to have in the circles she was hoping to travel!" Before she gets out of this town, she thinks, she might be able to "capitalize . . . on the hookworm"

(35). Sitting at her typewriter and thinking in terms of jargon she has learned from a creative writing class, she proceeds not to write but rather to fantasize about her story, which will apparently owe something to the Erskine Caldwell school of poor white fiction: "there would have to be some quite violent, naturalistic scenes, the sadistic sort of thing one read about in connection with that class" (36). Finally, however, she grows frustrated with her "subject" and turns to one which she knows even less about than she does sharecropping: "The Irish!" whom she begins to imagine as "full of spirit—red-haired, with broad shoulders and great, drooping mustaches" (41).

While much of the story is farcical and most obviously points to exactly how not to write, there is at least one moment when O'Connor places Miss Willerton squarely in a scene where she has the smallest glimmer of vision about the depths of the world in which she actually lives. Pulled from her typewriter to go to the grocery store, she wanders through it sulking:

> Silly that a grocery should depress one—nothing in it but trifling domestic doings—women buying beans—riding children in those grocery go-carts—higgling about an eighth of a pound more or less of squash—what did they get out of it? Miss Willerton wondered. Where was there any chance for self-expression, for creation, for art? All around her it was the same—sidewalks full of people scurrying about with their hands full of little packages and their minds full of little packages—that woman there with the child on the leash, pulling him, jerking him, dragging him away from a window with a jack-o'-lantern in it; she would probably be pulling and jerking him the rest of her life. (40)

Such is, of course, exactly the sort of scene in which O'Connor herself would have seen the mysterious depths of creation and the setting of a drama with eternal significance for the souls of its participants—all while remaining faithful to the concrete details of place and character. Instead, Miss Willerton worries about "*self*-expression" (my emphasis) and returns to her typewriter to daydream about a place and people she has never seen.

O'Connor further developed such types of the angelic artist later, most famously in "The Enduring Chill." Asbury Fox is in many respects a more sophisticated Miss Willerton, one whose self-absorption has a clearly religious dimension not developed in "The Crop." Fancying himself a version of Joyce's Stephen Dedalus, he has attempted to escape from "the slave's atmosphere of home" (his small town of Timberboro) to "liberate my imagination, to take it like a hawk from its cage" in New York (CS, 364).[51] But he has failed to produce anything there, and the story is concerned with his reluctant return home in the face of what he thinks is a deathly illness. His New York friend Goetz has encouraged him to see both death and life as an "illusion," but Asbury now must confront the horrible "thought of death *here*," on the all-too-real farm where he was raised (358–9). Out of a concern for his art, which apparently is to have a social dimension like that of Miss Willerton, and a desire to upset his mother, he makes a self-centered attempt to strike up a "friendship" with the two black men who work for her: "Last year he had been writing a play about the Negro and he had wanted to be around them for a while to see how they really felt about their condition, but the two who worked for her had lost their initiative over the years" (368). The "for a while" qualification is highly significant: Asbury is not interested in the lives of these two men, but in the "issue" of "the Negro," and their actual characters prove to be unsatisfactory to his purposes. The story is ultimately concerned with Asbury's spiritual awakening to these and other realities, including the final reality that he must not die but rather live "*here*." Whether or not this awakening will invigorate his sterile art, however, O'Connor does not suggest.

"The Partridge Festival" is a late story in the same vein, one that pairs two young would-be writers in their gross misconception of the violent events that have marred the spring Azalea Festival of the small town of Partridge. A man named Singleton has shot five local dignitaries during the opening ceremonies and has subsequently been imprisoned in the local jail. While the townspeople label Singleton a "maniac" and concern themselves with the incident's desultory effect on "the festive spirit" and sales, a young man named Calhoun imagines Singleton as a heroic nonconformist who has rejected the town's bourgeois values. Calhoun has been working as a salesman but thinks of himself as a "rebel-artist-mystic" and—when asked by his aunts about his future plans—pompously announces, as if to himself: "I think I shall write" (CS, 424). When he begins to prowl about the town, berating the "materialism" of its citizens and envisioning Singleton as a victim of its warped mores, he is unexpectedly joined by Mary Elizabeth, a young scholar intending to write a

51. See David Aiken, "Flannery O'Connor's Portrait of the Artist as a Young Failure," *Arizona Quarterly* 32 (1976): 245–59.

"non-fiction" study of the killer as "a Christ-figure" (435). "Stunned" by her insight, Calhoun enviously announces that his novel based on Singleton will be superior to her study because "the novelist is not interested in narrow abstractions" but rather in "concrete findings" and "the mystery of personality" (435–6). Although Calhoun's ramblings here superficially resemble O'Connor's own thoughts on fiction, the limitations of his vision of the real are revealed when he and Mary Elizabeth finally confront Singleton himself. The gifts they bring for their presumed savior—"a Modern Library *Thus Spake Zarathustra*, a paperback *Revolt of the Masses*, and a thin decorated volume of Housman"—suggest their own allegiance to an inherently illogical (but consistently "angelic") combination of views: self-generated Nietzschean morality, rigorously theoretical politics, and purely self-indulgent aesthetic sensibility (441). Singleton, unfortunately, is not interested in such high-minded gifts, not only because he is uneducated but also because he is a maniac after all, a perverse and lecherous old man who breaks away from his guards and chases the two "writers" out of the jail by threatening to expose himself.

O'Connor herself called "The Partridge Festival" a "farce" and was not completely happy with the finished story, but it is obviously the culmination of a pattern that runs from the beginning to the end of her career. For if "Parker's Back" was, as suggested at the beginning of this chapter, an exploration of the highest possibilities of art, "The Partridge Festival" is the final installment of a series of stories dealing with the utter impossibility of substantial art issuing forth from an angelic sensibility. It is possible to read this story, as Irving Malin has, as revealing the profound limitations of art itself. Calhoun's "pod-shaped" car—which contrasts with the flowering azaleas that recur throughout the story—suggests his ongoing isolation from creation, as does the single-mindedness reflected in his idol's name; such images reflect Calhoun's insistence upon looking "at reality from his warped, selfish perspective" and his refusal "to understand that he cannot simply break through jails of self-conception, that he cannot triumph over natural creation." To a degree, O'Connor would agree with Malin's conclusion that art by its very nature "can never completely capture spiritual worlds," that "it always tries to capture the invisible, underlying pattern of life, but it is doomed to failure."[52] Yet she

52. Irving Malin, "Singular Visions: 'The Partridge Festival,'" in *Critical Essays on Flannery O'Connor*, ed. Melvin J. Friedman and Beverly Lyon Clark (Boston: G. K. Hall, 1985), 185.

would doubtlessly contend that Calhoun, like Miss Willerton and Asbury, will not only fail but fail abysmally as an artist precisely because he has no sense whatsoever of a spiritual—or even a natural—world existing independently of his own sensibility and theories.

Whereas O'Connor provides us with a few taut stories entirely focused on the flawed artist, Percy more subtly scatters throughout his novels portraits of the flawed artist, portraits inevitably bound up with the larger themes of the works themselves. The pattern begins with *The Moviegoer*, which, like much of Percy's work, might be read as presenting a dialectic between abstracted romantic theorizing and holistic concrete living. The novel is concerned with Binx Bolling's shift from what he calls the lonely "vertical search"—during which he reads "only 'fundamental' books, that is, key books on key subjects" both literary and scientific, and engages in meaningless sexual relationships—to the "horizontal search" in which he begins to look for meaning in the world and people around him (59–60). Binx's initial life, then, is one characterized by angelism-bestialism, while his new search—unbeknownst to him—will lead him, through his understated conversion and marriage to Kate Cutrer, toward a richly sacramental life.

In doing so he overcomes his own penchant for romanticism, which he explicitly connects with a seemingly antithetical scientism. Scorning his own youthful Korean War letters as those of "a regular young Rupert Brooke," he recalls that similar sentiments led his father, who was shot down over Crete with a copy of Housman's *The Shropshire Lad* in his pocket, to join the RCAF in 1940: "Oh the crap that lies lurking in the English soul. Somewhere it, the English soul, received an injection of romanticism which nearly killed it. That's what killed my father, English romanticism, that and 1930 science." For it was paradoxically his father's faith in science that fostered his sentimentality, as Binx muses in his journal: "Explore connection between romanticism and scientific objectivity. Does a scientifically minded person become a romantic because he is a leftover from his own objectivity?" (76).

The novel is, accordingly, concerned with romanticism in many forms. The subject is initially explored in terms of not writing but reading, for *The Moviegoer* is as much concerned with books as it is with movies, as Binx's description of his vertical search suggests (59–60). His Aunt Emily, whom he largely ends up defining himself against, professes a detached Stoicism but is in fact romantic in her own fatalism. She is a high-minded reader of Platonic philosophy and Eastern religion, a woman "of the loftiest theosophical pan-Brahman sentiments"; but she has probably also read too much of Sir Walter Scott (whom Percy, following Mark Twain, linked with upper-class southern romanticism), as her lament for the passing of southern chivalry suggests (94, 196).[53] Her romanticism, like that of Binx's father, is also connected to science in her vision of "the new messiah, the scientist-philosopher-mystic who would come striding through the ruins with the *Gita* in one hand and a geiger counter in the other" (159). In his own day-to-day life, Binx is pleased to see that his secretary Sharon is a devotee of a more tawdry romanticism: he takes her reading of *Peyton Place* to be "a good omen" regarding his prospects for seducing her (58).

But the most damning assessment of romanticism in the novel comes near its conclusion, just before Binx's pivotal last confrontation with Aunt Emily, when he, returning from a trip to Chicago with Kate, encounters a young man reading Stendhal's *The Charterhouse of Parma*. Binx immediately identifies him as "a romantic": "His posture is the first clue: it is too good to be true, this distillation of all graceful slumps" (188). The intensity of the description that follows makes clear that the situation of "the romantic" is one Binx himself knows well (and perhaps it bears upon the future of his own relationship with Kate):

> The poor fellow. He has just begun to suffer from it, this miserable trick the romantic plays upon himself: of setting just beyond his reach the very thing he prizes. . . .
>
> Upon completion of his second trimester and having enough credits to graduate, he has lit out for New Orleans to load bananas for a while and perhaps join the merchant marine. . . . For a while, he says. He means that he hopes to find himself a girl, the rarest of rare pieces, and live the life of Rudolfo on the balcony, sitting around on the floor and experiencing soul-communions. I have my doubts. In the first place, he will defeat himself, jump ten miles ahead of himself, scare the wits out of some girl with his great choking silences, want her so desperately that by his own peculiar logic he can't have her; or, having her, jump another ten miles beyond both of them and end by fleeing to the islands where, propped on the

53. For Percy on Scott, see "Stoicism in the South," *SSL*, 85.

rail of his ship in some rancid port, he will ponder his own loneliness. (189–90)

Such reflections, like those in *Lost in the Cosmos*, bear on life more than art, but their connection to art is suggested not only by the young man's choice of fiction but also by their juxtaposition with Binx's description of Sam Yerger, the writer whom he and Kate encountered just before leaving for Chicago. Yerger is not as overtly ridiculed as O'Connor's flawed writers are, but he is clearly a laughable figure and, like Miss Willerton, Asbury, and Calhoun, a slave to literary fashion. He has been a journalist, and despite the commitment to verisimilitude one might expect from such a writer, he has chronicled his world in books that read like a list of clichés. Each is coolly rattled off by the wry Binx: "In the 1930s he wrote a humorous book about the French-speaking Negroes called *Yambilaya Ya-Ya* which was made into a stage show and later a movie." After serving as a war correspondent and moving to Mexico (where he apparently ruminated on more universal themes, writing "a novel called *The Honored and the Dishonored* which dealt, according to the dust jacket, with 'the problem of evil and the essential loneliness of man'"), Yeager returned to Louisiana, "where he wrote a nostalgic book called *Happy Land* which was commended in the reviews as a nice blend of a moderate attitude toward the race question and a conservative affection for the values of the agrarian South. An earlier book, called *Curse upon the Land*, which the dust jacket described as 'an impassioned plea for tolerance and understanding,' had not been well received in Feliciana" (148–9).

Although Yerger's political commitments have apparently shifted with the prevailing winds, it is clear that in each of his phases he has failed to capture his world, and the South, as it is. This pattern apparently continues in his life as well as his fiction, for he sees Kate Cutrer not as the profoundly troubled woman that she is, but rather as a type of "the Southerner who is so curiously like the old-style Russian gentry." To him she is not actually Kate but rather Tolstoy's "Natasha Rostov" (150). Such inclinations identify Sam as not the realist he likes to think himself but rather a romantic, just as do his tales of exotic adventure: "on the dark porch in Feliciana he told us once of the time when he made a journey up the headwaters of the Orinoco and caught a fever and lay ill for weeks," only to hear one night "an incredibly beautiful voice [a vacationing Austrian] sing the whole of *Winterreise*." Enthralling as such stories are, Binx finds that their extraordinary settings and obsessive emphasis on the aesthetic arouse "in me an appreciation so keen and pleasurable that it bordered upon the irritable" (158). Though he is occasionally amused by Yerger, the ironic narrator is certain of one thing: such a purveyor of cliché, forever gyrating between his own exquisitely romantic sensibility and appeals to political fashion, can tell him nothing about his search or the world he lives in.

In Binx's assessment of Yerger, more than anywhere else in the novel, we can assume that his voice is that of Percy, for the pattern of the flawed artist continues throughout Percy's oeuvre. In *The Last Gentleman*, Will Barrett confronts not only Forney Aiken, a white northern journalist who has dyed his skin black in order to penetrate the "cotton curtain" and capture the "reality" of southern racism (107)—the irony of an artificial black man doing so is self-evident—but also Mort Prince, author of a novel called *Love* "which was about orgasms, good and bad, some forty-six." When the narrator of *Love* has at last been physically satiated, he utters final words that are not only heretical, from Percy's point of view, but also suggest to any sober reader the shallowest sort of greeting-card romanticism: "And so I humbly ask of life that it grant us the only salvation, that of one human being discovering himself through another and through the miracle of love" (112). Even Will Barrett's suicidal father is later presented as the victim of a sort of romantic defeatism not unlike that of Aunt Emily, a defeatism suggested by his habitual recitation of the bleakest lines of Matthew Arnold's "Dover Beach": he posits a world that seems "To lie before us like a land of dreams" but "Hath really neither joy, nor love, nor light, / Nor certitude, nor peace, nor help for pain" (243).

In *The Second Coming,* an older Will Barrett has befriended a more likable flawed artist, Lewis Peckham. He is a University of Virginia graduate "of old Tidewater stock," a Vietnam veteran, and a discontented golf pro: "Maybe books had ruined him. . . . He thought he was a good poet but he was not. He thought books could tell him how to live but they couldn't. He was a serious but dazed reader. He read Dante and Shakespeare and Nietzsche and Freud. He read modern poetry and books on psychiatry. He had taken a degree in English, taught English, fought in a war, returned to teach English, couldn't, decided to farm, bought a goat farm, managed a Confederate museum in a cave on his property, wrote poetry, went broke, became a golf pro." His poetry is "not good. There was one poem called 'Moon over Khe Sanh,' which was typed in the shape of a new moon" (and is actually typed out in the text). But Percy suggests that there might be hope for Peckham, precisely because "he knew a great deal he hadn't learned from books. The trouble was he didn't set store by it." If he only gave up on his "bookish" notions about literature and turned to the world around him, he might become a decent writer: "How could he read signs and people so well, yet want to be a third-rate Rupert Brooke with his rendezvous with death at Khe Sanh? Why would he even want to be a first-rate Rupert Brooke?" (137–8).

Love in the Ruins and *The Thanatos Syndrome* lack such a figure—though literature is again an important influence on characters—but in *Lancelot* the flawed artist is central to the plot, here as filmmaker.[54] There are actually two versions of the figure here, the codirectors of the movie being made at Lance Lamar's Belle Isle mansion: Merlin and Jacoby. Merlin, who is clearly a half-baked Hemingway gone to pot, is the more likable of the two. Even though he has cuckolded Lance, the vengeful husband allows this "poor old man" to leave Belle Isle for his beloved Africa, where he hopes to make a film "about a man and a woman who are good comrades, go on a hunt, and then have good sex together" (217).[55] Jacoby, by contrast, is at once foolish—"he had been an actor too and so didn't know who he was" (115)—and despicable. His detachment from reality is indicated by his constantly shifting accents, his pretentious jargon—he makes films in accordance with his own "communication theory"—and his clichéd and superficial vision of the southern society he is filming. Though his film will depict sharecroppers (along with "a Klan type, a beautiful half-caste but also half-wit swamp girl, [and] a degenerate river rat"), his knowledge of them is on a par with Miss Willerton's: Lance

54. In *Love in the Ruins*, Dr. Thomas More believes that his wife has been ruined by books, "not by dirty books but by clean books, not by depraved books but by spiritual books." Convinced that only "transcendental religion could rescue Western materialism," she believes (in an angelic counterpoint to Mort Prince's bestial vision) that love should be purely "spiritual" and therefore rebuffs her husband's interest in sex. She wants to escape to some "lake isle of Innisfree" where she can rise above the restrictions of her mundane life—though Ayn Rand and Herman Hesse, not Yeats, seem to be her primary mentors (62–4, 68).

55. For more on Percy's extensive and complicated reaction to Hemingway, whose family history of suicide and advocacy of stoicism spoke directly to Percy's own most profound concerns, see William Rodney Allen, "All the Faces of Death: Walker Percy and Hemingway," *Mississippi Quarterly* 36:1 (Winter 1982–3): 3–19.

must point out to Jacoby that the plot's turning on a greedy aristocrat stealing oil-rich land from a sharecropper is problematic because "the land could not belong to the sharecropper if he was a sharecropper" (27). Such remarks emphasize Jacoby's clownishness, but in a darker moment Lance portrays the warping of reality accomplished by Jacoby's "movie people" as almost demonic. Under their influence the "town folk" begin to act "as if they had lived out their entire lives in a dim charade, a shadowplay in which they were the shadows and now all at once to have appear miraculously in their midst these resplendent larger-than-life beings. . . . What was nutty was that the movie folks were trafficking in illusions in a real world but the real world thought that its reality could only be found in the illusion. Two sets of maniacs" (161).

Lance, of course, is not completely sane himself, but his assessment of the impact of the flawed artist is accurate here. When a Jacoby or a Calhoun succeeds in communicating his twisted vision of the real, both Percy and O'Connor would agree, the flawed artist becomes not a figure of fun but rather one to be feared. For if art not only is dependent upon an adequate vision of the real but also is to be understood ultimately as a vehicle for conveying truth, it is to be taken very seriously indeed. In O'Connor's and Percy's satire of the flawed romantic artist—that angelic sensibility which has disconnected itself from reality—we see not only a dramatization of their "theories of fiction" but also an exploration of their most profound thematic concerns as Catholic artists striving to capture the depths of the real and mysterious world in which they live.

PERCY'S DESCRIPTION of O'Connor in *Lost in the Cosmos*—his claim that she saw "both creation and art as . . . dense and mysterious, gratuitous, anagogic, and sacramental"—bears a final reexamination, for its emphasis on both art and *creation* reminds us that for O'Connor and Percy alike, a sacramental vision is not merely the basis for a "theory of fiction": it is necessary for any adequate grasp of the reality in which we dwell. Accordingly, in their fiction the ability of characters to attain such vision is of central thematic importance. And insofar as that vision is necessarily ahistorical, grasping the presence of the eternal in a portion of the created world at any given moment, it is precisely this theme that enabled them to write of their contemporary South in a manner alien to their great predecessors in the Renascence.

In *The Last Gentleman,* Ed Barrett shifts smoothly from reciting "Dover

Beach" to telling stories of "the grandfather and the days of great men" (243). In his case, as with other destructive father figures in Percy's fiction, romanticism is linked with nostalgia, a certain inordinate fascination with the past and with his own perceived inability to live up to its standards of heroism. Certainly such a theme is not new to southern fiction; indeed, as depicted in Faulkner's Compson family and elsewhere, it is the theme par excellence of the Southern Renascence. What is new in Percy's fiction is Will Barrett's tentative response to the despairing vision of his father. In what is perhaps the most crucial passage of the novel, the intermittently amnesiac Will stands outside his old house and—as he recalls his father's suicide—simply touches "the warm finny whispering bark" where an oak tree has grown around an old hitching post: "*Wait.* While his fingers explored the juncture of iron and bark, his eyes narrowed as if he caught a glimmer of light on the cold iron skull. *Wait.* I think he was wrong and that he was looking in the wrong place. . . . *Wait.* He had missed it! It was not in the Brahms that one looked and not in the sad old poetry but—he wrung out his ear—but here, under your nose, here in the very curiousness and drollness and extraness of the iron and the bark . . ." (260). Percy later described this passage as representing the highest aspirations of his art, both as exemplifying fiction's possibilities as "a cognitive instrument for exploring an unknown terrain" and as providing "a kind of counterstatement" to a scene in Sartre's *Nausea* wherein Roquentin sees in a tree the apparent emptiness and repulsiveness of reality. Will, by contrast, has "in terms of traditional metaphysics . . . caught a glimpse of the goodness and gratuitousness of created being" (*SSL*, 219, 221). In doing so, he arguably provides as much of a counterstatement to Quentin as he does to Roquentin.

And certainly O'Connor's work is filled with such glimpses—or, more accurately, with occasions for such glimpses, which her characters frequently ignore until violence forces them to open their eyes. Not only Parker of "Parker's Back," who upon seeing a tattooed man first begins to sense that there is something "out of the ordinary about the fact that he existed" (*CS*, 513), but even Haze Motes at the beginning of *Wise Blood* almost sees something like what Will Barrett sees: even over the grim postwar city "the black sky was underpinned with long silver streaks that looked like scaffolding and depth on depth behind it were thousands of stars that seemed to be moving very slowly as if they were about some vast construction work that involved the whole order of the universe and would take all time to complete" (*TFO*, 18). Like the residents of Taulkinham who stare in the shop windows instead of at the stars, many of the women who populate O'Connor's short fiction are generally less despairing than Ed Barrett about the passing of the old southern order and more complacent about what they have gained from its legacy. But their complacency is inevitably shattered by sudden insight into the depths of the here and now: often the attainment of such a vision requires violence, like that inflicted upon the grandmother in "A Good Man Is Hard to Find," but "the goodness and gratuitousness of created being" is always present in something as mundane as the peacock in "The Displaced Person" or the hogs at the end of "Revelation." For all O'Connor's sense of the shortcomings of her contemporary world, she sees it as not empty but shot through with a rarely grasped significance—one that is merely veiled by selfish shortsightedness and romantic nostalgia alike. She would therefore be able to write about that contemporary world with faith in its inherent meaning.

Because Percy lived longer than O'Connor did and favored the urban and suburban settings in which he in fact lived, his vision of postwar southern society makes for the more jarring comparison with the world of the Renascence writers. The extent to which his sacramental view of reality was responsible for his conviction that meaning could be found even in the most seemingly empty corners of the postmodern world is suggested in a letter he wrote to Foote as the latter—ironically—neared completion of his great history, The Civil War: A Narrative. What Percy is working on is not a novel about the past but a supposedly "futuristic" one that in fact satirizes a contemporary American society rent apart "worse than the Civil War." Yet Love in the Ruins will also be a celebration "of the goodness of God, and of the merriness of living quite anonymously in the suburbs, drinking well, cooking out, attending Mass at the usual silo-and-barn, the goodness of Brunswick bowling alleys (the good white maple and plastic balls), coming home of an evening, with the twin rubies of the TV transmitter in the evening sky. . . ."[56] Such a superficially superficial postmodern world holds as much meaning as Antietam—or Yoknapatawpha—precisely because, as he tells his relentlessly agnostic friend, it is the setting of "what we Catholics call the Sacramental Life." The here and now is worth writing about because God is present in it, and Percy's characters, like

56. Percy to Foote, January–February 1967, in Tolson, Correspondence of Foote and Percy, 129.

O'Connor's, are essentially struggling to glimpse such a presence in a world whose connections with the past have been largely severed. But such speaks directly to their themes, to the paradoxical hopefulness—the coexisting sense of the apocalyptic and the Edenic—of the end of the modern world as depicted in their work, and it deserves full treatment in itself.

CHAPTER 4

Postwar America and
the End of the Modern South

Catastrophes, Castaways, New Worlds

Where you come from is gone, where you thought you were going to never was there, and where you are is no good unless you can get away from it. Where is there a place for you to be? No place.

—FLANNERY O'CONNOR, *Wise Blood*

Belle Isle is gone and I couldn't care less. . . . As gone with the wind as Tara and as good riddance. No, that's not the mystery. The mystery lies in the here and now. The mystery is: what is one to do with oneself?

—WALKER PERCY, *Lancelot*

O'CONNOR AND PERCY alike radically critiqued both decaying southern traditions and the triumphant American culture that was replacing them, but their fiction derives much of its power from its placement at the precise cultural moment when such a conflict was occurring in the wake of World War II. By way of introducing such concerns, it seems appropriate in this chapter especially to begin by considering portions of the fiction itself, to work backward, as it were, to themes by examining the protagonist of one work by each from the early 1960s—from Percy's first novel and what would have been O'Connor's last.

By 1962 O'Connor had long been interested in writing about "folks" rather than "freaks," and in her third novel she had committed herself to doing not "what I know I can do well" but rather "the larger things I need to do now."[1] The drafts that survive and the fragment that has been published suggest that

---

1. Quoted in Sally Fitzgerald, introduction to *Three by Flannery O'Connor* (New York: Penguin, 1983), xv, xxii.

Why Do the Heathen Rage? was indeed going to be a departure for O'Connor; its protagonist, a careful study of the manuscripts reveals, is "*not* grotesque, *not* perverse, and *not* violent." Walter Tilman is "superficially quite normal," an intelligent young man of "mild and ironic" temperament.[2] Rather than descending from a line of fundamentalist preachers, as did Hazel Motes and Francis Marion Tarwater, Walter has been brought up in an affluent and religiously indifferent atmosphere. His Laodicean mother, Mrs. Tilman, is deeply disappointed in him, not because of his failure to endorse a rigorous Christianity but rather because he rejects the values that have traditionally served her family well in southern society, as her comments in the published fragment suggest. Specifically, it is Walter's reluctance to take over the family land and "make Negroes work" that enrages her. When Walter tells Mrs. Tilman, whom he has called "the last of the nineteenth century," that she is better suited to manage than him because "a woman of your generation . . . is better than a man of mine," she sinks into a deep meditation on his shortcomings:

> She remained standing there, rigid, her eyes on him in stunned disgust. Her son. Her only son. His eyes and his skull and his smile belonged to the family face but underneath them was a different kind of man from any she had ever known. There was no innocence in him, no rectitude, no conviction either of sin or election. The man she saw courted good and evil impartially and saw so many sides of every question that he could not move, could not work, he could not even make niggers work. Any evil could enter that vacuum. God knows, she thought and caught her breath, God knows what he might do!
>
> He had not done anything. He was twenty-eight now and, so far as she could see, nothing occupied him but trivia. He had the air of a person who is waiting for some big event and can't start any work because it would only be interrupted. . . . He amused himself writing letters to people he did not know and to the newspapers. Under different names and using different personalities, he wrote to strangers. It was a peculiar, small, contemptible vice. Her father and her grandfather had been moral men but they would have scorned small vices more than great ones. They knew

2. Marian Burns, "O'Connor's Unfinished Novel," in *Critical Essays on Flannery O'Connor*, ed. Melvin J. Friedman and Beverly Lyon Clark (Boston: G. K. Hall, 1985), 179.

who they were and what they owed to themselves. It was impossible to tell what Walter knew or what his views were on anything. (*CS*, 485–6)

In all these respects Walter not only counters his mother's "nineteenth-century" character but also, as we shall see, embodies the predicament of the southern (and to some degree, the American) self at this cultural moment as seen by O'Connor and Percy.

Indeed, Walter's character may have partly been drawn from that of Percy's Binx Bolling. O'Connor had been aware of Percy throughout the 1950s and admired his nonfiction; she eagerly anticipated reading his first novel and responded to it with unusual enthusiasm. Since she read *The Moviegoer* in January 1962 and began work on *Why Do the Heathen Rage?* a few months later, the possibility of influence certainly exists, especially if she was looking for a model to write about a nongrotesque southerner approaching the Catholic Church.[3] The "pervasive self-irony" of Walter is much more characteristic of Binx than of Tarwater, and Mrs. Tilman's assessment of Walter seems to echo Aunt Emily's central condemnation of Binx in Percy's novel. Emily Cutrer thinks that Binx's particular brand of irresponsibility is a "novelty . . . something new under the sun": "[I]s it not true that in all of past history people who found themselves in difficult situations behaved in certain familiar ways, well or badly, courageously or cowardly, with distinction or mediocrity, with honor or dishonor? They are recognizable. . . . Your discovery, as best I can determine, is that there is an alternative no one has hit upon. It is that finding oneself in one of life's critical situations one need not after all respond in one of the traditional ways. No. One may simply default. Pass. Do as one

3. Walter was ultimately on his way to becoming a monk, and as such he would have been O'Connor's only treatment of a contemporary agnostic moving toward Catholicism (Burns, 173). Because of Walter's specific attraction to pre-Reformation Christianity and his epistolary endeavors, Burns briefly juxtaposes him with another character created by a Catholic southerner in the early 1960s: John Kennedy Toole's Ignatius Reilly. Toole could have read the fragment of "Heathen" published in *Esquire* in 1963, and he did admire O'Connor immensely, traveling to her grave in Milledgeville immediately before his 1969 suicide; see Patrick Samway, *Walker Percy: A Life* (New York: Farrar, Straus and Giroux, 1997), 334. For O'Connor's reading of Percy in the 1950s, see chapter 2 here; see *HB*, 442, 460, 501, for her admiration of *The Moviegoer* specifically. She wrote Percy to congratulate him on winning the National Book Award for this novel and on the strength of it alone began to recommend him to friends as a significant Catholic novelist (see note 31).

pleases, shrug, turn on one's heel and leave" (*M*, 192–3). Aunt Emily's rant here broadens to take in all of contemporary society and locates Binx's failing not in religious apathy—Emily Cutrer is no Christian—but in his failure to live up to the aristocratic "heritage of the men of our family," whose nobility encompassed "the only good things the South ever had and the only things that really matter in this life" (196). He spends his time in trivial diversion (sometimes writing letters to the editor) and seems to believe that "the purpose of life" is "to go to the movies and dally with every girl that comes along." When Aunt Emily asks, "[W]hat do you love? what do you live by?" he is silent—he has no answer (198).

The question of influence is an interesting one (though over the years Percy obviously had much more opportunity to be influenced by O'Connor than vice versa) but is not crucial to my central concern here: the fundamental similarity of Walter Tilman and Binx Bolling. Certainly, disquieting change—the decay of traditional manners and mores—is no innovative theme in southern literature, but in the characters of these protagonists it is taken to a final extreme. Both are fundamentally "new men," each of whom is not haunted by his family and regional past but radically severed from it; not merely rejecting but in fact failing even to consider seriously the codes of their ancestors, they are essentially valueless and live trivial lives devoid of direction in a seemingly empty present.[4] In the passages above, their characters are powerfully condemned by spokeswomen for certain traditional values of an older South. But those values themselves are also profoundly critiqued in O'Connor and Percy's work. For she had certainly developed similar themes in more violent and grotesque form in her earlier work, and he devoted his life to writing about variations on Binx. Mrs. Tilman is accurate in her observation that her son is "homeless here" on the family land and "homeless anywhere," just as Binx is a self-defined "seeker" who prefers living in an anonymous New

4. Scott Romine's *The Narrative Forms of Southern Community* (Baton Rouge: Louisiana State University Press, 1999) concisely captures the novelty of Binx's character: "While an uneasy ambivalence toward traditional modes of social order would dominate mid-century fiction—one thinks of Jack Burden's attitude toward Burden's Landing in *All the King's Men*, for example, or any number of works by Eudora Welty—it would remain for Walker Percy to confront reflexivity as a given. In broad terms, where Quentin Compson and Jack Burden find that they can no longer sustain the tacit dimension of a traditional culture, Binx Bolling appears on the first page of *The Moviegoer* without having that dimension available, even as an option" (199).

Orleans suburb to his aunt's Garden District home. But while these southern matriarchs see such wayfarers as radically displaced and therefore hopeless, O'Connor and Percy see their homelessness as the necessary condition for escaping despair. Their collapsing tradition and the postwar society taking its place are both finally insufficient.

The contemporary world itself, however, is paradoxically hopeful, for it provides the conditions wherein such seekers as Walter and Binx might not just escape the past but live *authentically* in the present. Generally, we are only given glimpses of such lives in the work of O'Connor and Percy. Much of their fiction is devoted to a satirical rejection of both traditional southern values and the complacent consumerism of postwar American culture, which are often placed in contention with each other only to exhaust themselves and point obliquely to the possibility of religious faith. O'Connor and Percy stage such dramas in settings and language that are often overtly apocalyptic, signaling the end of the modern world and an older southern order alike, but also revealing the eternally new heaven and earth that underlie the often banal surfaces of their contemporary world. Their craft—their fundamental commitment to the concrete—demands that in doing so they remain true to the particularities of their place and cultural moment, a task that both accomplish so well as to merit a place at the forefront of southern satirists. But their similar commitment to a transcendent Christian truth finally makes their satire—unlike, say, that of Mark Twain—of the most radically optimistic sort.

O'CONNOR AND PERCY'S Catholicism shaped their vision of the predicament not only of Western humanity generally during the "Age of Anxiety" and its aftermath, but also of southerners caught up in the most cataclysmic social changes to affect the region since Reconstruction, southerners who found themselves more and more part of a unified and materially prosperous United States. Such thematic considerations deserve more contextual introduction. The distinctive nature of O'Connor and Percy's apocalyptic vision needs to be explored; furthermore, we need to better understand their place within the postwar American culture that they saw replacing more traditional southern communities and that they critiqued so profoundly even as they refused to mourn fully the loss of the old ways.

Apocalypse has been a recurring theme in American literature—one befitting a New World culture—since its beginnings, and critical studies of apocalypticism have proliferated since midcentury. John R. May has traced the theme from Puritan New England through the work of John Barth, Thomas Pynchon, and Kurt Vonnegut but is careful to distinguish different types of apocalypse in the American novel: while the theme's ultimate source in our tradition is obviously Judeo-Christian, most recent manifestations have used Christian imagery only superficially, and the most overtly secular treatments of the theme range from black humor to a forthright "apocalypse of despair." The "patently Christian" imagination of apocalypse, in contrast, is distinguished by its openness "to a future that is genuinely new," and its greatest recent practitioner is Flannery O'Connor.[5]

It might seem ironic that the theme that had its roots, for Americans, in the Reformation—that "age of apocalyptic expectation," as May puts it— should be professed in its most orthodox form by a twentieth-century Catholic such as O'Connor. But Percy has been similarly described in an attempt to define him as an "American" writer. J. Donald Crowley sees in Percy's professed attempt "to write as if he were the first man on earth ever to set pencil to paper" an unexpected participation in the "Adamic impulse" of the nation's literature: "And this time it comes, most curiously, from a Mississippian, a Papist no less. There is in Percy—such are the swirling transformations in American history and culture—a newfangled version of the antinomianism of those original Puritans, a reversal in terms of their rebellion against authoritarianism. Paradoxical, to be sure, and tricky, but in the post-Christian technological world as Percy sees it, true."[6] While rebellion against tradition and authority might seem fundamentally Protestant, in the view of Percy and O'Connor alike the reigning authority of their own age—a post-Christendom dominated by shallow scientism and materialism—is illegitimate. And their radically sacramental faith in the goodness of creation itself allows them to hope in what is to come: an age, or even a moment, when that goodness might be recognized again for what it is.

In *Writing the Apocalypse: Historical Vision in Contemporary U.S. and Latin American Fiction*, Lois Parkinson Zamora considers apocalypticism in a more

5. John R. May, *Toward a New Earth: Apocalypse in the American Novel* (Notre Dame, IN: University of Notre Dame Press, 1972), 229, 213–4.

6. J. Donald Crowley, "Walker Percy: The Continuity of a Complex Fate," in *Critical Essays on Walker Percy*, ed. J. Donald Crowley and Sue Mitchell Crowley (Boston: G. K. Hall, 1989), 263.

broadly defined New World literature (and the development of the theme in cultures that are thoroughly Catholic, if not pre-Christian). But in pairing Gabriel García Márquez with his self-proclaimed master, Faulkner, she makes a distinction that is helpful in discussing southern literary history. She claims that both *One Hundred Years of Solitude* and *Absalom, Absalom!* are apocalyptic novels, but of a certain sort: "Their narrators share in the modernist thirst for myth, for explanatory masterplots which may justify their individual plots. [But] With the loss of belief in the sacred masterplot of apocalypse in which the secular leads to and is recuperated by the sacred, Quentin, Aurelian and the rest are left to create their own fictions of apocalypse." Accordingly, all these narrators have "after the ends of the world they describe" is "the description itself." Percy's orthodox belief, however, leads to a very different vision: "in the Christian existentialist context of his fiction, the end becomes something present and potential in every moment of his characters' lives. Apocalypse is the symbol and the means of renewal in the present." Insofar as his characters glimpse the depths of the present in which they live, they are saved from the tragedy of a Quentin who eternally attempts to reconstruct a collapsed past. And when we consider Zamora's definition of an orthodox apocalyptic vision as entailing a God who "breaks" into history to reveal, to uncover, what is already there, we see how such a vision might be shared by O'Connor (whom, incidentally, Zamora identifies as virtually the only female American writer concerned with apocalypse).[7]

Zamora is right to note that just as "biblical apocalypse grows out of, responds to, and describes metaphorically the historical context that surrounds it," so too do "the contemporary apocalyptic fictions . . . of Pynchon and Barth and Percy reflect the malaise of contemporary U.S. culture."[8] For Percy and O'Connor as apocalyptic writers must be distinguished from other twentieth-century American writers not only by the Christian orthodoxy of their vision (which is precisely how Zamora distinguishes Percy from Barth and Pynchon), but also by their precise historical moment. Though Percy began publishing long after O'Connor and outlived her by a quarter century, we have seen the roots of their mature thought in a particular postwar Catholic intellectual

---

7. Lois Parkinson Zamora, *Writing the Apocalypse: Historical Vision in Contemporary U.S. and Latin American Fiction* (New York: Cambridge University Press, 1989), 45, 6–7.

8. Ibid., 13.

milieu; furthermore, both shared the experience of the South's rapid integration into a newly unified, triumphant, and wealthy United States after World War II. Whatever apocalyptic sense they had was profoundly shaped by how their own changing culture measured up against their religious visions.

Their broadest vision of the state of Western culture in the wake of World War II—and their own particular sense of a nascent postmodern world—was communicated to them by such Christian existentialists as Marcel and, perhaps most profoundly, by the theologian Romano Guardini. Despite its foreboding title, Guardini's *The End of the Modern World* pronounces, as its author says, "no facile apocalyptic." Rejecting "that cheap disposition which revels always in prophesying collapse or destruction," the study is concerned neither with "a longing for a romantically envisioned Middle Ages [n]or with an advance into a glorified utopia of the future"; its stated purpose is "neither to repudiate nor to glorify . . . it is to understand the modern world, to comprehend why it is coming to an end," and to speculate on the nature of the epoch to follow it.[9] For all of these reasons, Guardini's work is perhaps best characterized by its subtitle: *A Search for Orientation*. Contemporary Western humanity, as he sees it, suffers from a profound rootlessness: in mastering nature, humankind has displaced itself from the universe and likewise left no "place" wherein God might be found. The age into which we are entering is one in which the last cultural remains of Christendom are vanishing and those "autonomous" selves, those thoughtful and sovereign souls that have not yet been made utterly complacent by the diversions of a mass technological society, are beginning to recognize their stark situation: lost in the cosmos, the postmodern self is at last beginning to "truly learn what it means to be cut off from Revelation."[10]

In Guardini's view, there is no possibility of turning back history to return

9. Romano Guardini, *The End of the Modern World: A Search for Orientation*, trans. Joseph Theman and Herbert Burke (New York: Sheed and Ward, 1956), 133, 69. Percy read this work not long after its publication and referred to it for the rest of his life; O'Connor sought it out upon its publication but did not read it any earlier than 1958 (See *HB*, 169, 296). Nonetheless, she read and admired Guardini's earlier work extensively, and this book is in many respects only the culmination of his thought.

10. Ibid., 123. A close reading of *Lost in the Cosmos* alongside *The End of the Modern World* reveals Percy's great debt to Guardini in this work particularly, e.g., in his emphasis on the late modern emergence of the "autonomous" self.

to the schema of the ancient, medieval, or modern world. A new epoch is beginning. His concern here is not with the material end of our civilization (e.g., in the possibility of nuclear war), nor is it with the Second Coming as described in the book of Revelation. In speaking "of the nearness of the End," he means not "nearness in the sense of time, but nearness as it pertains to the essence of the End, for in essence man's existence is now nearing an absolute decision." Furthermore, he believes that in the age to come, complete immersion in the "fogs of secularism" will paradoxically make clear the desirability of faith once again—and so the end of the modern world is an occasion for hope.[11]

Percy's essential embrace of such an understanding is indicated in his epigraph from Guardini at the beginning of *The Last Gentleman*, which emphasizes the bleakness of the coming age but also asserts its possibilities: though "love will disappear from the face of the public world, . . . the more precious will be that love which flows from one lonely person to another." Similarly, O'Connor emphasized the difficulty of faith during her age of thoroughgoing "nihilism"—"in or out of the Church, it's the gas you breathe"—but in her fiction she emphasized the final possibilities of rebirth in such a world (*HB*, 97). Less likely than Percy to depict personal love as integrating itself with a rejuvenated Christian faith, she nonetheless in stories such as "A Good Man Is Hard to Find" dramatized a vision of a stark and loveless present that nonetheless ends with a final glimpse of hope. In a story that is nothing if not cataclysmic on the most intimate level, the Grandmother's sense of the "nearness of the End" is precisely what finally moves her to reach out in love to another lonely person.

GUARDINI, THEN, provides not only a specific understanding of apocalypticism but also a Catholic Revival definition of the postmodern, and in examining how his vision informs that of O'Connor and Percy, we are reminded again of their difference from those southern modernists who were intellectually engaged with Catholicism. We have already considered the extent to which their visions differ from those of Tate and Gordon, who appropriated neo-Thomism in a manner consistent with their earlier concerns. Similarly, Paul Giles argues, for "Katherine Anne Porter, Catholicism operates as an aesthetic

11. Guardini, 133.

fiction, a beautiful idea" imaginatively affiliated with "the edenic, but necessarily spoiled, innocence of childhood and the old southern order"; O'Connor and Percy, in contrast, "negotiate that postmodern fragmentation and discontinuity more characteristic of the post-1945 era" in "literature and theology" alike.[12] Though they absorbed Maritain's aesthetic theory and parts of his cultural critique of modernity, I would maintain that their vision of their immediate historical moment owed much more to Guardini.

That moment is hopeful precisely insofar as those who dwell in it are aware of its bleakness and their own need of a "search for orientation." For disorientation is indeed the experience of the seekers who populate O'Connor and Percy's fiction, who exist in a numb complacency from which they are jolted only to recognize their own radical displacement in both a collapsed southern social order and the universe itself. In O'Connor's fiction, the subject is often enough the jolt itself; in Percy's, it is the search that follows. Both might be discussed in terms of Guardini's new age, as Percy suggested in a 1983 interview:

> I think if [my] novels have found any response it's because anybody who has any sense at all finds himself in this culture in a state of confusion; that is, as Guardini would say, we're living in the post-modern world. The world has ended in a sense. We're living in one of these times that hasn't been named yet . . . the end of Christendom as we know it. [S]o I think the normal state for a man to find himself in is in a state of confusion, spiritual disorientation, drawn in a sense to Christendom, but also repelled

12. Paul Giles, *American Catholic Arts and Fictions: Culture, Ideology, Aesthetics* (New York: Cambridge University Press, 1992), 353–4. Giles argues that "the creative tension between analogy and difference" in O'Connor's work anticipates the thought of late-twentieth-century Catholic theologians such as Karl Rahner, David Tracy, and David Burrell, who reemphasized Aquinas's own notion that "the differences and dissimilarities between God and the world are . . . equally as significant as those similarities upon which the analogical traditions in Catholic theology have insisted." Hence, "O'Connor is, to be sure, a 'Catholic' writer, but not just along the lines of narrower neo-scholastic orthodoxies, for the grotesque forms of her texts are charged also with the multiple uncertainties and discontinuities of postmodern literary and theological thought" (366–7). Giles's analysis of Percy is consistent with the claim developed in chapter 2 here: Percy's neoscholastic interests are counterbalanced by his engagement with the anxious "juggling of doubt and belief" more characteristic of the existentialists and proto-existentialists, especially Marcel, Kierkegaard, and Blaise Pascal (371).

by the cultural nature of Christendom. . . . I think the search is the normal condition. I think that's the one thread which unites all of my characters, that they're at various stages of disorder, and are aware of it, and not necessarily unhappy about it. . . .[13]

O'Connor likewise tended to judge her characters in regard to their complacency or lack thereof. In a statement reminiscent of Percy's Kierkegaardian epigraph to *The Moviegoer* ("The character of despair is precisely this: it is unaware of being despair"), she claimed: "At its best our age is an age of searchers and discoverers, and, at its worst, an age that has domesticated despair and learned to live with it happily. The fiction which celebrates this last state will be the least likely to transcend its limitation," for without at least a sense of "religious need . . . the sense of mystery vanishes" and "the whole range of feeling is dulled. The searchers," however, "are another matter" (*MM*, 160). O'Connor and Percy's mutual vision of the human self as spiritual wayfarer, as displaced person, as postmodern castaway, gave them a perspective on their contemporary southern society—whose members and traditions were being uprooted at an unprecedented rate—that was both historically apt and deeply penetrating (consider how O'Connor's first story, "The Geranium," which focuses on displacement in an almost sociological manner, lacks the depth of the religious reworking of the same theme in the late story "Judgement Day").

At the same time the nation as a whole entered a period of its history in which it excelled at "domesticating despair," one that O'Connor's and Percy's convictions led them to critique, and therefore to capture, profoundly. The America that came into being during this period was perhaps foreshadowed in Faulkner's *Go Down, Moses* (1942): not only is the Delta forest steadily being cut down throughout the novel, but at the end of "Pantaloon in Black," the

13. *Conversations with Walker Percy*, ed. Lewis A. Lawson and Victor A. Kramer (Jackson: University Press of Mississippi, 1985), 280–1. See also the essay "Why Are You a Catholic?" for evidence that when Percy says *postmodern*, he is usually thinking in Guardini's terms: "we live in a postmodern as well as a post-Christian age which as yet has no name" (*SSL*, 309). The modern "Age of Enlightenment" ended with "the catastrophes of the twentieth century," and with it went the already hollowed-out and perfunctory "Christendom" that had been in decline for centuries; but in the age to come there is hope that the "language of the Judeo-Christian religions"—"decrepit" and "abused" as it has become—might be renewed (306).

wife of a Mississippi lawman cuts off his tale of a black man's tragedy with a curt remark: "I'm going to the picture show." While Faulkner certainly knew how to search out despair, it was O'Connor and Percy who most fully captured such innovative mechanisms for domesticating it, which emerged in force in the wake of World War II. Native southern illusions might themselves be means of doing so, but in the postwar South these had to contend with, and were often subsumed by, newer and more technologically sophisticated illusions that were now being mass-produced for public consumption. In their nonfiction Percy and O'Connor alike reviled both "Hollywood and Madison Avenue"—the Ur-sources of Baudrillard's "hyperreality"—as the generators of such illusion, and their fiction took to task even more harshly the generally shallow faith in "the American Way of Life" that dominated the public mind for nearly two decades after the war.[14]

Jon Lance Bacon's *Flannery O'Connor and Cold War Culture* has recently defined this faith as a sort of secular mythology that O'Connor's radical Catholicism compelled her to dissent from and attack. His placement of O'Connor against the backdrop of what he calls the general "Cold War consensus" in the United States is an invaluable addition to O'Connor scholarship, properly crediting her vision as essentially religious but placing it within a very specific American historical and cultural context; and, while Bacon does not mention him, Percy certainly should be considered under a similar rubric. For he, like O'Connor, not only attacked the complacent consumerism of the era but also drew on and transformed the underlying anxieties it masked. Bertram Wyatt-Brown has suggested as much in his commendation of *The Moviegoer* as capturing "Southern—indeed American—materialism and shallowness after World War II." Recalling Jean Stafford's National Book Award citation of the novel (she deemed it essentially "truthful . . . with shocks of recognition and spasms of nostalgia for every—or nearly every—American"), Wyatt-Brown sees Percy's first novel as "well-suited to the mood of the day, a vague uneasiness in the midst of American domination of world events during the Cold War." Percy's "evocation of life in the 1950s," he writes, is particularly strong in its examination of "WASP culture as if it were a Polynesian tribe with

14. See Percy, "The Culture Critics," *SSL*, 264; O'Connor, "The Catholic Novelist in the Protestant South," *MM*, 200.

peculiarities of special notice rather than a normative standard by which other ethnic cultures in America should be judged."[15]

While O'Connor and Percy would never have described themselves as "ethnic" Catholics, Wyatt-Brown's implication that Percy conceived of his Catholicism as placing him outside the American mainstream is correct (a fact that Stafford, herself a Catholic convert, doubtlessly appreciated). As Bacon outlines in detail, anti-Catholic sentiments were very much still a part of American life in the 1950s, even though Catholics themselves in this era tended, in the face of Marxist atheism, to stronger patriotic sentiments than ever before. Some American Protestant leaders and secular liberals alike went so far as to compare the Vatican with the Kremlin and to argue that membership in a "totalitarian" Church of definitively international dimensions naturally inclined its members to Communist sympathies.[16] O'Connor surely had more opportunity to encounter such sentiments in Milledgeville than Percy did in southern Louisiana, but he certainly recalled his ancestors' battles with the rabidly anti-Catholic Mississippi Klan in the earlier part of the century.

Underlying such divisions was a profound shift in American religious life. Bacon suggests that in the wake of World War II, "capitalism, as the recognized source of national prosperity, seemed synonymous with the American way" and the American Way became, in effect, the "national religion" into which most mainstream denominations were subsumed.[17] In what Ralph Wood calls the "stifling ethos" of the Eisenhower era (when the president declared, "Our government makes no sense unless it is founded in a deeply felt religious faith—and I don't care what it is"), a professed concern for religious pluralism in fact masked a diluted American religiosity that subordinated itself to "suburban consumerism, the chief marks of which were the triumph of both advertising and the automobile."[18] Insofar as the churches helped to define the United States as the antithesis of the Communist threat, they were a useful

15. Bertram Wyatt-Brown, *The House of Percy* (New York: Oxford University Press, 1994), 320, 322. For the Stafford citation, see Samway, 22.

16. Jon Lance Bacon, *Flannery O'Connor and Cold War Culture* (New York: Cambridge University Press, 1993), 73–5.

17. Ibid., 61.

18. Ralph Wood, "Flannery O'Connor's Strange Alliance with Southern Fundamentalists," *Literature and Belief* 17 (1997): 76–8.

part of a culture that actively touted prosperity, convenience, and sunny optimism—all of which, of course, actually bore a profoundly problematic relationship to the central messages of the Gospel. But in this era, at least, a contemporary sociologist saw a few "hold outs" whose orthodoxy made them resistant to such notions: "Catholics who refused to let their traditional creeds 'be dissolved into an over-all American religion,' and Protestants who espoused the 'religions of the disinherited,' or the 'many holiness, pentecostal and millenarian sects of the socially and culturally submerged segments of our society.'"[19]

O'Connor, in critiquing the new consensus, often dramatized the fervent faith of the latter group (she once said that if she were not a Catholic, she would be not Episcopal but Pentecostal Holiness), but she obviously professed the faith of the former. In doing so she agreed to some extent with the secular critiques of a conformist consumer society advanced in such works as Vance Packard's *The Hidden Persuaders* (1957) and David Riesman's *The Lonely Crowd* (1950), but she certainly shared Percy's sense, expressed clearly in his 1959 essay "The Culture Critics," that these books generally did not go far enough; while condemning suburbia, they proposed nothing in its place.[20] O'Connor and Percy, by contrast, had definite beliefs about what was missing. Their intense and informed Catholicism, shaped by an intellectual movement that was international in scope, gave each an outsider's perspective on postwar America that went beyond that of the secular critics. While neither had any sympathy whatsoever for the Soviet Union (O'Connor refused to let her work be published behind the Iron Curtain because "they would probably use The Misfit to represent the Typical American Business Man"), Percy undoubtedly agreed with O'Connor's view that "the Communist world sprouts from our sins of omission."[21] As late as 1983, Percy proposed that Marxists and Western capitalists were essentially similar types of the "impoverished self," although the latter were adequately wealthy to spend enough money on pets to cover "the food costs of the entire Third World" (*LC*, 82). He and O'Connor finally

19. Will Herberg, *Protestant—Catholic—Jew: An Essay in American Religious Sociology* (Garden City, NY: Doubleday, 1955). Quoted in Bacon, 61.

20. Percy, *SSL*, 264.

21. O'Connor, *HB*, 151, 450. O'Connor's fiction in particular criticizes American nationalism as inherently provincial and often based on crude materialistic desires; see "The Displaced Person" especially.

had more in common with Alexander Solzhenitsyn, who emerged defiant from the Soviet gulag only to savagely critique Western materialism, than with most native American critics.

O'Connor and Percy's placement in the postwar milieu also informs the apocalyptic imagery so prominent in their fictions. Bacon argues that O'Connor's portrayal of "the Invaded Pastoral" is best understood in light of cold war anxieties about foreign invasion, often expressed in her contemporary popular culture through science fiction films; in O'Connor's world, however, invasion—and the accompanying disaster—often turns out to be for the good of the invaded.[22] Certainly Percy's thought was informed by such currents. One science fiction novel that Bacon draws upon in making the seemingly strange connection between Catholicism and a postapocalyptic world is Walter M. Miller Jr.'s A Canticle for Leibowitz (1960), which Percy strongly admired and drew upon in creating his "Space Odyssey" at the conclusion of Lost in the Cosmos. O'Connor and Percy's apocalyptic sense, like that of so many of their contemporaries, was also undeniably informed by their awareness of the real possibility of nuclear war. O'Connor said late in life that "so far as I am concerned, a bomb on Hiroshima affects my judgment of life in rural Georgia"; she also asked a friend who had moved to Los Alamos in 1949 what it was like to live "in a place completely Post Bomb."[23] Percy himself briefly lived in Santa Fe in 1946, and while there he visited the site of the first nuclear explosion at Alamogordo; he depicted scientists from Los Alamos in a vignette in Lost in the Cosmos and considered two alternative titles for The Last Gentleman: these were Ground Zero and The Fall Out, either of which might well befit a novel ending in the New Mexico desert.[24]

O'Connor and Percy differed from their Southern Renascence predecessors in their engagement with such postwar themes, but they also differed from many of their American contemporaries in their refusal to depict the end of the world as finally "absurd" (as R. W. B. Lewis in 1965 described the

22. Bacon, 8 ff.

23. O'Connor, MM, 134; HB, 18. In "Some Aspects of the Grotesque in Southern Fiction" she also mentions, in the context of a general critique of modern scientism, that she lives "in the first generation to face extinction because of" scientific "advances." MM, 41.

24. Jay Tolson, Pilgrim in the Ruins: A Life of Walker Percy (New York: Simon and Schuster, 1992), 191. See Percy, LC, 127 and following.

apocalypticism of Barth, Pynchon, Ralph Ellison, and Joseph Heller).[25] And by placing such themes in their native region, both came to write a new kind of southern fiction, as the first novel of each made clear. O'Connor's *Wise Blood* and Percy's *The Moviegoer*, radically different as they are in tone and character, are definitively postwar southern fictions both in their protagonists (Hazel Motes is a veteran of World War II, Binx Bolling of the Korean War) and in their profound engagement with a new American culture that was beginning to dominate the South. Each critique of that culture—its rabid consumerism as communicated through pervasive advertising and embodied most fully in the automobile, its complacency under the sway of Hollywood and soothing media messengers of the public good—is presented in a setting characterized by an underlying apocalyptic mood. That mood is established partly by a broad appeal to contemporary American anxieties and partly by a regional awareness of the demise of an older South, but it is resolved with a religiously grounded sense of the possibility of meaningful life in the here and now. In O'Connor's work this sense is stark, nagging, pitiless; in Percy's it is subtle, easily overlooked, almost mundane. But in neither case is it backward-looking, or absurd.

In *Wise Blood*, Hazel Motes has returned from World War II to find his rural Tennessee crossroads town abandoned in a manner that suggests not mere economic decline but rather destruction of biblical proportions. Coming into what was once Eastrod, he sees no people; instead he sees "in the dark the store boarded and the barn leaning and the smaller house half-carted away, the porch gone and no floor in the hall" (*TFO*, 9). Where his family lived he finds an even bleaker scene: "The house was as dark as the night and open to it and though he saw that the fence around it had partly fallen and that weeds were growing through the porch floor, he didn't realize all at once that it was only a shell, that there was nothing here but the skeleton of a house" (12). Such desolation underscores the irony of the novel's first line of dialogue, in which a woman on a train says to Haze, "I guess you're going home" (3). Hazel Motes has no home, and in this way he seems to personify

25. See R. W. B. Lewis, "Days of Wrath and Laughter," in *Trials of the Word* (New Haven, CT: Yale University Press, 1965), for a consideration of some of Percy and O'Connor's American contemporaries in whose work "the end of the world" becomes "not only imminent and titanic, but also . . . absurd" (184).

the final culmination of "the modern consciousness, that thing Jung describes as unhistorical, solitary and guilty" and that O'Connor saw as characterizing "the contemporary situation" in the Western world (*HB*, 90). More immediately, Motes exemplifies a social type O'Connor returned to throughout her career: the rural southerner whose traditional world has collapsed and who is destined for a deracinated life in the postwar—and emergently postmodern—city.

When he arrives in Taulkinham, he is immediately besieged by a new and alien culture: "as soon as he stepped off the train, he began to see signs and lights. PEANUTS, WESTERN UNION, AJAX, TAXI, HOTEL, CANDY. Most of them were electric and moved up and down or blinked frantically" (*TFO*, 14). Such is the first instance of a pattern of obtrusive advertising that runs throughout the novel and is emphasized by O'Connor's cartoonish descriptions, as Bacon has noted. Haze and his comical counterpart, Enoch Emery, both encounter garishly described salespeople whose appearances merely mirror the advertising that surrounds them; yielding their own reality to the marketing image, they have become little more than the products they sell. Enoch, who has a certain "fondness for supermarkets" and spends his afternoons browsing in them (66), is more subject to the sway of the advertisers than is Haze, as his utter inability to resist the lure of movie posters indicates (71).[26] Together, the mass media and consumer goods become the focal point of the postwar American life that O'Connor portrays here, and the basis for a kind of secular creed, as suggested both by Enoch's daily reading of the comics "like an office" and by Haze's encounter with a vendor who sells potato peelers atop his own "altar" (99, 18).

Complacency and religious indifference are the natural accompaniments to such an environment. Hazel Motes's "integrity," as O'Connor puts it in her preface to the 1962 edition, lies in the fact that he is incapable of such indifference: he is and remains a searcher after the truth despite himself. Though he preaches the "Church Without Christ," he is initially distinguished

26. Bacon traces the pervasiveness of advertising in Enoch's world and sees him as exemplifying the "public helplessness" that renowned Catholic communications theorist Marshall McLuhan observed among citizens confronted with the twentieth-century media (118–23); for O'Connor's reading of McLuhan's *The Mechanical Bride*, see *HB*, 173–4. McLuhan was also a major influence on Baudrillard's notions of hyperreality and simulacra and therefore of postmodernity itself.

from his unwilling listeners not so much by his atheism as by his passion. The rebuke he delivers to the crowds might almost be O'Connor's own: "'Leave!' Hazel Motes cried. 'Go ahead and leave! The truth don't matter to you. Listen,' he said, pointing his finger at the rest of them, 'the truth don't matter to you. If Jesus had redeemed you, what difference would it make to you? You wouldn't do nothing about it. Your faces wouldn't move, neither this way nor that, and if it was three crosses there and Him hung on the middle one, that one wouldn't mean no more to you and me than the other two'" (72). Haze attempts to proclaim his own indifference here, stating that his church is "the church peaceful and satisfied," but he continually reveals his burning commitment to preaching the truth, even if it is "that there ain't no truth." He is utterly enraged by the self-serving "Church of Christ Without Christ" preached by his foil, Onnie Jay Holy, with its consoling, "up-to-date" message about humanity's essential "sweetness."[27] Unlike Haze, Holy (alias Hoover Shoats) preaches for money and is cozy with the mass media: he is both "a preacher and a radio star" who has hosted a program called "Soulsease, a quarter hour of Mood, Melody, and Mentality" (80). His soothing message for "the whole family" fosters both American self-satisfaction and self-determination: his church is trustworthy, he says, because "there's nothing foreign connected with it. You don't have to believe nothing you don't understand and approve of" (78). O'Connor's Catholicism clearly fuels her satire of the American civil religion here, as it does Haze's initial interview with his landlady. Inquiring as to his profession, she learns that he is a preacher of the Church Without Christ: "'Protestant?' she asked suspiciously. 'Or something foreign?'" (55). In all such reactions to Haze's "church," O'Connor suggests that what matters in the churches of Taulkinham is neither Christ nor even some other "truth," but rather nationalistic self-assurance.

Hazel Motes, of course, battles such complacency not with Catholicism but with his own perversely nihilistic fundamentalist rhetoric, and he does so in front of a meeting place more popular than the church: the movie theater. His battles with Onnie Jay Holy and his disciple take place in front of theaters, as does his first night of preaching: "[Haze] parked the Essex in front

27. Bacon identifies Norman Vincent Peale's postwar "gospel of self-realization" in *The Power of Positive Thinking* (1952) as a contemporary analogue for Holy's preaching (64).

of a movie house where he could catch the drain of people coming out from the picture show. The lights around the marquee were so bright that the moon, moving overhead with a small procession of clouds behind it, looked pale and insignificant" (53). Given the general religious significance of celestial objects in O'Connor's fiction, it is clear that what is being drowned out by the theater is not an attractive view but rather a sense of the divine (consider the role of the sun in "Greenleaf" and "A Temple of the Holy Ghost"; similarly, as "The River" most clearly demonstrates, in O'Connor's work those who know nothing of Nature—and, accordingly, of human frailty—can know nothing of God, and vice versa). The image also recalls Haze's first night in the city, when he walks beneath "thousands of stars" that move "very slowly as if they were about some vast construction work," even while "no one was paying any attention to the sky. The stores in Taulkinham stayed open on Thursday nights so that people could have an extra opportunity to see what was for sale" (18). The mass images peddled by "Hollywood and Madison Avenue" in this world threaten to obscure not only the cosmos but also any proper sense of self: Enoch Emery is utterly unable to control his moviegoing compulsions and devotes himself to watching hopelessly inane films about mad scientists, penitentiary life, and "a baboon named Lonnie who rescued attractive children from a burning orphanage" (71). His enthrallment to such "stars" leads to his encounter with "Gonga," a similar character played by a man in an ape suit who insults the flustered fan. Although most critics have interpreted Enoch's subsequent theft and donning of the ape suit as indicative of his descent into a bestial state, Bacon argues convincingly that the masquerade more accurately reflects Enoch's envy of the "star" and his desire for "a new and improved self," one fit for the big screen.[28]

Haze is not a moviegoer, but he is a lover of cars. Soon after his arrival in Taulkinham, he acquires an Essex, which he envisions as more than a means of transportation: "I wanted this car mostly to be a house for me . . . I ain't got any place to be" (37). Haze in fact prefers having a "home" that is fundamentally mobile, and his attachment to the car, which he also uses as a platform for preaching, recalls that of Mr. Shiftlet in "The Life You Save May Be Your Own": "The body, lady, is like a house: it don't go anywhere; but the

28. Bacon, 123.

spirit, lady, is like a automobile: always on the move . . ." (*CS*, 152).[29] Insofar as such sentiments identify Haze as a searcher, they might, in O'Connor's eyes, be to his credit. But insofar as they indicate his attachment to·a consumer good that offers him a false sense of self-sufficiency, they are damning. Haze's belief that "[n]obody with a good car needs to be justified" is clearly indicative of his susceptibility to the same identity-based advertising to which Enoch falls prey (*TFO*, 58). Accordingly, it is the wreck of Haze's car that is most responsible for his final conversion. After he has used the Essex to murder the false "Prophet" who works for Shoats, he reassures himself that "nobody with a good car needed to be worried about anything" but nonetheless is stopped by a mysterious policeman, who destroys the vehicle (106–8).

Deprived of the machine that has served as his "home" and his source of identity, Haze is forced to settle down and begin his bizarre penance, the asceticism and self-blinding that will lead to new vision. The profoundly countercultural nature of his actions in the final chapter is emphasized in the comments of his landlady, Mrs. Flood: she views his penance as "something that people have quit doing—like boiling in oil or being a saint or walling up cats. . . . There's no reason for it. People have quit doing it." In fact, she "wouldn't be surprised if you weren't some kind a agent of the pope or got some connection with something funny" (116). Such comments suggest O'Connor's sentiment that "Catholicism is opposed to the bourgeois mind" (*CW*, 862) and that such a mind was being more rigorously developed in postwar America than ever before. She claimed that "no one but a Catholic could have written *Wise Blood* even though it is a book about a kind of Protestant saint," one whose fundamentalist commitment—learned from his circuit-riding preacher grandfather in Tennessee—makes him such a radical critic, first as nihilist and finally as Christian *malgré lui*, of the complacent postwar culture springing up in the cities of the newest New South.

The end of *Wise Blood* succinctly emphasizes the essential difference between O'Connor's novel and *The Moviegoer*. Itself a somber departure from the slapstick action that dominates the novel, the last chapter almost ends with a strange marriage between Haze and Mrs. Flood, who sadly realizes

29. Brian Abel Ragen has chronicled O'Connor's use of "the automobile as an emblem for the philosophies celebrating the individual's absolute freedom and autonomy" that dominate American culture. *A Wreck on the Road to Damascus* (Chicago: Loyola University Press, 1989), xvi.

that she actually wants to marry "a blind man and a sick one. If we don't help each other, Mr. Motes, there's nobody to help us. Nobody. The world's a empty place" (118). But Haze dies before she can convince him of this, and appropriately so, for we cannot imagine Haze settling down to a quiet domestic life in Taulkinham. O'Connor's great strength, as her disparaging remark about the bourgeoisie indicates, lies in her vicious satire of middle-class mores; Percy, by contrast, in *The Moviegoer*, "knew how to make the middle-class suburbanite look foolish without being unduly malicious"—"his dissection of his times was coolly anthropological."[30] Accordingly, Percy's novel ends with a marriage and the beginning of a life that seems outwardly conventional. There are no crusading fundamentalists in *The Moviegoer*, and here (more so than in some of his later fiction) Percy's few Catholic characters seem almost indistinguishable from the other "bourgeoisie"; but his critique of the new national order was no less penetrating or devastating than O'Connor's and in fact shared a number of essential similarities with it.[31]

Binx Bolling is, as noted earlier, a "new man" of sorts; though he is scion of an aristocratic southern family, he is as detached from their values as Haze Motes is from those of his plain upcountry grandfather. The Bollings have their roots in rural Feliciana Parish, but after returning from the Korean conflict, Binx settles neither there nor in the New Orleans Garden District home where his aunt attempts to maintain the family's heritage. He chooses instead "Gentilly, a middle-class suburb of New Orleans" that "one would never guess . . . was part of New Orleans"; he prefers its anonymity to "the old-world atmosphere of the French Quarter or the genteel charm of the Garden District" (3). Whereas Haze came home to find his traditional world destroyed, Binx elects to leave his and dwell instead on a street that might as well be in Los Angeles, one lined with "shopping centers and blocks of duplexes and bungalows and raised cottages" (6).[32]

---

30. Wyatt-Brown, 322.

31. Again, O'Connor had eagerly anticipated reading Percy's first novel and understood it from the start. When her acquaintance Robert Drake, a writer and professor of English, told her that he had not liked *The Moviegoer*, she told him he had been mistaken: " 'You'd better read it again,' O'Connor said in her simple but absolutely authoritative way" (Tolson, 324).

32. Though never a chronicler of suburban life as was Percy, O'Connor also made note of this new—and definitively postwar—environment. Taulkinham is seedy and urban, but Haze drives through its even more alien suburbs: "he went past long blocks of gray houses and then blocks

In Gentilly Binx never thinks of himself as the scion of an old aristocratic family, but rather as "a model tenant and a model citizen," a "veteran with all his papers in order" (4, 106). More educated, self-aware, and ironic than any of the characters in *Wise Blood*, he forthrightly posits that his identity is bound by the terms of contemporary American culture: "It is a pleasure to carry out the duties of a citizen and to receive in return a receipt or a neat styrene card with one's name on it certifying, so to speak, one's right to exist. What satisfaction I take in appearing the first day to get my auto tag and brake sticker! I subscribe to *Consumer Reports* and as a consequence I own a first-class television set, an all but silent air conditioner and a very long-lasting deodorant. My armpits never stink" (4). Though he seems canny about the limitations of the shallow culture he associates himself with here, Binx essentially lives on its terms and engages in a life of hedonism. His sole discernible talent, he says, is "the trick of making money" as a small-time stockbroker, a profession in which he also excels at seducing his secretaries. His ability to combine "love" with business, as well as his moviegoing habit and placement in the Eisenhower era, are all suggested in his successful ploy to impress Sharon Kincaid as he plays the "role" of a cunning but also caring broker who takes the time to write personal letters to his clients. He acts the part of a tough, no-nonsense boss as she takes dictation: "Dear Mr Fontenot: Glancing over your portfolio, it occurs to me that you are not in the best position to take advantage of the dawning age of missiles . . ." (92).

In the process of doing so, Binx imagines himself as several different movie stars, as he does throughout the novel. His eponymous habit is introduced immediately after his discussion of his identity as a citizen-consumer: "In the evenings I usually watch television or go to the movies. . . . Our neighborhood theater in Gentilly has permanent lettering on the front of the marquee reading: Where Happiness Costs So Little" (4). Though Binx again seems ironic here, he admits that he is in fact "quite happy in a movie, even a bad movie," generally preferring such mass-produced illusions to a seemingly dreary world. The impoverishment of individual personalities in Binx's society is suggested by his observation of a star, William Holden, encountering a young

---

of better, yellow houses. . . . He went past blocks of white houses, each sitting with an ugly dog face on a square of grass" before passing into that semi-urban stretch that precedes the true country, a highway "ragged with filling stations and trailer camps and roadhouses" (38).

northern tourist in the French Quarter. Holden, Binx thinks, carries "an aura of heightened reality," and the tourist "can only contrast Holden's resplendent reality with his own shadowy and precarious existence." Only when the tourist succeeds in offering the star a cigarette light does he feel certified: "He has won title to his own existence, as plenary an existence now as Holden's" (12–13). Whereas Enoch failed in his casual encounter with Gonga and comically resorted to stealing his identity, the tourist here effects a successfully discreet siphoning off of Holden's apparent "reality."

Binx also immerses himself in other forms of the mass media that actively promote good citizenship. "I pay attention to all spot announcements on the radio about mental health, the seven signs of cancer, and safe driving"; he finds Holden's announcement enlisting listeners to fight litter particularly compelling (4). He is also a devoted listener to Edward R. Murrow's "This I Believe," a radio program devoted to proclaiming the values of a liberal democratic society. Even as Binx testifies that he tunes in to the show daily, even religiously ("monks have their compline, I have 'This I Believe'"), he suggests that its humanist platitudes are somehow insufficient: "Everyone on 'This I Believe' believes in the uniqueness and the dignity of the individual. I have noticed, however, that the believers are far from unique themselves, are in fact alike as peas in a pod." The vague and diluted values espoused here, though professing to honor individualism, are ironically bound up with a kind of conformity, and those guests who repeatedly drone "I believe in freedom . . . and the brotherhood of man" clearly subscribe to the civil religion attacked by O'Connor; they are more educated and high-minded versions of Hoover Shoats. The self-satisfaction and sentimental sense of "sweetness" engendered by their creeds are suggested by Binx's final comment after the show ends: "I switch off my radio and lie in bed with a pleasant tingling sensation in my groin, a tingling for Sharon and for all my fellow Americans" (94–6).

For even as Binx thoroughly chronicles his own immersion in his society, he is aware and ironic enough to critique it. One of the best examples of his doing both simultaneously is in his description of his experiences with automobiles as he takes his secretaries on dates:

When I first moved to Gentilly, I bought a new Dodge sedan, a Red Ram Six. It was a comfortable, conservative and economical two-door sedan, just the thing, it seemed to me, for a young Gentilly businessman. When

I first slid under the wheel to drive it, it seemed that everything was in order—here was I, a healthy young man, a veteran with all his papers in order, a U.S. citizen driving a very good car. All these things were true enough, yet on my first trip to the Gulf Coast with Marcia, I discovered to my dismay that my fine new Dodge was a regular incubator of malaise. Though it was comfortable enough, though it ran like a clock, though we went spinning along in perfect comfort and with a perfect view of the scenery like the American couple in the Dodge ad, the malaise quickly became suffocating. We sat frozen in a gelid amiability. Our cheeks ached from smiling. (106)

Fortunately, Binx has acquired a new MG in which to court Sharon, a car that he thinks is "immune" to the malaise because it allows them to sit "out in the world, out in the thick summer air between sky and earth." His lingering fears about malaise, however, are not dispelled until the unexpected happens: a minor accident that renders him and Sharon newly aware of one another and the world.

Such is the manner in which catastrophe usually functions in Percy's work, and in fact *The Moviegoer* as a whole might be read as an expansion of the incidents described above. For the society Binx inhabits generally mirrors his experience with the Dodge: despite the promises of American freedom and happiness offered by ads—or "This I Believe"—he finds that most conversations seem to be "spoken by automatons who have no choice in what they say" and, even more grimly, that "everyone is dead" (86–7). As in *Wise Blood*, this postwar society professes not atheism but rather a superficial religiosity that is, in Percy's view, even more deadly. Binx reports this phenomenon in language that wryly bespeaks his society's bland consensus: "as everyone knows, the polls report that 98% of Americans believe in God and the remaining 2% are atheists and agnostics—which leaves not a single percentage point for a seeker" (10). The novel depicts Binx himself becoming such a seeker, and here, as with Haze, lies his integrity, though he is not fixated on the "wild ragged figure of Jesus" as O'Connor's hero is. He is more like those in Haze's crowd who seem unable to respond to Christianity at all, as he suggests in a journal entry regarding his search: "The only possible starting point: the strange fact of one's own invincible apathy—that if the proofs were proved and God presented himself, nothing would be changed. Here is the strangest fact of all. Abraham saw signs of God and believed. Now the only sign is that all the signs in the world make no difference. Is this God's ironic revenge? But I am onto him" (128–9). Furthermore, Binx's capacity for the search is inherently connected to his sense of catastrophe: "the first time the search occurred to me," he says, was while he lay wounded beneath a bush in Korea (7).

But the possibility of catastrophe affects Binx's suburban life as well. The reality of the atomic age hangs over Gentilly: within the first few pages of the novel, Binx speaks of a "TV play about a nuclear test explosion" in the desert and fantasizes about meeting a girl in the ruins of a bombed-out city. Near its conclusion he reads a headline over a commuter's shoulder: "SCIENTIST PREDICTS FUTURE IF NUCLEAR ENERGY NOT MISUSED" (5, 9, 167).[33] While the apocalyptic tone in *Wise Blood* is established by the disappearance of Eastrod and the very urgency of Haze's preaching, in *The Moviegoer* it comes from such technological imagery—and from Emily Cutrer's sense of a lost South. Aunt Emily's despairing sense of the decline of southern (and, on a larger scale, Western) civilization, is expressed in powerful romantic rhetoric and cannot but affect Binx. Early in the novel she tells him: "I no longer pretend to understand the world. . . . The world I knew has come crashing down around my ears. The things we hold dear are reviled and spat upon. . . . It's an interesting age you will live in—though I can't say I'm sorry to miss it. But it should be quite a sight, the going under of the evening land. That's us all right. And I can tell you, my young friend, it is evening. It is very late" (45). Such sentiments no doubt contribute to Binx's tendency (common to Percy's heroes generally) not to fear apocalypse so much as to relish it: in an age where "malaise has settled like a fallout" already, he thinks, "what people really fear is not that the bomb will fall but that the bomb will not fall" (200).

Binx's search ends, however, not in despair, but rather with a vision of a new heaven and a new earth glimpsed in his own age. In the epilogue he has not only given up his life of self-centered hedonism and convenience to marry the troubled Kate Cutrer; he has also undergone an understated conversion that enables him to speak with his young step-siblings about the goodness of

33. This commuter's reading material bespeaks all the worst features of Binx's society: he reads a "TECHNIQUE IN MARRIAGE" column and highlights passages about "the gradual convergence of physical science and social science" (166–70).

"the last day"—on which their handicapped and dying brother, he tells them, will be raised up and made whole (210). Yet the day on which Binx tells them this seems good as well, and his search—which he is reticent about partly because the very word *"religion"* is "peculiar," "something to be suspicious of"—seems, if not quite finished, then at least to have found a clear and hopeful new orientation (208). Unlike O'Connor, who in Haze Motes's penance conveys a vision of the present that is radically hopeful but only in the starkest sense, Percy conveys for Binx and Kate a more understated hope in the possibility of living an authentic—and sacramental—life that, by all outward appearances, seems quite "normal."[34] Percy's depictions of religious life changed to some extent in his later novels, with prophetic characters like Val Vaught and Father Smith, and perhaps show a greater debt to O'Connor's vision; but her great admiration for *The Moviegoer* speaks to the extent to which she herself saw it as essentially agreeing with her own critique of the "Cold War consensus," whatever the novel's radical differences from *Wise Blood* in character, tone, and sensibility.

OTHER SOUTHERNERS writing in the postwar era—Donald Davidson, for example—were also registering their own dissent from the American Way of Life, of course. And Percy and O'Connor's critique of the spiritually sterile mass culture that was overtaking their region bears at least a superficial resemblance to that mounted by the Agrarians earlier in the century: certainly insofar as both attacked unchecked technology and a homogeneous mass society that threatened individualism, they participated in a long-standing southern tradition. To a certain degree, each *did* frame a critique of contemporary

34. Indeed, with the exception of the handicapped youth Lonnie, all of Percy's Catholic characters (Uncle Jules Cutrer, the Smith family, even the middle-class Negro whom he sees on Ash Wednesday) in *The Moviegoer* are so apparently "normal" as to seem almost indifferent. As a guest at mass, Sharon is struck by the Smiths' "heroic unreligiousness"—though they do attend unfailingly, and other sections of the novel suggest that their faith is deceptively deep (141). In fact, they are distinguished from Aunt Emily, Sam Yerger, Kate, and Binx himself precisely by their solidity, stability, and refusal to take themselves too seriously. Binx sees the Smiths as pleasantly ordinary compared to the Bollings and Aunt Emily: "As a Bolling in Feliciana Parish, I became accustomed to sitting on the porch in the dark and talking of the size of the universe and the treachery of men; as a Smith on the Gulf Coast I have become accustomed to eating crabs and drinking beer under a hundred and fifty watt bulb" (135).

American culture in regional terms.[35] But finally O'Connor and, especially, Percy found this sort of approach insufficient: while each might draw upon traditional regional values as a means of taking the measure of the postwar world, each finally presented a radical critique of the South as well, one that drew upon religious convictions as the ultimate standard of judgment. Indeed, to a large extent their fictions are built upon a conflict between contemporary consumerism and traditional southern mores in which both exhaust themselves and point obliquely toward the possibility of a Christianity truly practiced.

In Percy's work this conflict may be clearly discerned. In the Kierkegaardian terms often and appropriately applied to his fiction, his protagonists tend to struggle out of a complacent "aesthetic" life devoted to pleasure-seeking—the life of the consumer—and toward a religious one, but they do so only in relation to a third possibility: that of the ethical life, the principles of which are derived solely from human reason and tradition rather than divine revelation. The most striking exemplars of such a life are inevitably what Percy called southern "Stoics," such as Emily Cutrer, Ed Barrett, and—more darkly—Lancelot Lamar (all modeled to some degree on the figure of William Alexander Percy). In *The Moviegoer*, for example, the moral critique most directly leveled against Binx comes not from the Catholic Church, but rather from Aunt Emily. What Percy finds most admirable in his own southern tradition is the strict Stoic code of its patrician leaders; but it is finally not good enough, for it is ultimately characterized by a secret self-absorption and despair. Yet Percy's best fiction arises from his struggle with its appeal, even though he knows that the code is passing or gone. Bertram Wyatt-Brown is correct in proclaiming that "Walker Percy is the last novelist in America to have made the southern ethic of honor a central concern of his work."[36] In

35. See chapter 1 regarding O'Connor's endorsement of C. Vann Woodward's notion of the potentially redemptive "burden of southern history" (which she interpreted in a more specifically theological sense than did Woodward). Also see Ralph Wood, "Flannery O'Connor, H. L. Mencken, and the Southern Agrarians: A Dispute over Religion More Than Region," *Flannery O'Connor Bulletin* 20 (1991): 1–21.

36. See Percy, "Stoicism in the South," *SSL*. Bertram Wyatt-Brown, "Will, Walker, and Honor Dying: The Percys and Literary Creativity," in *Looking South: Chapters in the Story of an American Region*, ed. Winfred B. Moore and Joseph F. Tripp (Westport, CT: Greenwood, 1989), 229.

doing so, certainly, he writes about not only the end of the modern world but also the end of the modern South.

O'Connor's appreciation of the southern tradition had little to do with such patrician codes, though she did value, to a degree, the manners most often associated with the aristocracy. While she saw manners as necessary for any meaningful social life, she believed that in her South "the old manners are obsolete" and that their "real basis of charity" must be rediscovered (*MM*, 234).[37] In her fiction the most elaborately mannered characters (e.g., the Grandmother of "A Good Man Is Hard to Find") lack the integrity of Percy's most exemplary Stoics; their essential selfishness tends to be utterly transparent, and even their alleged commitment to southern traditions actually blends easily with postwar consumerism. The concern for etiquette and propriety voiced by O'Connor's matrons, in contrast to the honor code advocated by Percy's usually male Stoics (Aunt Emily being the great exception), is most often revealed to be an utter facade.

In a completely different vein, we have seen how O'Connor does value the biblical tradition preserved by her backwoods southern Protestants: whereas Percy's standard foil to the postwar consumer is the honorable aristocrat, hers is usually some brand of country fundamentalist. But such characters are generally more "Christ-haunted" than "Christ-centered," as she famously labeled the entire region (*MM*, 44). Sometimes this is because they, like Haze Motes, have actively tried to put Christ behind them, but to some extent O'Connor saw such problems as inherent in fundamentalism itself: "Wise blood has to be these people's means of grace—they have no sacraments. The religion of the South is a do-it-yourself religion, something which I as a Catholic find painful and touching and grimly comic. It's full of unconscious pride that lands them in all sorts of ridiculous religious predicaments" (*HB*, 350). She does, on the one hand, "accept the same fundamental doctrines" as the truest of these believers (forthrightly stating that old Tarwater in *The Violent Bear It Away* essentially speaks for her), but she also implies in *Wise Blood* and numerous stories, on the other hand, that fundamentalism may contain the seeds of nihilism within itself. Although such characters as the Misfit, Mr. Shiftlet ("The Life You Save May Be Your Own"), and Rufus Johnson ("The

37. Both O'Connor's discussion of manners here and Percy's discussion of Stoicism are significantly bound up with their reactions to the growing racial tension in the 1950s South.

Lame Shall Enter First") show evidence of their roots in biblical tradition and even, in a sense, talk good moral talk, these Christ-haunted characters finally profess and practice beliefs that are far removed from those of O'Connor. "The Displaced Person," as we shall see, is perhaps her single clearest exploration of the dangers of fundamentalism.

Finally, O'Connor and Percy alike critiqued the South by critiquing the virtues associated with the Southern Renascence itself—or, rather, by critiquing the cliché that they threatened to become. Although both had the greatest admiration for most of their acclaimed predecessors in twentieth-century southern letters, they also saw the danger that "southern literature" would become institutionalized and falsified. In 1962 Percy wrote forthrightly of these matters in "Virtues and Vices in the Southern Literary Renascence": "The virtues of the Southern renascence provide clues to its faults. If Southern writers are blessed with a kind of historical perspective, as Louis Rubin called it, and a sense of place, as Thomas Daniel Young called it, they are also more likely to fall prey to genre and mannerism. It may be true that one needs the past in order to understand the present, but one can also be trapped by it, like Mark Twain's river boat which got locked up forever in a bayou when the river changed course."[38] O'Connor likely had such sentiments in mind when she made her well-known statement regarding her relationship to Faulkner: when she said, "nobody wants his mule and wagon stalled on the same track the Dixie Limited is roaring down," she was concerned about her own ability to avoid doing "what has already been done to completion" in a literature where "there are many writers all employing the same idiom" (*MM*, 45). Her statement may seem to bespeak anxiety of influence, but the fuller context of the remark, her essay "Some Aspects of the Grotesque in Southern Fiction," reveals that she is actually concerned with the same larger issues of truth and falsehood that Percy is, with the writer's ultimate duty to capture the essence of (southern) life in the here and now.

It is appropriate that Percy's statement ends with reference to Twain, for in his own sense that the southern aesthetic of memory might become cliché, he joined the nineteenth-century writer in satirizing the region's obsession with a romanticized past. But by the middle of his own century, that native

38. Walker Percy, "Virtues and Vices in the Southern Literary Renascence," *Commonweal*, May 11, 1962, 181.

obsession—so powerfully explored in the literature of the three preceding decades—had been appropriated by and subsumed into an increasingly powerful national media, so that mass-produced images of the South suddenly became more prominent in the new hyperreal consumer culture of the United States and the region itself than had previously been possible. Such "southern simulacra"—superficial copies of images that had often been false to begin with—were among Percy's primary concerns throughout his career, and he confronted them most directly in *Lancelot*. O'Connor preceded him in doing so, not in *Wise Blood* but in her first short story collection, *A Good Man Is Hard to Find*. The collection clearly deserves consideration as a short story cycle, for O'Connor asserted the thematic unity of these "nine stories about Original Sin"; they are no less nine stories about a region riddled with self-delusion and only dimly aware of its own ongoing upheaval in a time when forces of cataclysmic social change were making themselves felt in the land.

The second story, "A Late Encounter with the Enemy," most clearly emphasizes the emergence of a new and nascently postmodern southern culture. The central character is an ancient man who seems a virtual embodiment of the South. George Poker Sash is in fact a Confederate veteran who was probably a foot soldier, but "he didn't remember what he had been; in fact, he didn't remember that war at all" (*CS*, 135). What he does remember is the Atlanta premiere of a Civil War film twelve years ago (approximately 1939, which makes *Gone with the Wind* the likely analogue) at which he was dressed up, surrounded by "pretty guls" from California, and wheeled onstage to be introduced as "General Tennessee Flintrock" Sash. Ever since, he has been loaned out by his granddaughter to be "displayed" at the local museum on Confederate Memorial Day and to lend atmosphere to the porches of plantation homes during the spring pilgrimage season; he has become, in effect, an image meant to promote tourism. Enjoying his new identity and the access it affords him to the goods of a newly prosperous society, one that places him—a neutered, comic figure now—at the center of "parades full of floats with Miss Americas and Miss Daytona Beaches and Miss Queen Cotton Products," the "General" seems content with the present. It is, ironically, his granddaughter who seeks to preserve him as proof to the contemporary world—"all the upstarts who had turned the world on its head and unsettled the ways of decent living"—of her own ties to the "old traditions" of "Dignity! Honor! Courage!" (134–5). Her cherished plan to wheel him onstage dressed in all his Hollywood finery during her college graduation is marred when, unbeknownst to all, he dies during the ceremony. In a final scene rich with irony, we last see the old man in the hands of his great-great-nephew, "waiting now, with the corpse, in the long line at the Coca-Cola machine" (144). Since Sally Poker Sash and the "General" himself conceived their traditions and history in the terms provided them by a Hollywood hit, it is fitting that he end in the careless hands of a forgetful descendant and beside a symbol of the twentieth-century South's own greatest financial success story.

"A Late Encounter with the Enemy" more accurately satirizes a false historical consciousness than historical consciousness itself, but the collection as a whole suggests that the false version seems to be all that is available in postwar southern culture. "A Good Man Is Hard to Find" is in part a similar critique of contemporary regional self-perception: the Grandmother, like Sally Poker Sash, praises her own vision of an Old South that she sees enduring, to some extent, in the present day. Choosing to perceive impoverished black children as "picturesque," fantasizing about plantation houses laden with "family silver" hidden from the Yankees, and reminiscing about gentleman callers seems to her not escapist self-indulgence but rather real commentary on the South as it is. But once again, her images are partly shaped by Hollywood—she too references *Gone with the Wind*. The Grandmother does have a sense that the region and the modern world alike are decaying: she believes "people did right then" ("in my time") more often than they do now and that "a good man is hard to find" these days. But she does not see that fault might lay in the South itself and its amoral complicity with a self-satisfied American consumerism, instead claiming that "Europe was to blame for the way things were now" (*CS*, 122). She is totally unaware of the irony implicit in her recollection of a suitor whom she would have done well to marry not only "because he was a gentleman" but also because he "had bought Coca-Cola stock when it first came out and had died only a few years ago, a very wealthy man" (120).

Her faith in money and manners alike is carried beyond its breaking point in her encounter with the Misfit; her offer to pay him and her plea that he refrain from shooting a "lady" (she has been encouraged by his country habit of calling her "ma'am") are in vain. The Misfit presents her with a stark vision of a world where her strain of traditional southern values, themselves inherently tainted by the self-seeking interests she tries to attribute only to the contemporary world, is completely inefficacious. But the Misfit's own apocalyptic sentiments, fostered in O'Connor herself largely by the vision of European writers ranging from Dostoyevsky to Guardini, are delivered in a manner consistent with southern tradition of another sort, that biblical tradition which emphasizes not secular history but rather final judgment and the sealing of the soul's eternal fate in a choice that might be made in a moment. Insofar as the Misfit's stance is that of the fundamentalist, albeit a perverse one, O'Connor here uses one "southern" tradition to depict the collapse of another. Although he has come down on the wrong side, the Misfit's essentially religious vision of the contemporary world—his stark sense that the choice offered by Christ between selfless love and self-centered "meanness" holds today as it has always—is a clearer and truer one than the well-mannered Grandmother's falsely nostalgic fantasy, a fact she grasps only in the last moment of her life.

The Misfit is only one of many O'Connor characters who, though they come from a religious tradition that emphasizes human moral agency and decries the secularism of the age, are themselves deeply flawed. Mr. Shiftlet of "The Life You Save May Be Your Own" succinctly exemplifies the type. When he strolls onto the Crater farm and is seen standing silhouetted against the sun like "a crooked cross," we are prepared for his identity as a sort of half Christian—one who believes in sin but not, apparently, in redemption. He is both southern and "religious," we might assume, in his belief that "the [contemporary] world is almost rotten" and has lost its sense of the spiritual: "'Lady,' he said . . . 'lemme tell you something. There's one of these doctors in Atlanta that's taken a knife and cut the human heart—the human heart,' he repeated, leaning forward, 'out of a man's chest and held it in his hand . . . and studied it like it was a day-old chicken, and lady . . . he don't know no more about it than you or me'" (CS, 146–7). Mr. Shiftlet, in O'Connor's view, is certainly correct both here and in his later passionate statement that he has "a moral intelligence!"—but he is unable to use it properly. Radically committed to his own autonomy, he steals Mrs. Crater's car and abandons her mentally handicapped daughter before he is able to pray: "Oh Lord! . . . Break forth and wash the slime from this earth!"—at which point a cloud begins to chase after *him* (156). He seems to reject the modern world and is to some degree informed by a native religious sense, but Mr. Shiftlet proves to be as rotten as the world he describes, to have let the best in his own southern tradition become as inextricably bound up with a flawed contemporary society as the Grandmother did with hers.

"The Displaced Person" is the longest story in *A Good Man Is Hard to Find* and perhaps also the most ambitious, for it most fully depicts both the impending demise of native traditions and their inherent inadequacy. The three major characters are Mrs. McIntyre, a strong matriarch who runs a southern farm and enforces its traditional rules; Mrs. Shortley, one of the white "help" who takes up the language of fundamentalist Christianity in the service of her own interests; and the Displaced Person, a Pole who has fled war-ravaged Europe and has been brought to the farm by a Catholic priest. The Displaced Person's arrival is the catalyst for the story's action, for though he proves to be an invaluable worker on the farm, he is, as Mrs. McIntyre says, "extra and he's upset the balance around here" (*CS*, 231). That his presence on this particular farm has bearing on the region as a whole is strongly suggested in a scene where Mrs. McIntyre confronts the Pole as he cuts a field "in a circular path to the center where the graveyard was" and her late husband is buried (221). "The Judge," whose resting place is now being threatened, is here blatantly associated with a sort of historical consciousness:

> Of her three husbands, the Judge was the one most present to her although he was the only one she had buried. . . . He was a dirty snuff-dipping Court House figure, famous all over the county for being rich, who wore hightop shoes, a string tie, a gray suit with a black stripe in it, and a yellowed panama hat, winter and summer. His teeth and hair were tobacco-colored and his face a clay pink pitted and tracked with mysterious prehistoric-looking marks as if he had been unearthed among fossils. . . . The three years that he lived after they had been married were the happiest and most prosperous of Mrs. McIntyre's life, but when he died his estate proved to be bankrupt. (218)

Such imagery suggests the Old South, but Mrs. McIntyre's rule of the farm makes clear that its legacy is honored in the present. In her dealings with her "help" (whom she, like Ruby Turpin in the later story "Revelation," divides into "white trash and niggers" [*CS*, 202]), her own precarious finances are her first concern, and her indoctrination of the Displaced Person into southern culture is essentially limited to one area: a proper understanding of local racial codes. When he first arrives, for example, "she was a long time explaining to the Pole that all Negroes would steal" (202). In the end her loyalty to such traditions is even more important than her immediate wealth, for despite the fact that the Displaced Person vastly improves the farm, she wants to get rid of him after he tries to arrange a marriage between his cousin and one of the blacks with whom he works. She "will not have my niggers upset," because she "cannot run this place without my niggers," as she tells him and later the priest (223). In these characters' uncomprehending response to Mrs. McIntyre's horror at the thought of miscegenation, O'Connor suggests the shortcomings of regional mores in comparison with the demands of both postwar American society and a Christianity truly practiced.[39]

In the character of Mrs. Shortley, however, O'Connor gives one of her darkest portraits of an impulsive and superficial Christianity that is twisted to serve personal ends. Although her son is in Bible school studying to be a preacher, Mrs. Shortley has not been particularly religious throughout her life; her vision of her own identity and struggles have been cast in purely socioeconomic terms, and her essential allegiance to the material promise of American culture is suggested by her strange reverence for an ad that promises the attainment of "regular" gastrointestinal habits (211). It is only the arrival of the Polish family that precipitates her first "inner vision" (200). Fearful for her husband's job, she suddenly has the "intuition" that these newcomers are allied with the devil. Their origin in Europe, "where the religion had not been reformed," suggests so (203, 205). Henceforth she begins to read her Bible "with a new attention": "She poured over the Apocalypse and began to quote from the Prophets and before long she had come to a deeper understanding of her existence. She saw that the Lord God Almighty had created the strong people to do what had to be done and she felt that she would be ready when she was called. Right now she felt that her business was to watch the priest. . . . Here he was: leading foreigners over in hordes to places that were not theirs, to cause disputes, to uproot niggers, to plant the Whore of Babylon in the midst of the righteous!" (209). Mrs. Shortley undoubtedly feels

---

39. O'Connor was not necessarily a radical progressive on matters of racial justice herself, as certain of her letters make clear. But in her fiction she clearly satirized self-centered racists, not only in "The Displaced Person" but also in such stories as "The Artificial Nigger" and "Revelation"; the latter again convincingly emphasizes O'Connor's knowledge of how supposedly "religious" convictions can become complicit in racism.

that her new convictions have been come by honestly, and they certainly do not lack intensity. But the narrator's very emphasis on "intuition" and feeling here clearly suggests the dangers O'Connor saw implicit in the "do-it-yourself" southern religion she so often admired and adapted to her own purposes. Given Mrs. Shortley's forthright anti-Catholicism—as well as the manner in which her theology supports a superficially sanctified but essentially Darwinian socioeconomic theory—it is clear that O'Connor does not endorse the capacity for *self*-justification evidenced in such "religion." The narrative does finally depict Mrs. Shortley in a sympathetic light: when she dies in the car as her family prepares to leave the farm, her children's forlorn confusion underscores this woman's own sad life of displacement, and at the moment of her death she is granted for the first time a vision of "the tremendous frontiers of her true country" (214). But in her life she lacked anything resembling it, making her less like the authentically religious Pentecostal Mrs. Greenleaf of "Greenleaf" than the self-serving "Christian" Ruby Turpin in "Revelation."

In one of O'Connor's most unambiguous endings, Mrs. Shortley's vision and Mrs. McIntyre's secular one alike—both "southern" in their own way— have collapsed. With the farm falling into ruin after the silent conspiracy to kill the Displaced Person has been carried out, an ailing Mrs. McIntyre, confronted with what Guardini called "the nearness of the End," is left alone with the priest, who comes regularly to "sit by the side of her bed and explain the doctrines of the Church" (235). While such an ending might, in the broader context of Western civilization, suggest the ultimate return to tradition, in this context it suggests a new beginning. Throughout the story the Displaced Person and the priest alike have been associated with the changes sweeping the postwar South, not only in challenging established religious patterns and social mores but even in the Pole's mastery of machinery: "Mr. Guizac could drive a tractor, use the rotary hay-baler, the silage cutter, the combine, the letz mill, or any other machine she had on the place. He was an expert mechanic, a carpenter, and a mason" (201). Such associations suggest that, while O'Connor often used regional traditions to critique postwar America, she finally saw her own ultimately religious critique as being, in a sense, progressive; in a stark postwar world, hope finally lay neither in a self-satisfied contemporary American culture nor in turning back the clock to revitalize certain aspects of southern tradition, but rather in a true religious commitment made in the here and now.

Lucinda MacKethan has indirectly suggested as much in her consideration of yet another story in *A Good Man Is Hard to Find*, "The Artificial Nigger." Here, she claims, O'Connor's "representation of a large modern metropolis satirizes and thus complicates the traditional southern agrarian denunciation of the city. Thus, she provides a paradigm for later, post-Southern-renaissance portrayals of the city, particularly those by fellow Catholics Walker Percy and John Kennedy Toole." MacKethan correctly demonstrates that the city represents for all three of these authors the essential moral complexity of contemporary life, particularly as it forces "salvific" encounters between the races that are alien to the more traditional southern countryside.[40] Mr. Head's epiphanic insight at the close of "The Artificial Nigger" comes at the expense of his traditional convictions, through an experience in a contemporary landscape that, I would add, is presented as densely sacramental even in its most sordid aspects. MacKethan notes the essential similarity of Binx's moment of grace in *The Moviegoer* as he watches a middle-class black man emerge from a suburban church on Ash Wednesday. O'Connor and Percy alike, then, affirm the new possibilities inherent in a deracinated contemporary life because of both their Catholic moral perspective on southern social change and their fundamentally sacramental vision of reality itself.[41]

For Percy, too, profoundly critiqued not only his region's immersion in contemporary consumer culture but also the honor code he identified as characteristic of the older southern aristocracy. I have already suggested how *The Moviegoer* juxtaposes Aunt Emily's Stoicism with Binx's hedonism: she speaks

40. Lucinda MacKethan, "Redeeming Blackness: Urban Allegories of O'Connor, Percy, and Toole," *Studies in the Literary Imagination* (Fall 1994): 29. Also, "The Artificial Nigger" once again depicts the ascendancy of southern simulacra: entering the city, Mr. Head and Nelson pass signs for "The Dixie Chemical Corp! Southern Maid Flour! Dixie Doors! Southern Belle Cotton Products! . . . Southern Mammy Cane Syrup!" (*CS*, 257). The latter image in particular bears heavily upon the story's title and the final "product" the protagonists confront here, the "artificial nigger" itself.

41. Percy was much more of an open progressive on racial issues than O'Connor was, as a number of his nonfiction essays indicate. In "Walker Percy, the Catholic Church, and Southern Race Relations, ca. 1947–1970," *Mississippi Quarterly* (Winter 2000): 67–88, I have argued that his racial progressivism is inherently bound up with his particular experience of Catholicism. The Ash Wednesday scene in *The Moviegoer* is particularly interesting, for example, given that in 1960 the Catholic Church had recently become the only integrated church in New Orleans.

to him of honor and tradition and sends him edifying selections from Marcus Aurelius. Percy's second novel again presented such a contrast even as it depicted a South further gone in accommodating itself to contemporary American culture. In *The Last Gentleman* (1966), Will Barrett returns from a sojourn in Princeton and New York to find his native region even more self-satisfied than the rest of the country:

> The South he came home to was different from the South he had left. It was happy, victorious, Christian, rich, patriotic, and Republican. . . . The happiness of the South was very formidable. It was an almost invincible happiness. It defied you to call it anything else. Everyone was in fact happy. . . .
>
> As he pressed ever farther south . . . he passed more and more cars which had Confederate plates on the front bumper and plastic Christs on the dashboard. Radio programs became more patriotic and religious. More than once Dizzy Dean interrupted his sportscast to urge the listener to go to the church or synagogue of his choice. "You'll find it a rich and rewarding experience," said Diz. Several times a day he heard a patriotic program which praised God . . . and advertised beans and corn. (150)

This superficial South is perhaps best exemplified by the wealthy Vaught family, who live in a suburban "castle fronting on a golf links" funded by Mr. Vaught's successful "Confederate Chevrolet" agency. Here, false historical images have been superimposed on an increasingly prosperous and complacent subregion of the United States that almost seems to have become a commodity in itself.

But Will, though beset with a recurring amnesia that bespeaks the near inaccessibility of the past to his generation, confronts his own older heritage when he returns to Ithaca and recalls his father's suicide. Ed Barrett's despairing sense of the essential bleakness of the universe and of his own personal inadequacy, in comparison with his "grandfather and the days of great men," stands in stark contrast to the values of the superficial South described above (243). His Stoic code is partly admirable in its emphasis on "character," as Val Vaught puts it—but her own commitment as a Catholic nun demands her rejection of its ultimate pessimism. She lives out that commitment at a site that emphasizes her distance from her family's New South suburban opulence and is, ironically, built upon the ruins of a country academy where Barrett's aristocratic ancestors once studied Greek and military science. Rejecting the false, easy religiosity of postwar southern society, she teaches the poorest of Alabama blacks at an isolated setting that her brother describes as resembling "one of those surviving enclaves after the Final War": "a raw settlement of surplus army buildings, Quonset huts, and one geodesic dome, stretching out into the piney woods. . . . It looked like a lunar installation" (295, 233). Though such imagery suggests the end of the world, Val's work suggests its beginning: she teaches mute children to speak, and when they "suddenly break through into the world of language," she says, "they are like Adam on the First Day" (237). Her vision radically opposes that of the complacent Vaughts on their golf links, surely, but perhaps even more so the backward-looking despair of Ed Barrett.

Val is no sentimentalist, and one scholar has argued that in her prophetic vision, rural isolation, skill with language, even her love of birds, she is no less than a fictional version of O'Connor herself.[42] It is certain that during this decade Percy was increasingly considering O'Connor, whom he had been "completely bowled over" by when they finally met in 1962, as a literary model. As early as 1963 he explicitly defended her work in an essay considering the place of sex and violence in southern literature; in 1968, in "Notes for a Novel about the End of the World," he affirmed her as an exemplar for the novelist who has "cast his lot with a discredited Christendom and . . . inherited a defunct [religious] vocabulary." Her habit of using "shock, comedy, insult," and drawing "bizarre characters" in order to reach a "near-blind" world, he claimed, was essentially continuous with his own predilection for "conjuring up catastrophe" (MB, 118).[43]

Percy's next novel, *Love in the Ruins*, was about the end of the world, but its successor *Lancelot*, in its reliance on shock, violence, and a fanatical protagonist, was his most O'Connoresque novel, as well as the one in which he most fully took his own southern tradition to task. For if Ed Barrett is a darker and sadder version of Aunt Emily, Lancelot Lamar is Aunt Emily gone mad, spokesman for a grotesque version of the Stoic code of honor. Though

42. Gary M. Ciuba, "The Fierce Nun of *The Last Gentleman*: Percy's Vision of Flannery O'Connor," *Flannery O'Connor Bulletin* (1986): 57–65.

43. See Samway, 227–8.

he, like Mr. Shiftlet, is a critic of the dying modern age and is in many respects nearly correct in his assessment of a contemporary world that is "almost rotten," he asserts his own moral intelligence only in a quest for evil. Here that quest is conceived in peculiarly southern terms that bear final, radical witness to the limitations of the gentleman's code of honor that Percy's Stoic characters cling to.

The novel is an exploration of three possible ways of living, as Lance puts it: according to the amoral hedonism of "this age," which he "cannot tolerate"; according to the ethical code that his great-great-grandfather best exemplified when he used a Bowie knife to kill a man in a duel; or according to the Christian love advocated by his friend, the priest whom he calls Percival (163–5). More accurately, the choice seems to lie between the first two, for Percival remains silent until the novel's end, and the reader is most directly presented with a damning portrait of the contemporary world as assessed by a newly inspired southern "gentleman."

Lancelot's mid-1970s South is much further advanced into postmodernity and much more fully commodified than is the South of A Good Man Is Hard to Find, and it is accordingly plagued by a false historical consciousness more extreme than that exemplified by Sally Poker Sash and the Grandmother. The novel's main action is set at Belle Isle, the ancestral home of the Lamar family, which, despite being surrounded by refinery smokestacks, has become a tourist trap frequented by gullible midwesterners (59). To promote Belle Isle's lucrative image, Lance relies on the help of black servants in contrived outfits that "satisfy the tourist's need for proper NBC guide and authentic Southern butler rolled into one" (96) and, occasionally, on Belle Isle "belles," complete with hoop skirts. Lance's wife Margot is fittingly introduced in this role, for she most fully embodies the new false historical consciousness. Though of West Texas stock, this daughter of "rich new oil people" upon arrival in New Orleans takes up the vocabulary and accents of local debutantes, joining the preservation society and the Daughters of the American Revolution (73–4); again, shallow talk about the value of southern traditions goes hand in hand with contemporary consumerism. Once she becomes mistress of Belle Isle, Margot goes even further. She invites in a film crew whose ludicrously unrealistic production about southern life virtually usurps the house, and she develops a passion for architectural restoration that Lance sees as almost sexual.

Her biggest project, Lance says, may well have been to restore the master of Belle Isle—himself, whom he identifies as "old broke River Road gentry," "Louisiana Anglo-Saxon aristocracy gone to pot" (74, 84). Cynical, intelligent, and aware of the farcical nature of the inauthentic posturing that he and his wife are immersed in, Lance has nonetheless been at least casually interested in the past himself. An amateur scholar—"Civil War, of course"—his primary interest during the course of the novel lies in recalling the history of his immediate family and extracting a moral code from the actions of his ancestors (25). Because such recollection takes place only as Lance sits in a mental institution and narrates Margot's infidelity and his own subsequent acts of violence, the veracity of his account of the past is itself necessarily suspect; his own life, he says, has been divided into "Before and After" the moment he discovered he was a cuckold.[44]

Beyond such recent events, however, lies a deeper family history that Lance ultimately draws upon in justifying his actions, one centered on a father who dreamed "not so much of a real past as what ought to have been and should be now and might be yet" (231). Maury Lamar was a writer of historical vignettes and a man for whom Robert E. Lee and the Army of Northern Virginia "had long become as legendary and mythical . . . as King Arthur and the Round Table" (122). It is from such notions of a past—which Lance cannot, of course, remember at all but must perceive in relation to the dreaming father whom he vociferously disdains—that his vision of honor is distilled. Although Maury Lamar was himself dishonorable (Lance recalls, with a perverse pleasure, discovering that his father took bribes), it is, ironically, from his lineage and his romantic vision of chivalry that Lance must draw his own notion of the "gentleman" who stands in opposition to the current age. For such images of the South existed, of course, long before film crews appropriated them. But whereas Margot's and the tourists'—and even his father's—purpose in

44. The whole narrative of *Lancelot* is an exercise in forced recollection. From the very beginning Lance—who, like Will Barrett, suffers from a kind of amnesia—says that "the past doesn't seem worth remembering" and that "I don't like to remember" (1, 7). Throughout, he periodically reflects on the unreliability and "strangeness" of memory. His view is certainly skewed by his personal engagement with the story and his perverse new "ethical" commitment; before he discovered Margot's infidelity, he says, "there was nothing to remember" (18).

recovering images of the past is aesthetic, Lance's is sincerely (albeit perversely) ethical.[45]

Positing that the Lamars "were an honorable family with an honorable name," a family that lived "from one great event to another, tragic events, triumphant events . . . we lost Vicksburg, got slaughtered at Shiloh, fought duels, defied Huey Long," Lance sees in such strength and self-sufficiency a rigid model of behavior that stands in stark contrast to contemporary moral flaccidity (42, 24). The code of the "gentleman" that he hopes to reimplement is "a stern code" characterized by "a gentleness toward women and an intolerance of swinishness, a counsel kept and above all a readiness to act, and act alone if necessary" (167). Such action, he says, may well be violent and will not be tempered by Christian forgiveness, which Lance sees as corrupting the true ideal of honor. He tells Percival, "[Y]ou have your Sacred Heart, we have Lee" and that the "new order" he will found in Virginia will depend upon "men who are strong and pure of heart, not for Christ's sake but for their own sake" (191). In Lance's mind, Christendom has let itself be absorbed into contemporary decadence, and the revitalization of his own ethical code, which he associates with the Confederacy and pagan Rome, is necessary.

Lance's code, an extreme version of the aristocratic Stoicism Percy dissected in his essay "Stoicism in the South," offers an alternative to contemporary American mores by drawing on a vision of southern history but is itself deeply flawed. What is most admirable in Lance's vision, as Percy might see it, is an apocalypticism that finally looks forward; for, unlike Quentin Compson, Lance is neither paralyzed nor destroyed by his struggle to recollect the past, but rather compelled to consider the possibilities of the present and future. Although Lance looks to implement an apocalypse—"it will be settled in Virginia, where it started"—he also believes that an apocalypse has already occurred: he and the woman in the adjoining cell might move to the Shenandoah Valley and share "a new life together . . . each stripped of the past, each aware that the end had come and that there had to be a new beginning" (235,

45. Kierkegaard distinguishes the man who dwells in the ethical sphere precisely by his failure to recognize both the transcendent nature of the true ideals and his final inability to live up to them unaided; dutiful though the ethical man may be, he inevitably lacks the humility, hope, and love that belong to the religious man.

272). Lance's conviction that "the past is absolutely dead" and "the future must be absolutely new . . . is true not only of me but of you and of everyone. A new beginning must be made" (66).[46] The destruction of Belle Isle somehow liberates him to contemplate the "mystery" of his present life, though, problematically, he finds himself still casting backward into the past for clues as to how to live.

The third way of living that Lance postulates as a possibility—neither the contemporary American way nor the old Stoic way—is not truly considered until the end of the novel, and it too is introduced in apocalyptic terms. When Percival begins to speak, however tentatively, at the end of the novel, he makes clear his agreement with Lance that contemporary mores are inadequate and that "there must be a new beginning." But he endorses neither Lance's gentlemanly code of violence nor his grand vision of a militant new order to be founded in the Shenandoah Valley as civilization collapses. Rather, Percival (recently returned from performing humanitarian work in Africa) is about to embark on what seems to Lance the most mundane of lives: "So you plan to take a little church in Alabama, Father, preach the gospel, turn bread into flesh, forgive the sins of Buick dealers, administer communion to suburban housewives? . . . So what's the new beginning in that? Isn't that just more of the same?" (277–8). Although Lance himself has earlier stated that the "mystery" of life lies in "the here and now" and the problem of determining "what . . . to do with oneself," he misses the fact that the priest's life as he describes it speaks profoundly to just such concerns (110). For Percival, such a seemingly ordinary world *is* new beginning enough, one renewed eternally and shot through with the goodness of an ever-ongoing Creation. The image of the Eucharist here, of a God who comes again and again into the mundane circumstances of contemporary lives, suggests as much. So does Percival's identity as a news-bearer. When he begins to speak in the conclusion, we—having read "The Message in the Bottle" and having noted Lance's obsessive habit of watching the nightly news in anticipation of some ineffable happening—are

46. John Desmond sees Lance and the Misfit in particular as embodying Percy and O'Connor's "shared apocalyptic sense [which reflects] not the apocalypse to come but the one that has occurred," a sense that "distinguishes them as religious writers from almost all other post-1950 Southern writers." See "Signs of the Times: Lancelot and the Misfit," in *At the Crossroads: Ethical and Religious Themes in the Writing of Walker Percy* (Troy, NY: Whitston, 1997), 87.

prepared to infer that his message is that of the Good *News,* news of the Word that has come into the world. This is certainly the news Percy's Percival brings to Lance as the novel ends, much like "The Displaced Person," with the priest beginning to speak in the ruins left by a clash between contemporary American culture and an imperfectly remembered southern ethos.

IT IS FITTING for our conclusion to begin with such a vision, for, bleak as both books may seem, *A Good Man Is Hard to Find* and *Lancelot* both finally seek to affirm the real possibilities of life in the here and now. Damning as O'Connor and Percy are in their satire of postwar society, they are at least as damning in their portrayal of characters who cling blindly to their inevitably flawed notions of the past and fail to see the potential of the present. We have seen how their own vision owes something to Guardini's sense that the "end of the modern world" in fact carries the potential for spiritual renewal; furthermore, their common sacramental vision places a profound value in the present, no matter how seemingly shallow it may appear. In a world where bread is turned into divine flesh to feed Buick dealers and suburban housewives, Buicks and suburbs themselves somehow gain in significance. Such a vision may be most clearly revealed in O'Connor and Percy's curious reaction to a phenomenon traditionally vilified in southern letters: technology. For, far from rejecting it out of hand, both finally accept it as an inevitable and potentially meaningful part of the contemporary landscape.

Such a claim may seem questionable given, for example, O'Connor's usual treatment of automobiles or Percy's portrayals of science's power to warp perception of the real. But Jeffrey J. Folks has argued extensively and convincingly that O'Connor essentially accepts the "post-modernist landscape" of a mechanized postwar South "as her necessary canvas." Indeed, to her "modernity is less alien and threatening than it had been to the Victorians and early modernists," and her profoundly comic mode actually "removes the treatment of the machine from the wasteland aesthetic by revealing the limitations of technology to affect more central and permanent human concerns." Folks is insightful both in this placement of O'Connor in the larger context of twentieth-century southern letters and in his description of her specific postwar milieu: "the concrete reality out of which she writes is the fact of sweeping social and physical change with all the dislocation, destruction, and excitement it brings about." I have already suggested how "The Displaced Person" ultimately presents such change positively, even associating its "Christ figure" with machinery; Folks provides convincing readings of other individual stories, especially in *Everything That Rises Must Converge,* which emphasize the potential goodness of mechanization.[47] In O'Connor's work, machines themselves are finally not inherently bound up with despair but are, rather, part of a radically hopeful contemporary landscape.

Folks does not explicitly connect O'Connor's acceptance of mechanization with her sacramental vision (though he does suggest that her theological commitment to the value of sense experience plays a role in her commitment to her "concrete reality"); indeed, in her work not technology but rather, as one would expect, nature is most often presented as "panting with a secret life," as she describes a cluster of hogs in "Revelation." Percy, I would contend, actually outdoes O'Connor in this regard—partly because he long outlived her, saw the collapsing rural world she depicted itself largely becoming cliché, and witnessed the rise of "a burgeoning Sunbelt of agribusiness, superdomes, condos, and high-rises" (*SSL,* 166). Although Folks claims that Percy "regresses" toward Victorian attitudes in his attitude toward mechanization, his presentation of contemporary landscapes in fact frequently emphasizes an essential mystery that is not diminished but perhaps even unexpectedly enhanced by technology. We might recall not only his description of Percival's world and his own letter to Shelby Foote about the value of a "Sacramental Life" lived amongst "Brunswick bowling alleys" and TV transmitters, but also descriptions such as the following from *The Moviegoer:*[48]

> Evening is the best time in Gentilly. There are not so many trees and the buildings are low and the world is all sky. The sky is a deep bright ocean full of light and life. A mare's tail of cirrus cloud stands in high from the Gulf. High above the Lake a broken vee of ibises points for the marshes; they go suddenly white as they fly into the tilting salient of sunlight. Swifts

47. Jeffrey J. Folks, *Southern Writers and the Machine: Faulkner to Percy* (New York: Peter Lang, 1993), 89, 100, 7, 86. Folks argues that even in "A View of the Woods," which opens and closes with ominous descriptions of construction machinery, the machine is not a "monster" but "appears as such to Mr. Fortune . . . because he has failed to humanize the machine by accepting it for what it is" (98).

48. Percy to Foote, January–February 1967, in *The Correspondence of Shelby Foote and Walker Percy,* ed. Jay Tolson (New York: Doubletake/Norton, 1997), 129.

find a windy middle reach of sky and come twittering down so fast I think at first gnats have crossed my eyelids. In the last sector of apple green a Lockheed Connie lowers from Mobile, her running lights blinking in the dust. Station wagons and Greyhounds and diesel rigs rumble toward the Gulf Coast, their fabulous taillights glowing like rubies in the darkening east. Most of the commercial buildings are empty except the filling stations where attendants hose down the concrete under the glowing disks and shells and stars. (63)

In the novel, as we have seen, Percy is often concerned with critiquing Binx's self-definition as mere consumer of the goods and services of an advanced technological society. But while his *moral* vision, like that of O'Connor, rejects the deflation of human identity to the limited terms dictated by and satisfied within the parameters of modern science, such rejection does not extend to the fruits of science; the shallow limitation of human identity is evil, not the "things" themselves—material objects or media images—that characterize contemporary experience. For surely the new world described in the passage above, with its delicate balance of nature and technology, is as densely beautiful and mysterious as the older South, whose passing earlier writers had mourned.

O'Connor and Percy's treatment of technology contains a clue to their broadest contribution to twentieth-century southern letters. Their own aesthetic and vision of a postmodern world was, as we have seen, shaped profoundly by the Catholic Revival. While such specific religious concerns may or (more often) may not be shared by later writers, the fictional vision that Catholicism fostered in O'Connor and Percy after midcentury clearly marks a turning point in southern literary history and provides a rich legacy for those writers who have come after them. Hence Folks can claim that O'Connor's work is "the beginning of the post-modernist Southern vision that is the starting point for such artists as Toni Morrison and Richard Ford."[49] Alice Walker would seem to agree in an assessment of O'Connor that praises both her broadly religious aesthetic and her satirical treatment of contemporary American culture. In O'Connor's view, she says, serious writing should tend ". . . away from sociology, away from the 'writing of explanation,' of statistics,

49. Folks, 101.

and further into mystery, into poetry, and into prophecy. I believe this is true . . . and not only do I believe it is true for serious writers in general, but I believe, as firmly as did O'Connor, that this is our only hope—in a culture so in love with flash, with trendiness, with superficiality, as ours—of acquiring a sense of essence, of timelessness, and of vision."[50] Walker's comments here suggest a link between O'Connor's vision and the magical realism that came into vogue nearly two decades after her death—a connection that may well have pleased a writer who defined a prophet as a "realist of distances," though O'Connor would insist that "magic" was to be found precisely in a fidelity to the real, to the immediate world she lived in. So would Percy, if we are to believe Eudora Welty's assessment of his fictional vision. "On first reading a novel by Walker Percy," she said in a 1990 tribute to him, "we might rather soon ask ourselves":

> "Where are we? Where in the world is he taking us?" We'd set off in a comfortably familiar world. . . . There was some real, everyday, but mysterious happening going on in the country around us—right up our road, in fact . . . [in] what was up until a moment ago a familiar time and place (even, perhaps, "Southern"). . . . In Percy novels, ordinary lives do get subjected to these occasional quick, glancing, comical, or metaphysical jolts. Thereby much goes on to be revealed.
>
> Where is Walker Percy taking us?
>
> But we are still at home. Home lies before us in a different light, and its face is turned toward a different perspective, but it is still where we live.[51]

Welty was the last great living writer associated with the Southern Renascence, and Alice Walker is one of the best writers to emerge from the region in the latter half of the century. What their observations here capture is the value of that vision—rooted in the here and now but penetrating the eternal— that O'Connor and Percy brought to southern letters even as the region saw

50. Alice Walker, *In Search of Our Mothers' Gardens* (New York: Harcourt Brace Jovanovich, 1983), 8.

51. Eudora Welty, untitled memorial, in *Memorial Tributes to Walker Percy* (New York: Farrar, Straus and Giroux, 1990). Limited edition held in Rare Books Collection, University of North Carolina at Chapel Hill.

wrenching changes that partly undermined the traditions underlying the historical vision of the great modernists. O'Connor and Percy's Christian existentialism, firmly focused on the essential moral decision they saw confronting a radically displaced humanity whose ties to a meaningful past had largely been severed, not only served them well in capturing the essential drama of southern life in the postwar era but also might provide a model for later writers focusing on often deracinated characters searching for meaning in a seemingly empty contemporary landscape.[52]

52. While I hope to have addressed the most profound commonalities between O'Connor and Percy, certainly there is more to be said about the relationship of these two writers. For example, I have not directly concerned myself with the question of Percy's *debt to* O'Connor, whom he cited frequently in interviews. Even in Percy's wide-ranging "bioethical novels," connections exist: Father Smith's interpretation of the Holocaust in *The Thanatos Syndrome* directly echoes O'Connor's comments on the Nazi death camps in her introduction to *A Memoir of Mary Ann* (see chapter 2, note 61).

CHAPTER 5

Languages of Mystery

Legacies of O'Connor and Percy in
Contemporary Southern Letters

We do not expect to find salvation in a Kmart or a mall or a downtown freeway, although Flannery O'Connor instructs us to look even there. Perhaps especially there.

— DAVE SMITH, "Speculations on a Southern Snipe"

[Walker Percy] was the writer who told me . . . that *everything* can be magic—a trunk in an attic, the ninth green of a golf course. We all go through hating the South, even though Quentin said, "I don't hate it, I don't hate it, I don't, I don't." Oh yes we did, a lot of us, for a long time. . . . Then Walker walked out on a golf course and the South—our South—came alive.

— MARY LEE SETTLE, in *Memorial Tributes to Walker Percy*

THUS FAR I HAVE focused on how O'Connor and Percy's Catholicism shaped their relationship to their immediate predecessors and contemporaries in southern literary history. Now I want to consider their relationship to their posterity, to those writers who followed them in the last quarter of the twentieth century. If, as Fred Hobson has suggested, O'Connor and Percy (along with Eudora Welty) have overshadowed Faulkner as models for this "third generation" of twentieth-century southern writers, their influence might be present in any number of ways.[1] Certainly for contemporary writers whose

---

1. Fred Hobson, *The Southern Writer in the Postmodern World* (Athens: University of Georgia Press, 1991), 8–9. Due to necessary limitations of scope, I am unable to speculate here regarding O'Connor and Percy's legacy outside the South. O'Connor clearly has the larger national reputation of the two and has impacted a vast number of writers, whether somehow "Catholic" (e.g., Tobias Wolff and Louise Erdrich) or resolutely secular (e.g., Joyce Carol Oates); her influence on

work is deeply informed by Christian convictions, the legacies of O'Connor and Percy alike seem virtually inescapable. But their vision—which emphasizes not the individual's immersion in a communal history but rather his or her sovereign moral freedom in an essentially mysterious present—has been partly communicated, I will argue, to a number of other writers of less explicitly religious inclination who nonetheless find much to admire in O'Connor and Percy's search for meaning in a postmodern South wherein the historical themes favored by Renascence writers often seem problematic. In fact, I will focus primarily on writers of the latter group, exploring O'Connor's legacy for such African American writers as Alice Walker and Randall Kenan and Percy's for such keen observers of the contemporary southern landscape as Josephine Humphreys and Padgett Powell. But first I allow myself a few generalizations, to provide a sweeping overview of different categories of writers who might share some kinship with O'Connor, Percy, or both as specifically "religious" writers. I briefly suggest a few specific examples among these who seem worthy of further investigation in terms of direct influence.

Religion has long been a central theme in southern literature and was, in its way, a pronounced influence on the writers of the Renascence: the Agrarian symposium was sparked by national ridicule of the "Bible Belt" in the wake of the Scopes trial, and early-twentieth-century writers from Jean Toomer to Tennessee Williams drew upon the Christian symbols that saturated the regional culture. But O'Connor and Percy's stance on religious matters radically departed from William Faulkner's statement (which might be extended to many of his contemporaries) regarding Christianity: "I assimilated that, took that in without even knowing it. It's just there. It has nothing to do with how much of it I might believe or disbelieve—it's just there." By contrast, both Catholic writers, in their lives and in their fiction, were engaged with religious

---

the American short story since her death has been overwhelming. Percy's *influence* is substantially lesser, but his work at least deserves further critical juxtaposition with that of Saul Bellow, whom he greatly admired and many of whose novels (from *Dangling Man* to *Herzog*) have striking similarities in tone and character to Percy's. Don DeLillo demands further analysis as a Catholic author who has affinities with and possibly owes a debt to O'Connor and Percy alike. See Vince Passaro, "The Unsparing Vision of Don DeLillo," *Harper's,* November 1997, 72–5; John F. Desmond, "Technology and the Other in Walker Percy and Don DeLillo," in *At the Crossroads: Ethical and Religious Themes in the Writings of Walker Percy* (Troy, NY: Whitston, 1997); and Richard Giannone, *Flannery O'Connor, Hermit Novelist* (Urbana: University of Illinois Press, 2000), 2–3.

questions in a profoundly self-aware manner. Even as the South itself grew increasingly secular after midcentury, O'Connor and Percy for the first time introduced into its fiction protagonists whose souls—like those of Hawthorne's characters, to use the most comparable American example—struggled to achieve a salvation conceived in orthodox Christian terms. In the nineteenth century, Mark Twain relied upon the integrity of an independent boy's individual conscience to ridicule the hypocritical mores of a southern "Christendom" (to use one of Percy's favored terms) that permitted slavery; but as the region moved into the second half of the twentieth century, O'Connor and Percy reversed Twain's terms and drew upon their religious convictions to satirize a society that increasingly glorified the autonomous self. Their brand of informed Christian existentialism—drawing deeply on earlier European literary influences such as Dostoyevsky as well as contemporary Continental philosophy—and social satire brought something new to southern literature which, for good or ill, writers of religious inclination have ever since had to come to terms with.[2]

At the forefront of O'Connor and Percy's admirers among contemporary southern writers of forthright Christian conviction is Doris Betts, though Betts, like O'Connor and Percy themselves, is hesitant about being labeled a "Christian writer." Presbyterian rather than Catholic, Betts has nonetheless been inspired by her two predecessors' intellectual interests; she once described herself as "the only French existentialist housewife in Sanford, North Carolina."[3] In her forthright homage to O'Connor in particular, Betts joins such older Protestant writers as Robert Drake and Madison Jones. Her novels and stories focus on plain folk of the upland South (she has written of her affinity with O'Connor as a "Piedmont" writer), though often enough in her fiction, as in *Souls Raised from the Dead* (1994), such folk have left the farm

---

2. Faulkner, quoted in Susan Ketchin, *The Christ-Haunted Landscape: Faith and Doubt in Southern Fiction* (Jackson: University Press of Mississippi, 1994), xii–xiii. Ketchin's title itself is drawn from O'Connor's essay "The Grotesque in Southern Fiction." The writers in this collection of interviews continually refer to O'Connor and Percy and make clear their familiarity with the fact that each understood "mystery" in the terms of their Catholic faith; and at least some of them seem to agree with Percy's understanding of "dogma" not as a threat to artistic freedom but rather as "a guarantee of the mystery of human existence and for the novelist . . . a warrant to explore the mystery" (*SSL*, 178).

3. Betts, quoted in Elizabeth Evans, *Doris Betts* (New York: Twayne, 1997), 26.

and are living in apartments outside of Chapel Hill.[4] Betts's indebtedness to O'Connor's forthrightly theological understanding of the southern grotesque can be seen in characters such as the deeply scarred Violet of "The Ugliest Pilgrim," as well as, ironically, the superficially attractive Christine of *Souls,* who primps her body meticulously even as she steadfastly avoids donating a kidney to her dying daughter. Betts's essay "Southern Writers and the Bible" indicates that she also shares O'Connor's admiration for the concrete religious language that has to some degree endured in the South.[5]

Betts has distinguished her vision from O'Connor's in certain ways, noting that the Georgia writer "draws these dark, stylized lines around people, like Rouault, and I really prefer ordinary people who are muddling through." Such "ordinary" characters, however, are thoughtful ones, whom Betts sees as being "like Walker Percy's characters who in some way are willing to ask questions, or to take a risk. They haven't settled down or given up."[6] Betts's kinship with Percy might also be seen in some of her contemporary landscapes that reflect a displacement of the real in the postmodern South: in *Souls Raised from the Dead,* North Carolina state trooper Frank Thompson lives in a cheap apartment complex named "Ramshead Chateaux" and has trouble distinguishing the actual wrecks he sees on the Carolina highways from those he watches on television.[7] The "real" and the artificial here are as hopelessly confused as they are in the world accepted by Binx Bolling and condemned by Lance Lamar.

At the same time there are contemporary southern writers who, though in some respects admiring the two Catholic authors, reject the often harsh satire they see stemming from the religious vision of O'Connor and Percy. Reynolds Price is perhaps the most eminent spokesman for this group. While deeply committed to exploring Christian themes himself, he regrets that in O'Connor's stories "the spectacle of belief is so radiant as to be potentially lethal. God in O'Connor seems almost like a nuclear plant out of control." He deplores her "mean streak" even as he posits that "of course, that's all part

4. See Betts, "Talking to Flannery," *Flannery O'Connor Bulletin* (1995–6): 77–81.

5. Betts, *The Bookmark,* vol. 53 (Chapel Hill, NC: The University Library and Friends of the Library, 1985). See Evans, 113.

6. Betts, quoted in Ketchin, 249, 246.

7. Betts, *Souls Raised from the Dead* (New York: Knopf, 1994), 50, 56.

and parcel of her gifts as a satirist" and places her, along with Percy, in rather elite literary company:

> I think she probably didn't want to be as much of a born satirist as she is. Satirists—great satirists like Swift and O'Connor—of necessity have to possess an awful lot of hatred. Walker Percy had heavy doses of hatred and rejection of the world in him. . . . There's a lot of Percy I never felt comfortable reading or knowing, in his reactions to certain things in the real world. It's very hard for a Christian to be a satirist, I think because you have to keep those fires of resentment and hatred really banked to keep on with good comic satire, with good denunciation; and that stoking is not really all that congenial with Christianity as we know it. . . .

Still, Price is able to admire O'Connor stories such as "Revelation" and to join other writers of more liberal theological sentiment—for example, Allen Gurganus, Gail Godwin—in finally admiring the Christian vision of both O'Connor and Percy.[8]

There continue to be a surprising number of figures who might be considered under the rubric of the "southern Catholic writer," although some have received only minor critical recognition and some are only problematically southern. Some of these authors write with a clear debt to O'Connor or Percy, or both; others might fruitfully be juxtaposed with them simply because of their participation in similar traditions. I have already mentioned northern Virginia's Richard Bausch, whose consistent exploration of the human capacity for self-deception—and spiritual renewal—is profoundly informed by his Catholicism. His short story "The Man Who Knew Belle Starr," which focuses on the destruction of a man's illusions as he falls victim to a roadside killer, clearly owes something to "A Good Man Is Hard to Find" (and might also be placed with other recent southern fiction focusing on journeys into the Ameri-

---

8. Price, quoted in Ketchin, 77–8. Price goes on to say that O'Connor's letters give a much more balanced picture of her faith than her stories, revealing that "this is a person who, in her own completely undemonstrative way, did an enormous amount of practical good and charity in her life" (79). See Gurganus's comments on O'Connor in Ketchin, 388. Two of Godwin's more recent novels, *Father Melancholy* and *Evensong,* focus on Episcopalian clergy and share with many of Percy's an explicit concern with both faith and psychological depression. Godwin discussed both novels and mentioned in passing her admiration for Percy in an interview on *Fresh Air, National Public Radio,* March 1, 1999.

can West). In *Real Presence* (1980), which, fittingly, abounds with images of the Eucharist, a backsliding priest is assigned to a small town in the Shenandoah Valley and unwillingly drawn into the lives of a hapless family whose patriarch finally commits murder. John Desmond has aptly described Bausch's particular concern with violence as bearing witness to "those invisible forces, benevolent and demonic, which so compellingly shape our lives," and in doing so links him as a Catholic writer to both O'Connor and Andre Dubus.[9]

Although Dubus spent most of his mature life outside the South, he might be associated with O'Connor and Percy in a number of ways. He claimed that O'Connor's fiction "frightens" him, but he essentially agrees with the views expressed in her essays and letters when he says, "[M]y Catholicism has increased my sense of fascination and my compassion. . . . I still think the main problem with the United States is that we lost God and we lost religion and we didn't replace God or religion with anything of value."[10] Despite the recurrent sinfulness of most of Dubus's characters, a Catholic vision profoundly informs his fiction, wherein, as John Updike once noted, "amid the self-seeking tangle of secular America, the Church still functions as a standard of measure, a repository that can give scale and structure to our social lives."[11] Dubus's last short story collection, *Dancing after Hours* (1994), bears witness to this observation, featuring erratically religious characters who struggle to find any semblance of enduring commitment in contemporary American life. His probing exploration of romantic relationships herein—of the many ways in which "love" can be misunderstood, destroyed, or fiercely maintained—might well be compared with that in *Lancelot,* which Dubus once praised as part of Percy's ongoing meditation on fundamental moral questions: "What is one to do on an ordinary afternoon? Therefore, what is time for? What is a human being for?"[12]

Dubus doubtlessly appreciated Percy's settings as well as his themes. Even *Dancing after Hours,* set primarily in Massachusetts, opens with "The In-

9. John Desmond, "Catholicism in Contemporary American Fiction," *America,* May 14, 1994, 10.

10. Patrick Samway, "An Interview with Andre Dubus," ms., quoted in *Contemporary Fiction Writers of the South,* ed. Joseph M. Flora and Robert Bain (Westport, CT: Greenwood Press, 1993), 106.

11. Updike, "Ungreat Lives," *New Yorker,* February 4, 1985, 94. See also 97–8.

12. Andre Dubus, "Paths to Redemption," *Harper's,* April 1977, 87.

truder," a story that seems to recall Dubus's own adolescence and thereby continues to place him in the unsurprisingly large contingent of contemporary Catholic writers connected with Louisiana. Percy encouraged and supported a number of such writers, including Berry Morgan, Sheila Bosworth, and (posthumously) John Kennedy Toole.[13] One writer who perhaps deserves more critical attention than she has yet received is Rebecca Wells, whose first novel, *Little Altars Everywhere* (1992), showed great promise; while her treatment of a dysfunctional Louisiana family through multiple narrators obviously owes a great deal to Faulkner, individual segments of the narrative show a debt to Percy—and O'Connor—as well. The composite novel's opening vignette, featuring a prideful Girl Scout whose cruel mockery of a freakish girl at camp ends in her abashed vision of the people around her as sacred "altars," seems to directly echo O'Connor's "A Temple of the Holy Ghost." And the most self-aware male character in the novel, Baylor, introduces himself by announcing that as an undergraduate at Louisiana State University he "read and re-read *The Moviegoer*" because Walker Percy "could take all those words like 'honor' and 'gentleman' and show you how fucking empty they are, but how underneath the emptiness there's something else, something that's real, not just some dream about the Old South."[14] Although Percy's legacy may not be quite so explicitly present in all contemporary fiction by Louisiana Catholics, it certainly bears further exploration.

That legacy may be seen even in genres often disdained by the academy, such as "crime fiction." Though John William Corrington and James Lee Burke have received relatively little critical acclaim, their work intersects with Percy's in important ways. Corrington is a lifelong Catholic, a friend of Percy's who arranged for him to teach at Loyola in the 1960s, and a novelist whose own fiction, as Terry Roberts has argued, attempts "to reply to a frightening

13. Morgan was directly indebted to Percy's example and instruction; see Flora and Bain, 321–3. Bosworth writes about Catholics but is wary of calling herself a Catholic writer: "I think that Walker Percy was a Catholic writer, and he took it to a level of genius, but unless you have that level of genius, watch out. Then you get into didacticism. . . ." Quoted in Ketchin, 163.

14. Wells, *Little Altars Everywhere* (New York: HarperCollins, 1998), 158, 161. Incidentally, Wells's second novel opens with an epigraph from contemporary Catholic theologian Henri Nouwen, who has been called Dubus's "spiritual mentor." See Lucy Ferris, "Never Truly Members," in *Southern Writers at Century's End,* ed. Jeffrey J. Folks and James A. Perkins (Lexington: University Press of Kentucky, 1997), 237.

postmodernist world" and seeks "to define a metaphysics of action appropriate to the twentieth century"; Corrington's reading of political philosopher Eric Voegelin, a thinker admired by Percy and O'Connor as well, informs his "legal" novels as well as his detective fiction.[15] Percy's fiction, with its consistent emphasis on a single protagonist's search for meaning in a fragmented society, is quite compatible with the latter genre. *Lancelot,* which is replete with allusions to the detective fictions of Poe and Raymond Chandler alike, and *The Thanatos Syndrome* in particular focus on the protagonist's search for evil; *The Thanatos Syndrome* even verges on being a philosophical "thriller," reflecting Percy's urge to reach a wider audience.

Given this strain in Percy, it is not too far-fetched to connect his vision with that of Burke, whose Edgar-winning novels on Cajun detective Dave Robicheaux often rise above the potential limitations of the popular genre. Even Burke's earlier work, William Bedford Clark and Charlene Kerne Clark have argued, shows an "all-consuming" concern with "the problem of evil— social, psychological, and metaphysical." Interpreting his later detective fiction as the antithesis of escapist literature, they describe him as a fundamentally "religious" writer whose scholastic training in the parochial schools of French Louisiana shaped both his vision of evil as the negation of a naturally good creation and his mature choice of form: "From the mid-sixties on, James Lee Burke was gradually shaping a distinctive vision to counter the sinister vacuity of postmodernity, and in hitting upon the fabulistic possibilities of the crime novel, he realized the perfect vehicle for articulating that vision. He stands as one of the most perceptive 'diagnostic' novelists writing at present, locating and probing the psychic and societal pathologies that abound in the latter decades of the apocalyptic twentieth century."[16] Given such an interpretation of Burke's vision, there is perhaps a case to be made for reading *In the Electric Mist with Confederate Dead* and *Dixie City Jam* alongside the stories of Lancelot Lamar and Dr. Tom More.

Cormac McCarthy, who graduated from Knoxville's Catholic High School

15. Jay Tolson, *Pilgrim in the Ruins* (New York: Simon and Schuster, 1992), 342; O'Connor, *HB,* 294–5, 297, 310, 316; Terry Roberts, "John William Corrington," in Flora and Bain, 83–5.

16. William Bedford Clark and Charlene Kerne Clark, "James Lee Burke," in Folks and Perkins, 61–3. Clark and Clark also note that Burkes's theological traditionalism has often allied him with causes that are, in American political terms, progressive—another commonality with Percy (65).

and bears the name of a medieval Irish king and patron of the Church, is most appropriately linked with O'Connor in both the setting and the characters of his early fiction. His own version of the Southern Gothic style most famously associated with O'Connor, however, offers little or no hope of redemption, especially in its depiction of Lester Ballard in *Child of God* (1973). The eponymous murderer and necrophiliac briefly considers the question of his own moral nature when he looks through the opening of his cave at "the hordes of cold stars . . . and wondered at what they were made of, or himself"; the novel ends, however, not with even the meager hope of spiritual conversion hinted at in the closing of "A Good Man Is Hard to Find," but rather with Ballard's dissection by medical students. If human beings have any spiritual capacity at all in this novel, it seems to be *only* for evil. As avatar of Original Sin, Lester Ballard outdoes O'Connor's worst characters and suggests McCarthy's final alliance with Melville—protesting God's inhumanity to man— rather than with his inherited religious tradition. During the flood of near biblical proportions prior to the novel's conclusion, an old man asserts that people now are neither better nor "meaner" than they ever have been: "I think people are the same from the day God first made one." The Deity's parental relationship to Ballard herein seems to bespeak not the creature's dignity but rather the Creator's depravity.[17]

The contemporary female writer whose Catholic vision most closely approximates that of O'Connor may be Annie Dillard. Dillard—who has only tenuous connections to the South and is best known for writing nonfiction of an essentially universal scope—may seem, in this context, a strange choice at first, but there are intriguing connections to be made between her and O'Connor. In 1963, during Dillard's first year as a creative writing student at

17. Cormac McCarthy, *Child of God* (New York: Vintage, 1973), 141, 168. A seemingly more orthodox vision of human sinfulness informs Mississippi-reared Donna Tartt's *The Secret History* (1992), a philosophical crime drama that—though set among classical scholars at a New England college—bears critical examination both as a southern fiction and in light of the author's religious convictions: she has recently stated that "as a novelist who happens to be a Roman Catholic, faith is vital in the process of making my work and in the reasons I'm driven to make it." Tartt's recent tribute to Willie Morris (who encouraged her to undertake her self-imposed exile from the South) bears witness to her ongoing sense of regional identity. See Tartt, "Spirituality in the Modern Novel," *Oxford American* (November–December 1999): 54–63; and "Willie Morris, 1934–1999: In Memoriam," *Oxford American* (September–October 1999): 108–10.

Hollins College, her instructor, Louis D. Rubin Jr., arranged for O'Connor to spend three days as the college's first writer-in-residence, which may well have made a lasting impression upon a young intellectual who was then developing the interest in theology that finally led her to join the Catholic Church.[18] Dillard's early poems in *Tickets for a Prayer Wheel* (1974) reflect that interest, and in *Pilgrim at Tinker Creek* (1974) she cites the thought of Jewish existentialist Martin Buber, Trappist monk Thomas Merton, and Jesuit paleontologist Pierre Teilhard de Chardin; the latter in particular profoundly influenced O'Connor.

While Dillard draws on a base of scientific knowledge in her reflections on nature and evolution, her finally mystical vision of the physical world—influenced by Teilhard de Chardin—links her closely to O'Connor, who took the title *Everything That Rises Must Converge* from the priest's work. In Dillard's nonfiction that vision focuses on the natural world rather than human action, but its affinity with O'Connor's is suggested throughout *Pilgrim at Tinker Creek*. Here Dillard asserts that "our life is a faint tracing on the surface of mystery"; meditating on the apparent cruelty of nature, she recalls witnessing a feeding frenzy of sharks that "roiled and heaved" in crimson waves—only to interpret the moment as a manifestation of divine "power and beauty, grace tangled in a rapture with violence." Her final vision of human mortality is essentially similar:

> I think that the dying pray at the last not "please," but "thank you," as a guest thanks his host at the door. Falling from airplanes the people are crying thank you, thank you, all down the air; and the cold carriages draw up for them on the rocks. Divinity is not playful. The universe was not made in jest but in solemn uncomprehensible earnest. By a power that is

18. O'Connor visited Hollins in October of 1963. See Jean W. Cash, "Flannery O'Connor as Lecturer," *Flannery O'Connor Bulletin* (1987): 1–15. See also Nancy C. Parrish, *Lee Smith, Annie Dillard, and the Hollins Group* (Baton Rouge: Louisiana State University Press, 1998), 55, on O'Connor's visit. For Dillard's study of theology at Hollins, see Parrish, 130 ff. She did not become a Catholic until much later, but see her interview with Ray Kelleher, "Pilgrim at Planet Earth," *Notre Dame Magazine* (Winter 1998–9): 24–6, regarding her undergraduate exposure to theology: "It was a system of meaning and beauty—just what I found in poetry, only I profoundly thought that *this is true*. After I graduated I kept reading theology and thought, if I go on this way I'm going to end up a Catholic" (26).

unfathomably secret, and holy, and fleet. There is nothing to be done about it, but ignore, or see. And then you walk fearlessly, eating what you must, growing wherever you can, like the monk on the road who knows precisely how vulnerable he is, who takes no comfort among death-forgetting men, and who carries his vision of vastness and might around in his tunic like a live coal which neither burns nor warms him, but with which he will not part.[19]

Dillard's frequent comparison with generally cheerier observers of the natural world—Emerson and Thoreau—is certainly justified, but the strain in her work highlighted above suggests that she may be at least as akin to O'Connor as she is to the transcendentalists. And her most recent publication, *For the Time Being* (1999), continues—in its opening meditations on birth defects and human suffering, its central reflection on Teilhard de Chardin, and its fascination with late-twentieth-century apocalypticism—to speak to themes of central importance to O'Connor (and, here, perhaps Percy as well). Herein she continues to engage Catholic and Jewish theology as part of her ongoing exploration of not pantheism but rather the deeply sacramental "Christian panentheism" (asserting not that all things are God but rather that God is *in* all things) that she first articulated at Tinker Creek, Virginia.[20]

WHAT IS LESS OBVIOUS than O'Connor's and Percy's legacies to professedly Christian writers is the extent to which other contemporary writers draw in somewhat unorthodox fashion upon the religious (vice historical) vision that the older writers developed in the context of the Catholic Revival. Investigation of this question necessarily requires some clear distinction among the patterns of influence attributable to each of the two writers. O'Connor, I believe, has a substantial legacy not only as a religious writer but as a *realist*

19. Annie Dillard, *Pilgrim at Tinker Creek* (New York: Harper's Magazine Press, 1974), 8–9, 270.

20. In Dillard's discussion with Kelleher, she "most vehemently" rejects the label "Woman Writer" ("it implies an agenda I don't have") but is more subtle in her consideration of the label "Catholic Writer": "Graham Greene said that to be categorized as a 'Catholic writer' is the kiss of death. I am a Catholic, and I am a writer. I write for secular intellectuals. I'm trying to lure 'em into the idea that not all religious people are ignorant. In a lot of my books I never show my hand" (25).

among a number of southern authors writing today; more intriguingly, her uncompromising belief in the supernatural might connect her with a number of contemporary African American writers.

Such a joint commitment to the real and the supernatural may seem paradoxical to the modern mind, but it is at the heart of O'Connor's work and marks her place in American literary history. The authors of *Since Flannery O'Connor: Essays on the Contemporary American Short Story* have observed that O'Connor "is at once a traditional realist and an experimental writer," a "realist of distances," as she herself said. She "produced the kind of realism in which the writer becomes a prophet, not by mirroring the modern world but by approximating it—that is, by showing us the grotesque, fantastic, often monstrously comic quality of modern life. . . ."[21] Furthermore, they note that since her death there has been a "split" in American fiction between traditional "realistic" stories and radical new "experimental stories," so that her legacy might extend in two entirely different directions—as I would contend it does in contemporary southern letters. After briefly delineating O'Connor's legacy for contemporary white writers engaged in a rather quotidian realism, I will explore her possible legacy for African American practitioners of a more magical realism.

Dillard's *For the Time Being* is dedicated to Lee Smith, a fellow Hollins graduate and a writer who draws on O'Connor in a different manner than we have yet considered. For if Dillard's vision of nature is informed by the religious tradition that shaped O'Connor's perception of the world and people around her, Smith is fascinated by the immediate world and people that appear in O'Connor's fiction. Although she has credited O'Connor with inspiring her "religious" novel *Saving Grace* and produces O'Connoresque satire of social scientists in *Oral History,* Smith is essentially not a religious writer in the sense that Dillard or even Betts is; rather, she is a realist who captures the daily lives of middle- and lower-class characters in her contemporary South.[22] As such she finds O'Connor an important exemplar, and she is not alone in doing so.

Smith has credited the Georgia writer, along with Mississippi's Eudora

21. Loren Logsdon and Charles W. Mayer, eds. *Since Flannery O'Connor: Essays on the Contemporary American Short Story* (Macomb: Western Illinois University Press, 1987), 7.

22. For Lee Smith's comments regarding *Saving Grace,* see "A Visit to Milledgeville," *Flannery O'Connor Bulletin* (1995–6): 102. For an assessment of O'Connoresque satire in *Oral History,* see Hobson, 25–6.

Welty, with enabling her to write about life in her Appalachian hometown of Grundy, Virginia: wonderful as O'Connor and Welty's stories were, "I realized that these writers hadn't been anywhere I hadn't been, and didn't know anybody I didn't know."[23] Smith's account of a 1994 visit to Milledgeville suggests that this aspect of O'Connor's legacy, a penchant for faithfully observing the social realities of small town and rural life, continues for her and other writers as well: "When Jill McCorkle and I walked downtown for lunch . . . we encountered a young couple coming along the sidewalk toward us: he, a gangling fellow with a grin all over his face; she, a sweet-looking goofy girl with *a wooden leg.* Jill and I stared at each other. But then we were at the restaurant, and as we entered, a man emerged with a huge wad of cotton sticking out of his ear. Oh, Lord! We sat down and laughed until we cried. It was perfectly clear: O'Connor didn't make anything up."[24] McCorkle's own account of this trip echoes Smith's observations, praising not only O'Connor's essays (particularly "The Nature and Aim of Fiction") but also her ability to capture real characters who "rise up and walk. Their voices are clear and true, perfectly pitched. They are people (odd though they often are!) that we have seen and heard in reality; we have seen and heard bits of them closer to home than we care to admit, I'd think."[25] Both writers here admire not O'Connor's religious vision per se, but rather her fidelity to the reality of southern life—particularly among whites of decidedly unaristocratic stripe—in the here and now.

To some extent, however, O'Connor's religious vision remains inextricable from her ability to capture such characters. Poet Dave Smith's observation regarding her legacy for contemporary southern writers suggests as much: "We do not expect to find salvation in a Kmart or a mall or a downtown freeway, although Flannery O'Connor instructs us to look even there. Perhaps especially there."[26] While Smith likely conceives "salvation" more broadly than O'Connor might, his remark suggests both that her vision depends upon a real sense of her characters' essential moral depth and that it is profoundly well suited to capturing meaning in a postmodern South where historical

23. Lee Smith, quoted in Parrish, 174.

24. Lee Smith, "A Visit to Milledgeville," 102–3.

25. Jill McCorkle, "Listening to Flannery," *Flannery O'Connor Bulletin* (1995–6): 127–8.

26. Dave Smith, "Speculations on a Southern Snipe," in *The Future of Southern Letters,* ed. Jefferson Humphries and John Lowe (New York: Oxford University Press, 1996), 148.

themes might seem increasingly problematic. His insight implicitly connects O'Connor's vision to what might seem an unrelated trend in recent southern fiction: the development of what has been derogatorily classified as "K-Mart Realism."

At its best, however, such fiction might include that of writers as accomplished as Bobbie Ann Mason. Appropriately, Linda Adam Barnes has interpreted Mason's *Shiloh and Other Stories* (1982) as O'Connoresque moral explorations of present reality: Mason sees that "the things that shake the foundations of the South in the 1980's" are not roadside shootings (which in fact seem commonplace enough) but rather the cumulative impact of "marriages breaking up, identity crises disrupting retirement years, and shopping centers taking over farmland." Mason's characters—only "mundanely" grotesque as befits their times, but grotesque nonetheless—live out their lives in settings that appropriately reflect, as O'Connor would have demanded, the "concrete reality" of their time and place: K-Marts, Crisco cans, episodes of "Charlie's Angels."[27] Barnes's argument here that Mason portrays modified grotesques seems essentially correct and might be extended to other writers, such as Larry Brown, who capture the moral lives of poorer southern whites in a manner that sometimes more directly reflects the Southern Gothic tradition most fully developed by O'Connor. As Fred Hobson has pointed out, changing conditions in the region have increasingly made such types (e.g., McCarthy's Ballard, some of Brown's or Barry Hannah's characters) more unrealistic, sociologically speaking, than O'Connor's (or Faulkner's, or Caldwell's) grotesques were earlier in the century.[28] If we recall, however, Louis D. Rubin Jr.'s early observation that O'Connor's fiction possessed a clearly moral dimension that Caldwell's lacked, we might see the promise her vision continues to hold for writers concerned with contemporary characters whose lives might be only superficially less grotesque.[29]

Southern Gothic itself may depend upon some sense of the supernatural; but the writer who has most fully endorsed not O'Connor's quotidian social

27. Barnes, "The Freak Endures: The Southern Grotesque from Flannery O'Connor to Bobbie Ann Mason," in Logsdon and Mayer, 133, 137–8.

28. Hobson, 7.

29. Rubin, "Two Ladies of the South," in *Critical Essays on Flannery O'Connor*, ed. Melvin J. Friedman and Beverly Lyon Clark (Boston: G. K. Hall, 1985), 25–8.

realism but rather her "magical" realism—and has, perhaps surprisingly, deemed it a valuable model for African American writers—is Alice Walker. Her remarks in this regard bear repeating in their full context:

> Flannery O'Connor has written that more and more the serious novelist will write, not what other people want, and certainly not what other people expect, but whatever interests her or him. And that the direction taken, therefore, will be away from sociology, away from the "writing of explanation," of statistics, and further into mystery, into poetry, and into prophecy. I believe that this is true, *fortunately true*, especially for "Third World Writers": Morrison, Márquez, Ahmadi, Camara Laye make good examples. And not only do I believe it is true for serious writers in general, but I believe, as firmly as did O'Connor, that this is our only hope—in a culture so in love with flash, with trendiness, with superficiality, as ours—of acquiring a sense of essence, of timelessness, of vision. Therefore, to write the books one wants to read is both to point the direction of vision and, at the same time, to follow it.

Although Walker does value O'Connor as a satirist who "destroyed the last vestiges of sentimentality in white Southern writing" and "caused white women to look ridiculous on pedestals," she above all relishes "the magic, the wit, and the mystery" of O'Connor's stories and, despite her own unorthodox religious views, acknowledges that such stories are profoundly shaped by their author's Catholicism.[30] On a separate occasion, Walker again linked O'Connor with García Márquez and African writers who "do not seem afraid of fantasy, myth, and mystery" and go "beyond the bounds of realism." O'Connor's willingness to do the same, Walker implies, makes her "to me, the best of the white southern writers, including Faulkner."[31]

Walker's remarks may seem strange when one focuses on the often plainly naturalistic surfaces of O'Connor's work and forgets those moments when the usually submerged but always present elements of the supernatural erupt—as,

30. Alice Walker, *In Search of Our Mothers' Gardens* (New York: Harcourt Brace Jovanovich, 1983), 8, 59, 57.

31. Alice Walker, quoted in "An Interview with John O'Brien," in *Alice Walker: Critical Perspectives Past and Present*, ed. Henry Louis Gates Jr. and K. A. Appiah (New York: Amistad, 1993), 337.

for example, in the visions afforded to Mrs. Shortley in "The Displaced Person," Ruby Turpin in "Revelation," O. E. Parker in "Parker's Back," and Francis Marion Tarwater at the conclusion of *The Violent Bear It Away*. It is perhaps with such visions in mind that Lois Parkinson Zamora draws on O'Connor to introduce her "Magical Romance/Magical Realism: Ghosts in U.S. and Latin American Fiction." Zamora does not make the case—though she might—that the South shares some characteristics with the postcolonial or "Third World" settings often deemed particularly conducive to magical realism, but she implicitly agrees with Walker's assessment of O'Connor. Zamora flatly states that "magical realists," including those Latin American authors such as Borges and García Márquez with whom the term is usually associated, "are what Flannery O'Connor calls 'realists of distance,'" and she goes on to describe O'Connor, Faulkner, and Texas writer William Goyen as the prime examples of "U.S. counterrealism" in the twentieth century.[32]

In her definition of a "literary ghost" as "a spiritual force that enters the material world of the fiction and expresses itself as such," however, Zamora briefly suggests a crucial distinction: between, on the one hand, "a symbolic repository of religious truth, a holy ghost" as exemplified by the stain on the ceiling in O'Connor's "The Enduring Chill," and, on the other, a ghost that is "an archetypal embodiment of cultural memory" such as is often seen in Faulkner.[33] This distinction seems to me an essential one in distinguishing the supernatural visions of Faulkner and O'Connor, which are, respectively, historical and suprahistorical. And despite Walker's remarks, I must admit that if there is among contemporary African American literature any legacy of magical realism deriving partly from white authors (and certainly within the African American tradition itself there are more than ample sources for that legacy: Charles Chesnutt, Jean Toomer, Zora Neale Hurston, etc.), it would seem such a legacy is primarily Faulkner's, not O'Connor's. But there are, perhaps, some important exceptions.

For example, Toni Morrison's *Beloved* (1987) is clearly concerned with exactly the sort of ghost, "an archetypal embodiment of cultural memory," that Zamora associates with Faulkner (whom Morrison forthrightly admires):

32. In *Magical Realism: Theory, History, Community,* ed. Lois Parkinson Zamora and Wendy B. Faris (Durham, NC: Duke University Press, 1995), 504, 518.

33. Ibid., 498–9.

in the novel itself Beloved becomes the spirit of not only Sethe's daughter but also all African Americans who died in slavery. There is little evidence of any O'Connoresque vision either in this ghost or in the unorthodox "preaching" of Baby Suggs. Where her legacy may indeed be present, however, is in the character who is the antithesis of all that Suggs preaches, the mind that would quash the souls of Sethe and her kin. For in Morrison's masterpiece the embodiment of slavery's worst evils is neither barbaric overseer nor decadent aristocrat—neither Douglass's Mr. Plummer nor Stowe's Simon Legree—but rather an educated middle-class man, a rationalist seemingly already on the cusp of the twentieth century. He is identified by only one name: "schoolteacher." Morrison has called O'Connor's "The Artificial Nigger"—which explores an abstract mind's construction of race—"brilliant," and her villain's name here suggests that he is similar not only to Mr. Head but also to Rayber of *The Violent Bear It Away*.[34] Just as Rayber, whose brain turns "every living thing . . . into a book or a paper or a chart," attempts to do a case study of old Tarwater for the "schoolteacher magazine," so Morrison's schoolteacher instructs one of his "pupils" to write a study of Sethe, putting "her human characteristics on the left; her animal ones on the right. And don't forget to line them up."[35] More Nazi physician than stereotypical southern slave owner, schoolteacher seems to embody "the binarisms, rationalisms, and reductive materialisms of Western modernity" that Zamora characterizes as antithetical to magical realism, which by contrast "works toward enlarging and enriching Western ontological understanding." O'Connor herself clearly saw that understanding as having become impoverished in the twentieth century, and although Morrison may not share O'Connor's exact view of the supernatural, she seems to share her view of its enemy.[36]

34. Toni Morrison, *Playing in the Dark: Whiteness and the Literary Imagination* (Cambridge, MA: Harvard University Press, 1992), 68. Elsewhere in the study Morrison derides previous critics for overlooking the "connection between God's grace and Africanist 'othering' in Flannery O'Connor" (14); her tone is hostile to the critics, but not to O'Connor. For more on Morrison and theology (especially in her novel *Paradise*), see "Loose Magic: A. J. Verdelle Interviews Toni Morrison," *DoubleTake* 4:3 (Summer 1998): 121–8.

35. O'Connor, *Three by Flannery O'Connor* (New York: Penguin, 1983), 134; Toni Morrison, *Beloved* (New York: Penguin, 1987), 193.

36. Zamora, 498. Schoolteacher's methods also indirectly call to mind the experience of the narrator of Ralph Ellison's *Invisible Man*, who becomes the subject of an ominous scientific examination during his brief hospitalization. This inhumane treatment finally transcends questions of

In speculating more positively upon O'Connor's influence in this regard, we might look to Walker's own fiction or the work of Leon Forrest, whose vision in novels such as *There Is a Tree More Ancient Than Eden* (1973) and *Two Wings to Veil My Face* (1984) has been linked to O'Connor's.[37] But the contemporary African American magical realist who seems most worthy of investigation in this connection is Randall Kenan, who has praised O'Connor in interviews. His first novel, *A Visitation of Spirits* (1989), abounds with exactly the sort of supernatural activity promised in the title; his second and more widely read work of fiction, the short story cycle *Let the Dead Bury Their Dead* (1992), has been described by Terry McMillan as a rich interweaving of "myth, folktales, magic, and reality" written by "our black Marquez."[38] While *Let the Dead Bury Their Dead* in its magical meditations upon the *history* of a small North Carolina community doubtlessly owes a great deal to the African American tradition—and also to Faulkner (especially in the story "Cornsilk")—in certain respects it also bears the unmistakable stamp of O'Connor.

It does so in its exploration of the ongoing presence of not the physically dead among the living (a historical theme, surely) but rather the spiritually

---

race when his tormentors ask, "WHAT . . . IS . . . YOUR . . . NAME?" and "WHO . . . ARE . . . YOU?" (New York: Vintage International, 1995), 238–40. Ellison's concerns here finally intersect with those of the existential movement that was so prominent as he wrote the novel; his particular debt to proto-existentialist Dostoyevsky, who provided the model for his narrator's underground lodgings, was in part what made his work so appealing to Percy. In the "Literature of Alienation" seminar that Percy designed at Louisiana State, he taught *Invisible Man* alongside both *Notes from Underground* and *Wise Blood,* suggesting the extent to which he saw O'Connor and Ellison alike as sharing his own sense of the latent threat of reductive rationalist theories (i.e., intellectual modernism) to a fully developed sense of selfhood in twentieth-century American society. Although such is not necessarily Morrison's first concern, the character of schoolteacher alone seems to suggest that it informs her thought as well.

37. Walker's short story collection that most strongly bears the stamp of O'Connor, *In Love and Trouble,* actually seems heavily indebted to her satirical and superficially naturalistic side in stories such as "Everyday Use," "Strong Horse Tea," and "Entertaining God." But "Diary of an African Nun" has strong elements of the supernatural (though it is finally anti-Catholic), and "The Welcome Table" has clear affinities with O'Connor's work. On Forrest and O'Connor, see John G. Cawelti, ed., *Leon Forrest: Introductions and Interpretations* (Bowling Green, Iowa: Bowling Green State University Popular Press, 1997), 2, 104–5.

38. Terri McMillan, outside front cover of Kenan's *Let the Dead Bury Their Dead* (New York: Harcourt Brace Jovanovich, 1992).

dead among the apparently living, in its satire of professing Christians who have a rigid sense of morality but no real sense of the supernatural (as in O'Connor's "A Temple of the Holy Ghost," "Revelation," and "Parker's Back") and, most specifically, in its reliance upon a clearly "holy" ghost in "Things of This World." For Chi, the mysterious and only apparently Asian character who in this story suddenly appears in the garden of John Edgar Stokes, is a "ghost" not from within but rather from outside of history. Like O'Connor's "Displaced Person," a Pole who becomes a figure of Christ, he is a stranger in a strange land, an utter outsider who does not fit into the racial patterns of the rural southern setting where Stokes, an elderly black man, is the under-dog in a running feud with the local white landowners, the Terrells. Chi—whose name suggests both the Eastern concept of Ch'i and the Greek letter symbolizing Christ—is more than a mere sociological anomaly, though, as is suggested from the story's beginning, where there are indications that he is an angel briefly fallen into human form for a particular purpose. The culmina-tion of this pattern of imagery comes as Stokes, after taking the stranger in, observes Chi performing his morning exercises. Stokes notes "the reverence with which he moved, with grace, yes, that's what it was, the grace of his movements. . . . Looked like a ritual of some kind. Was he casting a spell? Praying?"[39]

Chi's quiet interest in his bachelor host awakens a sense of wonder in Stokes that has long been absent from the old man's life, but the quiet story-telling that the two enjoy is shattered by the slaughter of Stokes's dog at the hands of the Terrell boys. With this act Stokes is thrown back into a familiar, bloody cycle of southern history: he exacts a violent vengeance himself, invok-ing the familiar "an eye for an eye" as he shoots the Terrell dogs and then awaits the retaliation he knows is inevitable. The subsequent standoff at his

39. Kenan, 33. Kenan masterfully plays on subtleties in the American racial consciousness in creating the confusion surrounding Chi's identity. Stokes first mistakes the man who falls into his garden for "one of them migrant workers. Mexican. Dead drunk" (25). As such, Chi would have been somewhat familiar in this corner of the New World (a tainted garden on a larger scale), in a South where Latino farm workers are an increasingly prominent part of rural culture—and so could have been easily placed on the socioeconomic ladder at a rung lower than even Stokes. But Chi's apparently "Asian aspect" bears witness to his humanity and not much more, and it makes him an utter stranger in backwoods North Carolina. Stokes is only able to vaguely compare him to "Chinamen" he has seen on TV (24, 26).

front porch is perhaps the most curious scene in the story, one in which all the familiar—even stereotypical—southern elements are present: the evil white landowner and his brood; the fat, corrupt sheriff who does his bidding; the pillars of the black community who confront them; the young Uncle Tom who betrays his race. In this setting, Chi seems more alien than ever. He almost disrupts the scene by his very unobtrusiveness: "the white men stood about the sheriff's car in the road; the black men on the porch, a strange Asian man in their midst. Chi said nothing, just looked from one group to another, seeming to drink it all into his Dead Sea–calm black eyes."[40] Kenan almost suggests that if everyone stopped to ask what this enigmatic stranger was doing here—if they merely paid attention to the wonder in their midst—this folly would come to an end.

But it continues. Stokes is unjustly sent to jail; bail affords him what will surely be only a brief respite from a long, losing legal struggle. In the moment of quiet he has with Chi at the end of the story, he expresses his immediate satisfaction with his deed but also his own weariness with the cycle of conflict and vengeance that he has been forced to enter (he at least regrets that the dogs had to die). And it is only in this final conversation, after Stokes admits, "I could die right now—content," that Chi's divine nature is most fully suggested.

For the sudden shift of perspective in the final paragraph, from dialogue to a detached description of Stokes's dead body, places all the preceding story in the background, and the reader is left with a grotesquely comic image of a death that raises more questions than it answers:

> When they found Mr. John Edgar Stokes he was sitting upright in a chair by his kitchen sink, his back straight as a swamp reed, not slouching one whit, clutching a large wooden spoon; his eyes stretched wide with astonishment, his mouth a gaping O—though his false teeth had held admirably to the gums—as if his last sight had been something more than truly remarkable, something wonderful and awesome to behold.
>
> They found no sign of the man called Chi.[41]

O'Connor's influence here is unmistakable. The description of the corpse not only calls to mind the beginning of *The Violent Bear It Away*, wherein old

40. Ibid., 43–4.
41. Ibid., 48.

Tarwater dies sitting rigid at the breakfast table, but also evokes the height-ened vision often granted to dying characters in her fiction; it directly turns upon the *as if* construction that marks so many of her most compelling images. And more broadly, the story as a whole recalls Walker's observation that O'Connor's own fictions, despite the fact that they are set in the intensely "*racial* culture" of the rural South, are refreshing precisely because they are on the most "*essential*" level about not race, but grace. Specifically, they are about "the impact of supernatural grace on human beings who don't have a chance of spiritual growth without it."[42] Similarly, "Things of This World" is certainly in some sense about *this* world, about racial identity and racial poli-tics in a particular sociological setting; but finally it depicts, through its "holy ghost," the presence of the divine in the midst of the profane. Stokes's final expression here is only the culmination of the growing sense of wonder that began overtaking him upon Chi's arrival, and it suggests that their dialogue ended with a final question and a gracious response that unexpectedly freed Stokes from the burden of his history in a manner beyond his imagining—and in a manner that O'Connor herself would have relished describing.

Let the Dead Bury Their Dead contains one more story that clearly depends upon "angelic" intervention: "What Are Days?" in which a mysterious young man arrives to provide lusty solace to a middle-aged widow whose life has become a routine of subdued grieving. While such a theme may owe some-thing to the African American tradition or perhaps to García Márquez, it—and the many probing portrayals of sexuality in the novel—surely owes little if anything to O'Connor; the same is true of the supernaturally informed medita-tions upon history in the fictional "Annotated Oral History" that closes the book. But in "Things of the World" and elsewhere (e.g., many of the tropes of "Clarence *And* the Dead"), this virtual tour de force of magical realist tech-niques demonstrates that there is—in a manner consistent with Alice Walker's hopes—a place for O'Connor's vision, however unexpectedly, among the many strands of supernatural vision that might inform a realism so broadly conceived. And so O'Connor's legacy endures not only in the various depic-tions of contemporary middle- and lower-class white life—and variations on the Southern Gothic—practiced by writers such as Smith and Mason, but also in a contemporary African American literature that often critiques modern

42. Walker, *In Search of Our Mothers' Gardens*, 53.

Western rationalism precisely by means of its own departure from the quotidian.

AS THE MOST consistently designated harbinger of a "new kind" of southern fiction, or even as the writer of novels about "the end of the South," Percy presents a clearer model of departure from regional tradition than does O'Connor.[43] In part, his distinctiveness in this regard can be explained simply by his longer lifespan. The "here and now" of his fiction is the South from the 1960s through the 1980s, and by the end of his life he was advising "the aspiring novelist in the Sunbelt" that "he can't go back" to either "Faulkner's Mississippi or O'Connor's Georgia" but must instead realize that "over there just beyond the interstate loom the gleaming high-rises of Atlanta" (SSL, 176, 184). Percy's own fiction provided one of the earliest models for writers interested in capturing such a South, where the affluent live "in tastefully restored shotgun cottages in New Orleans or carriage houses in Savannah or condos and villas on the golf course, or even in an A-frame on Grandfather Mountain and have cable TV" (SSL, 166).

But it is one thing simply to write a fiction portraying such contemporary settings; it is another to capture that world meaningfully. In distinguishing how Percy did so—and how he influenced other writers—in a manner altogether different from the great figures of the Renascence, no writer has been more straightforward than Mary Lee Settle:

> I did not know him well—but I stood in a very private relation to him, one that I never told him. I was his pupil, and I never would have dared say so to him. Whether he wanted to call himself so or not, he was a writer to whom Southerners who were also writers could look for a kind of—oh, I hate the word 'courage'—guts. He taught us that we could love the South and tell the truth at the same time. This is not easy for any of us. He did it with a panache, with a sense of magic, with a feeling for things as they are.
>
> For me he was the writer who told me . . . that *everything* can be magic—a trunk in an attic, the ninth green of a golf course. We all go

43. See Hobson, 8. Also Richard Gray, *Writing the South: Ideas of an American Tradition* (Baton Rouge: Louisiana State University Press, 1997), 251 and passim.

through hating the South, even though Quentin said, "I don't hate it, I don't hate it, I don't, I don't." Oh yes we did, a lot of us, for a long time. . . . Then Walker walked out on a golf course and the South—our South— came alive. An old greenhouse became a castle. A cave became not more than a cave but the true cave of man's self-deception and death. . . . This is such reality, and this is how I've always thought Walker Percy taught me to write—not the mundane thing of learning to write, but simply learning that the work is too hard to do anything but try to tell the truth and see its lights and see its magic.[44]

Settle's statement, delivered at a 1990 memorial service following Percy's death, is all the more interesting because she is in fact a writer *of his generation*. Her best-known works are contained in *The Beulah Quintet*, a series of historical novels that concludes in 1970s West Virginia; but since finishing that series, Settle, at least partly under the influence of Percy, has shifted from historical novelist to chronicler of late-twentieth-century life. *Celebration* (1986), set in contemporary England and featuring a couple struggling toward renewed spiritual life (with the aid of an African Jesuit), exemplifies how Settle, as Doris Betts has written, "has steadily moved the boundaries of her region out to encompass the human spirit."[45] She returned to contemporary Beulah in *Charley Bland* (1989), which explores the suicide of a member of the country club set. The copy she presented to Percy suggests the extent to which he inspired her not just to write about golf courses, but to do so with a more focused spiritual vision, one no doubt shaped in part by her 1987 conversion to Catholicism.

There are a number of contemporary writers who, while not sharing Percy's particular religious sentiments, share his commitment to a kind of *moral realism* of the here and now. In *The Future of Southern Letters*, Jefferson Humphries and John Lowe suggest that "the elegant patterns of malaise charted by the late Walker Percy have found a more pedestrian expression in the recent and creative neorealism of writers such as Bobbie Ann Mason, Valerie Sayers, Larry Brown, Richard Ford, and Josephine Humphreys."[46] Again, my own thought is that despite sharing a life in the "Sunbelt" South with Percy,

44. Settle, untitled memorial, 18–19, in *Memorial Tributes*. See chap. 4, note 51.

45. Betts, review of *Celebration, America*, October 18, 1986, 211–2.

46. John Lowe, introduction to Humphries and Lowe, 9.

Mason and Brown are more indebted to O'Connor for their subject matter and moral vision of contemporary society. But Ford and Humphreys are another matter altogether, and Fred Hobson—followed by a number of other critics—has suggested their debt to Percy.[47]

I will have more to say regarding Humphreys myself, but by way of introducing her I want to mention another writer, one who has perhaps given the most comprehensive account of what Percy might mean to the third generation of twentieth-century southern writers. Madison Smartt Bell, raised outside of Nashville by Vanderbilt-educated parents who practiced an "agrarian way of living," became in college a self-professed "specialist in the *we told you so* theory of Southern literary criticism" and initially saw himself as a writer in the Fugitive-Agrarian mold. He knew Allen Tate and Andrew Lytle from childhood on and spoke with them often as he moved into mature intellectual life.[48] But finally, he found that the concerns of their generation were not his own. By contrast, "the person who in my reading brought me into the second half of the 20th century was Walker Percy. . . . The interesting thing about Walker Percy as a Southern writer was that he didn't write about the past. He tended to write science fiction, instead. He was interested in teleology, how the present was going to form the future. According to Percy, it's all spelled out in the message of the Bible."[49] Percy's broad reading in philosophy, science, and religion spoke directly to Bell, particularly in its concern with apocalypse and displacement; he has credited Percy's essays for their "discussion of what it is like for us to be living in the last days" and further asserted that Percy's vision has informed his own depictions of profoundly homeless "spiritual pilgrim[s]" seeking an "escape hatch from the unthinkable situation of human beings at the end of our twentieth century."[50] Bell's own work approaches such concerns from a variety of perspectives and has meditated upon

47. See the chapter "Richard Ford and Josephine Humphreys," in Hobson, 41–72.

48. Madison Smartt Bell, "An Essay Introducing His Work in a Rather Lunatic Fashion," *Chattahoochee Review* 12.1 (Fall 1991): 5–6; Mary Louise Weaks, "An Interview with Madison Smartt Bell," *Southern Review* 30.1 (January 1994): 6–7.

49. Justin Cronin, "A Conversation with Madison Smartt Bell," *Four Quarters* 9.1 (Spring 1995): 20. Bell personally conveyed his gratitude for Percy's essays in their conversation after the elder author's 1989 Jefferson Lecture in Washington. See Patrick H. Samway, *Walker Percy: A Life* (New York: Farrar, Straus and Giroux, 1997), 407.

50. Bell, "An Essay," 4–7.

everything from "New Age mysticism" to alchemy. But his comments indicate the extent to which Percy's vision in particular has helped to bring about a paradigm shift in southern literature, one that has brought a new sort of understated "religious" concern—if we define the term in the broadest possible manner—to bear on characters whose concern is not so much history as it is what Bell describes as the "sense of estrangement," that feeling of being "on a very extended visit" to a strange land that characterizes Percy's protagonists.[51]

But while Bell has most often explored such concerns in settings not at all southern, Humphreys—along with Padgett Powell—has brought Percy's vision to the South Carolina Lowcountry. Humphreys' relationship with Percy has been remarked before, but it has not been explored in exactly the manner that I wish to suggest here. For although *Dreams of Sleep* (1984) is indeed a novel of satirical social commentary that meditates in its own subtle manner upon the past, and although it is certainly the work of a female sensibility and may even in some sense parody Percy's cerebral male characters, it is also a novel about a character who is—in Percy's terms—*onto* something she has not fully noticed before about the reality of her here-and-now world.[52] It is a novel in which the characters, especially the protagonist, Alice Reese, speak a language of mystery, a language of signs and portents.

Humphreys herself has placed such a language—or rather, the conditions

51. The fruit of Percy's influence might be seen most explicitly in three of Bell's books as he has described them: "*Waiting for the End of the World* is basically about Eastern Orthodox Christianity, and . . . [*Straight Cut*] is about philosophical Christianity under the aegis of Kierkegaard. *The Year of Silence* is a novel about life in a world *without* religion, based on the ideas of French existentialism." Cronin, 14. *Dr. Sleep* is concerned with "hermetic Gnosticism and the writings of Giordano Bruno," whose work Bell came to via "a long and twisted path" that began with his reading of Jacques Maritain at the recommendation of Tate. "An Essay," 9.

52. See Hobson, 58–72. His suggestion that Humphreys has nearly written a "novel of ideas" in the tradition of Percy and Warren perhaps comes closest to the approach I am interested in here. For compelling feminist readings, see Susan H. Irons, "Josephine Humphreys' *Dreams of Sleep*: Revising Walker Percy's Male Gaze," *Mississippi Quarterly* 47:2 (Spring 1994): 287–300; and Kathryn B. McKee, "Rewriting Southern Male Introspection in Josephine Humphreys' *Dreams of Sleep*," *Mississippi Quarterly* 46.2 (Spring 1993): 241–54. Elinor Ann Walker, "Cold Parody and Subtle Historian: Reading Walker Percy's Legacy in *The Firemen's Fair*," *Southern Literary Journal* 31:1 (Fall 1998): 51–69, most fully explores the possibility that Humphreys is (at least in this later novel) actually parodying Percy. Humphreys herself has in interviews expressed nothing but the

that produce it—among her most profound commonalities with Percy. In addition to noting their social affinity (*The Last Gentleman*, she has noted, "was the first southern novel I had ever read that seemed real, that seemed about my South," not the "rural South" of Welty or O'Connor) and her great admiration for Percy's style and humor, she has also responded thoughtfully to the suggestion that her characters are, like his, engaged in "looking for signs in the world":

> I think that's probable. I don't know why they do that, but many of Percy's characters are religious in the traditional sense, in what you call the Christian South. None of my characters are churchgoing members and yet they all have a religious—what I think of as a religious longing for meaning and they don't know where to look for that. They really don't know how to find it. They have no road map to turn to, so they turn to things that are, I think, unreliable, like the weather and little signs like that because it is the only thing they've got.[53]

And indeed they do. In the opening paragraph of *Dreams of Sleep*, Alice Reese, trained as a mathematician, observes the sunbeam piercing her window and falling upon her bedroom floor, "its cool path stamped by the shadow of mullions, squares stretching to rhomboids of clear fall sun. . . . She loves the quiet of light and its mutable geometry, as those wizards did who chinked and slit their stones to let in messages from the sun gods."[54] The light, she thinks, carries a "message" for her, and suggests that the world she lives in is a mysteriously meaningful one.

Other events in her life follow this pattern. In the opening chapter alone she ponders not the cause of her withdrawal from the world, which is "no mystery: knowledge, a cankerous little node of it concerning her husband and his receptionist"; the "mystery," by contrast, "is what will happen next." And there are "more mysteries: her two children," whose uncommon delicacy suggests to Alice some hidden meaning: "*Why* are they so fragile?" After reflecting on her family and house in terms that reflect her radical displacement ("this

---

greatest admiration for Percy and even his often troubled "cerebral males." See Alphonse Vinh, "Talking with Josephine Humphreys," *Southern Quarterly* 32:4 (Summer 1994): 131–40.

53. Humphreys, quoted in Vinh, 138–9.

54. Josephine Humphreys, *Dreams of Sleep* (New York: Penguin, 1984), 1.

marriage is like a place where the language is not her native tongue"; "she does not feel at home, here at home's center"), Alice nonetheless asserts an understanding of her life that suggests its deeply hidden but fundamental meaningfulness:

> At one time she thought that math would clarify the world for her. She knew her link to real things was weak: she had never been able to catch a softball; couldn't remember the colors of eyes, or years in which given events occurred; lost valuable pieces of jewelry (heirlooms that other people had kept safe for years). She had hoped knowledge of mathematics, the world's rules, might strengthen her hold. But it did not. The world turned opaque and medieval, its every event mysterious. Now she used a private mathematics, one made from omens and signs and dreams.

In short, Alice seems to embody Percy's ideal of the postmodern protagonist, a character whom the author joins in setting forth as "a stranger in a strange land where the signposts are enigmatic but which he sets out to explore nonetheless" (MB, 102).[55]

Or, of course, she sets out to explore. I do not mean to suggest that Humphreys' vision is entirely derivative of Percy and generally agree with Kathryn B. McKee's conclusion that in Dreams of Sleep Humphreys ultimately "rewrites" from a female perspective the "introspective Southern male" type, of which Percy's characters are only part of a long line. I would claim, however, that the openness to the "future" that McKee rightly sees Alice achieving at the conclusion—and the novel's "larger theme of possibility" itself—are, while indeed antithetical to Quentin Compson's despairing obsession with the past, finally consistent with Percy's own comic vision. For Percy, that vision is bound up with his sacramental understanding of the world, whereas Humphreys' characters seek, and seem to find, meaning outside of any clear theological framework.[56] Humphreys turns to traditional religious imagery only

---

55. Ibid., 3–4, 8 (my emphasis). For an account of Percy's substantial influence on a documentary filmmaker in this regard, see Ross McElwee, "The Act of Seeing with One's Own Eyes," in *The Last Physician: Walker Percy and the Moral Life of Medicine* (Durham, NC: Duke University Press, 1999), 16–37.

56. McKee, 253–4. Elinor Ann Walker sees Humphreys' comparatively secular stance as advantageous, or at least as providing a valuable counterpoint to Percy: "[*The Firemen's Fair*] makes its own subtle argument in spite of (because of?) the lack of a more visible philosophical or religious context" (68).

once, to suggest the richness of Alice's final reconciliation with her husband. As they lie in bed on Sunday morning, their conversation is punctuated by church bells from multiple steeples: "together they played a medley that wound together strands of half-familiar hymns, and the effect was of a pure music, uncorrupted by words or tune."[57] It is a scene that also calls to mind, by contrast, the end of *Rabbit, Run,* wherein Harry Angstrom (a philandering husband like Will Reese, but unregenerate) lies with his prostitute-lover looking at the darkened church window across the street. If Rabbit lies half-anguished by the possibility of a seemingly defunct faith, Percy's and Humphreys' characters achieve something more: behind the signs, Christian or secular, that mark their lives, as well as in the signs by which they communicate with others, they find not absurdity but *mystery,* not a world devoid of meaning but one that invites investigation because its meaning grows ever deeper as they seek.

By way of turning to similar concerns in the novels of Padgett Powell, whose best work has been set along the coast just south of Humphreys' Charleston, I want to review more carefully Percy's own "language of mystery." I have already dwelt at length upon Will Barrett's discovery of the gratuitous goodness of creation in the oak tree he grasps while pondering his father's suicide—a scene that suggests the fundamentally extrahistorical character of the mystery Percy is most concerned with—but there are a number of such scenes in Percy's oeuvre, many of which are concerned with the debilitating effect a scientific mind-set can wreak upon the mysterious sense of the fullness of Being that Will achieves here.[58] He is a sort of scientist or at least technician himself, an "engineer" who, like Alice Reese, once thought life would be "elegant as algebra" (*LG,* 15). But Binx Bolling is the character through whom Percy first explored such concerns. In *The Moviegoer,* Binx

57. Humphreys, 230.

58. See my discussion of this scene in chapters 3 and 4. In Humphreys' world, as in Percy's, the past is not the locus of meaning. At the beginning of *The Firemen's Fair,* Rob Wyatt sees, in the wake of a hurricane that has swept through his island home, "sunk in the mud marsh across the street, listing but upright . . . a white piano, by now not a strange sight among the herons and the barn swallows—for now, and here, one saw extraordinary things" (1). Such a postapocalyptic vision, signifying if not the actual aftermath of history then at least Rob's freedom to break with his own past, is for this protagonist the beginning of a search (and Percy's own work abounds with meditations upon the liberating effects of hurricanes; see *Lancelot* especially).

explains his failure (as Aunt Emily sees it) to go into scientific research by recalling, in terms that bear upon his "horizontal" search throughout the novel, his failed role in a summer study project. All was going well as he and a partner ran their experiment on pH levels in pig blood:

> But then a peculiar thing happened. I became extraordinarily affected by the summer afternoons in the laboratory. The August sunlight came streaming in the great dusty fanlights and lay in yellow bars throughout the room. The old building ticked and creaked in the heat. Outside we could hear the cries of summer students playing touch football. . . . I became bewitched by the presence of the building; for minutes at a stretch I sat on the floor and watched the motes rise and fall in the sunlight. I called Harry's attention to the presence but he shrugged and went on with his work. He was absolutely unaffected by the singularities of time and place. His abode was anywhere. . . .
>
> He was actually like one of those scientists in the movies who don't care about anything but the problem in their heads—now here is a fellow who does have a "flair for research" and will be heard from. Yet I do not envy him. I would not change places with him if he discovered the cause and cure of cancer. For he is no more aware of the mystery which surrounds him than a fish is aware of the water it swims in. He could do research for a thousand years and never have an inkling of it. By the middle of August I could not see what difference it made whether the pigs got kidney stones or not (they didn't, incidentally), compared to the mystery of those summer afternoons. (43)

Such is only one of the lengthier passages in *The Moviegoer* meditating upon the "mystery" of the seemingly everyday world of Binx's present. Throughout the novel Binx catalogs those who fail to see it: not only scientists, but also the grandiosely nostalgic Aunt Emily herself and businessmen like the one who, "cogent as a bird dog," sees "[n]o mystery here! He understands everything out there and everything out there is something to be understood" (14). He also, however, finds those who do see and speak of it, whether in the explicitly religious language of Lonnie Smith or the more subdued tones of Kate Cutrer, which finally echo those of Binx himself.

Binx's experiment seems particularly appropriate here in part because Padgett Powell, like Percy himself, earned a B.A. in chemistry—what he has called a "poet's degree in chemistry"—and his fiction clearly reveals other affinities with Percy. When his first novel, *Edisto,* appeared in 1984, it not only led Saul Bellow to place Powell at the "top" of the "list of the best American writers of the younger generation" but also drew direct praise from Percy himself. Since Powell had written the novel under Percy's sometime colleague Donald Barthelme, the older author was perhaps prepared to like it, but his assessment went beyond the dutiful: Percy hailed the novel as "truly remarkable . . . both as a narrative and in its extraordinary use of language. It reminds one of *The Catcher in the Rye,* but it's better—sharper, funnier, more poignant."[59] Its adolescent narrator, Simons Manigault, has been compared to Huck Finn as well as to Holden Caulfield, but in certain respects he has a great deal in common with Binx Bolling and Will Barrett. For *Edisto*—as becomes clearer in *Edisto Revisited* (1996)—not only relies upon a language of mystery that owes a great deal to Percy, but also introduces its own version of the cerebral and "well-educated young southern white male," a comic one nearer to Percy's than to Faulkner's, Warren's, or Tate's renditions of the type.[60]

For though Simons Manigault is indeed, like Huck Finn, not particularly well-mannered, his manners are in fact a function of his eccentric but elaborate education at the hands of his mother, an English professor who brought him home from the maternity ward to a "bassinet bound by books" and then enrolled him in the local "podunkus" public schools so that he could gather "material" for his future novels. Simons and his mother, called "the Duchess" by the local blacks, live on as-yet-undeveloped Edisto Island, on what he calls a "Southern barony" reduced "to a tract of clay roads cut in feathery herbaceous jungle of deerfly for stock and scrub oak for crop, and the great house is a model beach house resembling a pagoda, and the planter's wife is abandoned by the planter." For Simons's father has left the family for a conventional life practicing law in nearby Hilton Head, leaving Simons in a

59. See Thomas M. Carlson, "Padgett Powell," in Flora and Bain, 371–81. Carlson also links Powell and Percy as writers who "move casually from science to metaphysics in their fiction" (375). Bellow's and Percy's comments are from the 1996 Henry Holt paperback edition of *Edisto*: Bellow on the outside front cover, Percy on the outside back. In the 1950s Barthelme actually published some of Percy's earliest work, including an essay on language and an early excerpt from *The Moviegoer*; see Tolson, 265, 287.

60. See Hobson, 77, 55.

relationship with his mother best characterized as that of "protégé and master." More like Binx's Aunt Emily than Huck Finn's father, the Duchess is an intellectual and a romantic who places great expectations upon the shoulders of this last scion of an old Southern family (though she does so in ways Aunt Emily never would: e.g., by encouraging him to frequent the local black nightclub, the Baby Grand).[61] And Simons himself has become a hypereducated truant, equally at home sipping malt liquor with the locals and making allusions to the *Odyssey*.

The plot centers on the arrival at Edisto of the unnamed man whom Simons designates "Taurus," a process server who comes in search of their black maid's daughter but who ends up becoming lover to the Duchess and mentor to the young boy. Taurus himself is, essentially, a figure of mystery, partly in the tradition of *Light in August* and *Absalom, Absalom!* in that his origins, racial and otherwise, remain unclear (despite his pale complexion, the maid is convinced that he is her grandson), but partly in terms that seem to owe more to Percy. Simons is amazed that "he lets me *name* him. He never corrected me. I called him Taurus from then on, fine with him. . . . He was controlling things, but like the elephant promised the monkey, he wasn't going to force it." Such self-conscious meditations on language throughout the narrative—which openly reflects on Gullah and African American dialects generally, the vocabulary of early childhood ("the best language was then," Simons thinks), the naming habits of white southerners—suggest the extent to which language here is not only medium but also theme, one of the aspects of *Edisto* that most appealed to Percy himself.[62] And Taurus's depiction as a being not subject to definitive classification but receptive to tentative epistemological approaches, to a naming that is accurate largely insofar as it is playful, squares with Percy's notions of language and being itself, a connection suggested more fully later in the narrative.

One of the most complex forms of naming is history, and *Edisto* is also subtly concerned with that theme, not only in the ultimately unresolved question of Taurus's identity but also in its satire of the Federal Oral History Program. When Taurus and Simons visit the program's Charleston office to view

61. Powell, *Edisto* (New York: Farrar, Straus and Giroux, 1984), 5, 9–10, 7. Simons's aristocratic lineage is more fully revealed in *Edisto Revisited*, as detailed below.

62. Powell, *Edisto*, 51. For other passages on language, see 48, 104, 66–7.

a tape of the now-fugitive maid Athenia weaving baskets, they are disgusted to learn that the historians plan to edit out a part of the tape that, unexpectedly, shows her wearing a sweet potato as a shoe. Such filtering of "history" through preconceived notions, however, is finally only part of their society's larger blindness to the essential mystery of the world, a mystery upon which Taurus, by contrast, keeps Simons focused. The passage that most emphasizes this aspect of their relationship—and that seems to me to be at the center of the novel—satirizes historians in terms that echo Percy's attack on scientists in *The Moviegoer* but in doing so relies on an image of "mystery" that seems rooted not necessarily in the past but in any given moment:

> That's the thing I learned from him in those days: you can wait to know something like waiting for a dream to surface in the morning, which if you jump up and wonder hard you will never remember, but if you just lie there and listen to the suck-pump chop of the surf and the peppering and the palm thrashing and feel the rising glare of Atlantic heat, you can remember all the things of the night. But if you go around beating the world with questions like a reporter or federal oral history junior sociologist number-two pencil electronic keyout asshole, all the answers will go back into mystery like fiddlers into pluff mud. You just sit down in the marsh and watch mystery peek out and begin to nibble the air and saw and sing and run from hole to hole with itself. Lie down and the fiddlers will come as close to you as trained squirrels in a park. And how did he teach me that? I don't know, but you don't need a package of peanuts or anything.

This is indeed the lesson Simons learns from Taurus, and the imagery used to evoke it here is repeated throughout the novel. Simons soon realizes that pursuing the "racial question"—a personal history—with Taurus would be "like charging into the marsh with a coffee can to catch the fiddlers, and they would have defended their secrets, waving their tiny ivory swords and backing into their holes." Even more significantly, by the conclusion of the novel Simons himself has become "as dumbly wise as a fiddler crab" and has adopted a new "motto": "never to forget that, dull as things get, old as it is, something is happening, happening all the time, and to watch it."[63]

63. Ibid., 84–5, 101, 181.

It is a motto that—though expressed here without the maturity of Percy's seekers—befits characters such as Binx and Will, who finally escape the burdens of their history and learn to watch and wait in a densely mysterious present. And it is well that Simons has acquired such a vision, for we leave him not on Edisto but with his father and in a new landscape, one akin to the "Paradise Estates" of *Love in the Ruins*: "pruned trees. Yards with grass in them. Heavy post fences. Private drives. Mercedes. Negro on a mowing machine cut a swath about eight feet wide. Hilton Head." Much as he regrets having to leave the world of his childhood behind, Simons ends by looking back on his life on Edisto and wondering, "what if *that's* the museum?"—one now, we might presume, full of ossifying artifacts of memory. It is in thinking of Taurus and his new motto that Simons is able to decide that there may be as much to provoke wonder in Hilton Head as there was in the marshes of Edisto: "Just because this place looks like a layout on a ping-pong table don't mean it ain't happening right here too."[64] Like many a Percy character who stumbles onto an unexpectedly rich life amid the anonymity of the suburbs, Simons ends with an eager receptiveness to the possibilities of his present world.

Although Percy's legacy is only implicit in *Edisto*, it becomes explicit in *Edisto Revisited*, which from its opening sentence cries out for an intertextual reading: "I, Simons Manigault, did not go to Harvard, following my mother's Quentin Compson, nor to Sewanee, following my father's footsteps and hopes."[65] The allusion continues, indirectly, when Simons states that, despite his frequent disillusionment with society, his early familiarity with "young suicide poets . . . bred enough contempt that I declared the route invalid." If we recall Percy's comment that he wrote about versions of "a Quentin Compson who DIDN'T commit suicide," we might recognize that Powell's most proximate model here is actually Percy, not Faulkner.[66] For, like Binx Bolling in particular, Simons has turned out to be not quite the genius his family ex-

64. Ibid., 165, 181.

65. Padgett Powell, *Edisto Revisited* (New York: Henry Holt, 1996), 1. The novel is littered with allusions. Hawthorne is also mentioned on the first page, and Thomas Wolfe is evoked—or parodied—throughout, as when Simons thinks, "You Can't Go to the Baby Grand Again" (8). His reasons for finally deciding that he *will* return to Edisto owe more to Percy: "I *can* go home again. It isn't home! What a pleasant surprise" (9).

66. Ibid., 3; Percy, *Conversations with Walker Percy*, ed. Lewis A. Lawson and Victor A. Kramer (Jackson: University of Mississippi Press, 1985), 299–300.

pected and, well into his twenties, is living a life of more or less unabashed hedonism. After he brings the reader up to date on his life since leaving Edisto, his story begins with his "Going Home to See Mother," which he expects will be a "scripted" affair involving roundabout discussion of his life goals via consideration of grand philosophical questions; as such, it recalls Aunt Emily's predictable summons for Binx at the opening of The Moviegoer. In the ensuing events the aristocratic heritage of the Manigaults is clearly suggested ("two hundred years ago we had more rice than the Kennedys have votes"), as is Simons's recognition that he does not know what to do with himself: "I do not have the big picture on life."[67] What most directly links Simons to Binx, however, is the manner in which he finally does begin to approach "the big picture," via his unexpected romantic involvement with a slightly unstable cousin, Patricia Hod, reminiscent of Binx's Kate Cutrer.

But Edisto Revisited lacks the understated tone of The Moviegoer, and though the mature Simons is, like Binx, ironic and self-centered, the antic tone of his subsequent flight from and eventual embrace of commitment more aptly recalls the travels of the young Will Barrett. Of course, Simons's picaresque adventures in the postmodern world between the Carolina coast and Texas are in most respects his own. But the novel's nod to Percy is cemented by the protagonist's lengthy detour in search of Taurus, whom he finds in the swamps outside of Covington, Louisiana. During his brief sojourn in the Achtafalaya Basin (a recurrent setting in Percy's novels), Simons uses a favorite metaphor of Will Barrett's in describing himself as "a kind of passive radio receiver of the signals of enigma swirling around" (96). When he finally returns to Edisto to settle into a job and marry his cousin, he declares (for once without irony) that "Patricia Hod is a girl from God," and it is difficult not to see in this statement an allusion to the elder Will Barrett's final question regarding Alison Huger at the conclusion of The Second Coming: "Is she a gift and therefore a sign of a giver?" (SC, 328).[68] Simons tells the reader that he still has "no idea what the big picture is," but the novel ends on a comic note as he and Patricia hold one another and dance along the coast of their island,

67. Powell, Edisto Revisited, 11–12, 36, 17.

68. Ibid., 116. Even the rhyme in Simons's phrasing suggests the childlike fascination with language that characterizes Alison herself.

where—in yet another characteristically Percyean scene—an impending hurricane serves only to heighten their joy.[69]

None of this makes Powell a religious writer in the sense that Percy was (though there is in *Edisto Revisited* a curious Christian subtext).[70] Indeed, in *Edisto* Simons recounts with adolescent irreverence his reasons for taking a big "slug" of wine while receiving communion during his semiannual visit to an Episcopal church: "I have to, because the bread of His body is stuck to the roof of my mouth like a rubber tire patch, and if I can't wash it loose by swishing His blood around, I'm going to have to dig it off with a finger, in slow motion, and possibly gag."[71] But such comical Huck Finn–like skepticism toward organized religion finally seems old hat to Simons, and perhaps to Powell, whose main satirical target in *Edisto Revisited* is, again, a certain kind of historian—in this case the "Southern Historian," who sounds a great deal like none other than Shelby Foote (whose unexpected celebrity from Ken Burns's Civil War documentary peaked in the years just before the publication of the novel). Simons mockingly longs for the opportunity "to sit before documentary cameras in my cozy, musty, Memphis study and relate lugubrious apocrypha about Rebel valor, with modest little tears in my wide delta face." And throughout the narrative Simons defines himself against this imaginatively recurring character, declaring himself the "worst enemy" of the Historian who would "apotheosize the Lost World, confident of discovering yet in it the last baby Confederate dinosaur alive."[72] The adolescent communion scene seems gentle beside this blistering—even savage—attack on the "histo-

69. For a more purely comical Percy legacy, see Simons's satirical remarks on Ohioans. Ibid., 133.

70. Beyond the "girl from God" comment at the conclusion, there is Simons's early—and uncharacteristically somber—allusion to O'Connor's Haze Motes: "I was once a student of literature. A character of whom I was fond makes a joke. . . . 'You do not have to be justified,' he says—he means it biblically—'if you have a *good car.*' Drunk in my own house, I see that a good car, a good building, a good career, a good woman, a good . . . *anything,* will not justify me" (15). Simons's first stop in his flight from Edisto is Corpus Christi, Texas, which he matter-of-factly describes as "named the Body of Christ" (63); when he finally returns home, he, his mother, and Patricia eat potato salad "Communion-style until we were Confirmed to the gills" (127).

71. Powell, *Edisto,* 150.

72. Powell, *Edisto Revisited,* 5.

rian," one that seems motivated not so much by progressive political sentiments as by a disdain for individuals who nostalgically turn to the past for
meaning.

For Simons asserts early on that he is "not a historian-archaeologist of
the South" but rather "an architect of no distinction," and that is—at least
superficially—what he remains at the novel's conclusion. In his new life with
Patricia Hod, he puts his college degree to work as a "coastal architect," a
profession in which he throws up beach homes modeled from the pages of
Southern Living. In short, he immerses himself in the often banal life of his
contemporary world, but ultimately he does not find it an altogether bad business, particularly when he shows up at the end of the day to talk with the
men who build his houses:

> But this is a nice moment in your dubious occupation, drinking beer and
> smelling the faint ammonia of the plans and the good salt air and the
> perennial whiff of pot on these guys who do the honest, hands-on beach
> mauling, driving their threepenny nails into your white, white spruce all
> the livelong day, sitting with you a moment in your respective philosophi-
> cal poses. You are not such a bad guy for a suit, and they of course are not
> such bad guys for grunts. A sunset under these conditions, glassy waves
> catching the last pink light, a green marsh turning chill and stopping even
> its fiddler ticking, and turning gray, can be a most agreeable thing.[73]

Simons finds in such a moment that even his seemingly superficial postmodern South, in which Edisto itself is now becoming another Hilton Head, is
imbued with a beauty and a mystery that the "Historian" misses but that he
and Patricia Hod will share. His adolescent motto still holds up well here, for
"something" well worth watching "is happening" along this beach, something
rooted in the present moment. Whether Simons, or Powell, would consider
such a moment to be bearing witness to the "sacramental" nature of the contemporary world is doubtful, but Percy, to whom they both owe so much,
certainly would.

ALTHOUGH IN CONSIDERING O'Connor and Percy's legacies, I might, perhaps, have concentrated on malaise or even aspects of the moral in contempo-

73. Ibid., 5, 136.

rary southern fiction, I have chosen to focus on mystery; but all three are finally intertwined. In the vision of O'Connor and Percy alike, the merits of society and of individuals lie most fundamentally in their responsiveness to the fundamental mystery at the center of reality and their consequent freedom from reductive ideologies—modern, "southern," or otherwise. Their identities as Catholic skeptics pointing to "those absences and lacunae lurking in the brave new world of humanist reason" provided them with a particularly advantageous perspective on their society, a vision finally open to the possibilities of existence in the here and now and "skeptical" toward not the wider world of created being, but rather the world of human preconceptions.[74] Such a vision also continues to make them worthy exemplars for contemporary writers, who, as Fred Hobson has noted, are at their best when they are "well aware of what has gone before but closely observing the here and now, keenly attuned to contemporary science, religion, language, trendiness, false gods of various sorts, and modernity in general."[75]

Perhaps the most daunting false god each had to face was the great legacy of the Southern Renascence, or the southern obsession with the past itself. Though O'Connor and Percy themselves were, to a degree, willing to explain their own "sense of mystery" in terms of the regional experience of loss, they finally looked for their understanding of such loss to a faith that ultimately transcended history. It was only in such faith that they found the ultimately comic mystery obliquely reflected in the "wonderful and awesome" vision of Kenan's John Edgar Stokes and the more understated mysteries glimpsed by Alice Reese and Simons Manigault. The particular Christian vision of O'Connor and Percy—as shaped by the writers of the Catholic Revival at midcentury—ultimately looked to the goodness and gratuitousness of created being in a contemporary world that, behind its facade of emptiness, remained eternally and radically mysterious. That vision finally complemented the Renascence's focus on the crossroads of place and time, and its focus on place and eternity remains the great gift of O'Connor and Percy alike to those southern writers who have followed them.

74. See Paul Giles, *American Catholic Arts and Fictions: Culture, Ideology, Aesthetics* (New York: Cambridge University Press, 1992), 525, on "Catholic skeptics," and see end of chapter 2 here.

75. Hobson, "Of Canons and Culture Wars," in Humphries and Lowe, 86.

Selected Bibliography

Bacon, Jon Lance. *Flannery O'Connor and Cold War Culture*. New York: Cambridge University Press, 1993.

Baudrillard, Jean. *America*. London: Verso, 1988.

———. *Symbolic Exchange and Death*. London: Sage, 1993.

Beck, Charlotte H. *The Fugitive Legacy: A Critical History*. Baton Rouge: Louisiana State University Press, 2001.

Betts, Doris. *Souls Raised from the Dead*. New York: Alfred A. Knopf, 1994.

Brinkmeyer, Robert H., Jr. *The Art and Vision of Flannery O'Connor*. Baton Rouge: Louisiana State University Press, 1989.

———. "A Closer Walk with Thee: Flannery O'Connor and Southern Fundamentalists." *Southern Literary Journal* 18 (Spring 1986): 3–13.

———. *Three Catholic Writers of the Modern South: Allen Tate, Caroline Gordon, Walker Percy*. Jackson: University Press of Mississippi, 1985.

Broughton, Panthea Reid, ed. *The Art of Walker Percy: Stratagems for Being*. Baton Rouge: Louisiana State University Press, 1979.

Cash, Jean. "Flannery O'Connor as Lecturer: '. . . a secret Desire to Rival Charles Dickens.'" *Flannery O'Connor Bulletin* (1987): 1–15.

———. "O'Connor in the Iowa Writer's Workshop." *Flannery O'Connor Bulletin* (1995–6): 65–75.

Cash, Wilbur J. *The Mind of the South*. New York: Vintage, 1991.

Christenbury, Tamara O'Hearn. "The Literary Relationship of Flannery O'Connor and Caroline Gordon." M.A. thesis, James Madison University, 1989.

Ciuba, Gary M. *Walker Percy: Books of Revelations*. Athens: University of Georgia Press, 1991.

Coles, Robert. *Flannery O'Connor's South*. Baton Rouge: Louisiana State University Press, 1980.

————. *Walker Percy: An American Search*. Boston: Little, Brown, 1978.

Collins, James. *The Existentialists: A Critical Study*. Chicago: Regnery, 1952.

Conkin, Paul. *The Southern Agrarians*. Knoxville: University of Tennessee Press, 1980.

Core, George, ed. *Southern Fiction Today: Renascence and Beyond*. Athens: University of Georgia Press, 1969.

Cowan, Louise. *The Fugitive Group: A Literary History*. Baton Rouge: Louisiana State University Press, 1959.

Crowley, J. Donald, and Sue Mitchell Crowley, eds. *Critical Essays on Walker Percy*. Boston: G. K. Hall, 1989.

Desmond, John F. *At the Crossroads: Ethical and Religious Themes in the Writings of Walker Percy*. Troy, NY: Whitston, 1997.

————. *Risen Sons: Flannery O'Connor's Vision of History*. Athens: University of Georgia Press, 1987.

Dillard, Annie. *Pilgrim at Tinker Creek*. New York: Harper's Magazine Press, 1974.

Dunaway, John M., ed. *Exiles and Fugitives: The Letters of Jacques and Raissa Maritain, Allen Tate, and Caroline Gordon*. Baton Rouge: Louisiana State University Press, 1992.

Fain, John T., and Thomas Daniel Young, eds. *The Literary Correspondence of Donald Davidson and Allen Tate*. Athens: University of Georgia Press, 1974.

Fitzgerald, Sally. "Flannery O'Connor: Patterns of Friendship, Patterns of Love." *Georgia Review* 52:3 (Fall 1998): 412–25.

————. "The Invisible Father." *Christianity and Literature* 47:1 (Autumn 1997): 5–20.

————. "A Master Class: From the Correspondence of Caroline Gordon and Flannery O'Connor." *Georgia Review* 33:4 (Winter 1979): 827–46.

————. "Rooms with a View: The Double Vocations of Thomas Merton and Flannery O'Connor." *Katallagete* 8.1 (Summer 1982): 4–11.

————. "Root and Branch: O'Connor of Georgia." *Georgia Historical Quarterly* 64:4 (Winter 1980): 377–87.

Flora, Joseph M., and Robert Bain, eds. *Contemporary Fiction Writers of the South*. Westport, CT: Greenwood Press, 1993.

Folks, Jeffrey J. *Southern Writers and the Machine: Faulkner to Percy*. New York: Peter Lang, 1993.

Folks, Jeffrey J., and James A. Perkins, eds. *Southern Writers at Century's End*. Lexington: University Press of Kentucky, 1997.

Friedman, Melvin J., and Beverly Lyon Clark, eds. *Critical Essays on Flannery O'Connor*. Boston: G. K. Hall, 1985.

Friedman, Melvin J., and Lewis A. Lawson, eds. *The Added Dimension: The Art and Mind of Flannery O'Connor*. New York: Fordham University Press, 1966.

Friedman, Melvin J., and Ben Siegel, eds. *Traditions, Voices, and Dreams: The American Novel since the 1960s*. Newark: University of Delaware Press, 1995.

Genovese, Eugene D. *The Southern Tradition: The Achievements and Limitations of an American Conservatism*. Cambridge, MA: Harvard University Press, 1994.

Getz, Lorine M. *Flannery O'Connor: Her Life, Library, and Book Reviews*. New York: Edwin Mellen Press, 1980.

Giannone, Richard. *Flannery O'Connor, Hermit Novelist*. Urbana: University of Illinois Press, 2000.

Giles, Paul A. *American Catholic Arts and Fictions: Culture, Ideology, Aesthetics*. New York: Cambridge University Press, 1992.

Gordon, Caroline. *How to Read a Novel*. New York: Viking, 1957.

———. *The Malefactors*. New York: Harcourt, Brace, 1956.

———. *The Strange Children*. New York: Scribner's, 1951.

Gordon, Caroline, and Allen Tate, eds. *The House of Fiction: An Anthology of the Short Story with Commentary*. 2d ed. New York: Scribner's, 1960.

Gray, Richard. *Writing the South: Ideas of an American Region*. Cambridge: Cambridge University Press, 1986.

Gretlund, Jan Nordby, and Karl-Heinz Westarp, eds. *Walker Percy: Novelist and Philosopher*. Jackson: University Press of Mississippi, 1991.

Guardini, Romano. *The End of the Modern World*. New York: Sheed and Ward, 1956.

———. *The Faith and Modern Man*. Trans. Charlotte E. Forsyth. New York: Pantheon, 1952.

———. *Freedom, Grace, and Destiny: Three Chapters in the Interpretation of Existence*. Trans. John Murray, S.J. New York: Pantheon, 1961.

Guinn, Michael. *After Southern Modernism: Fiction of the Contemporary South*. Jackson: University Press of Mississippi, 2000.

Haddox, Thomas. "Contextualizing Flannery O'Connor: Allen Tate, Caroline Gordon, and the Catholic Turn in Southern Literature." *Southern Quarterly* 38:1 (Fall 1999): 173–90.

Hardy, John Edward. *The Fiction of Walker Percy.* Urbana: University of Illinois Press, 1987.

Hawkins, Peter S. *The Language of Grace: Flannery O'Connor, Walker Percy, and Iris Murdoch.* Cambridge, MA: Cowley, 1983.

Hobson, Fred. *The Southern Writer in the Postmodern World.* Athens: University of Georgia Press, 1991.

Hobson, Linda Whitney. *Understanding Walker Percy.* Columbia: University of South Carolina Press, 1988.

———. *Walker Percy: A Comprehensive Descriptive Bibliography.* New Orleans: Faust, 1988.

Howland, Mary Deems. *The Gift of the Other: Gabriel Marcel's Concept of Inter-subjectivity in Walker Percy's Novels.* Pittsburgh: Duquesne University Press, 1990.

Huff, Peter. *Allen Tate and the Catholic Revival: Trace of the Fugitive Gods.* New York: Paulist Press, 1996.

Humphreys, Josephine. *Dreams of Sleep.* New York: Penguin, 1984.

———. *The Firemen's Fair.* New York: Viking, 1991.

Humphries, Jefferson, and John Lowe, eds. *The Future of Southern Letters.* New York: Oxford University Press, 1996.

Kazin, Alfred. *God and the American Writer.* New York: Alfred A. Knopf, 1997.

Kenan, Randall. *Let the Dead Bury Their Dead.* New York: Harcourt Brace Jovanovich, 1992.

Ketchin, Susan. *The Christ-Haunted Landscape: Faith and Doubt in Southern Fiction.* Jackson: University Press of Mississippi, 1994.

King, Richard. *A Southern Renaissance: The Cultural Awakening of the American South, 1930–1955.* New York: Oxford University Press, 1980.

Kinney, Arthur F., ed. *Flannery O'Connor's Library: Resources of Being.* Athens: University of Georgia Press, 1985.

Labrie, Ross. *The Catholic Imagination in American Literature.* Columbia: University of Missouri Press, 1997.

Lawler, Peter A. *Postmodernism Rightly Understood.* Lanham, MD: Rowman and Littlefield, 1999.

Lawson, Lewis A. *Another Generation: Southern Fiction since World War II.* Jackson: University Press of Mississippi, 1984.

———. *Following Percy.* Troy, NY: Whitston, 1988.

———. *Still Following Percy.* Jackson: University Press of Mississippi, 1995.

Lawson, Lewis A., and Victor A. Kramer, eds. *Conversations with Walker Percy.* Jackson: University Press of Mississippi, 1985.

———. *More Conversations with Walker Percy.* Jackson: University Press of Mississippi, 1993.

Lewis, R. W. B. *Trials of the Word.* New Haven, CT: Yale University Press, 1965.

Logsdon, Loren, and Charles W. Mayer, eds. *Since Flannery O'Connor: Essays on the Contemporary American Short Story.* Macomb: Western Illinois University Press, 1987.

Lukacs, John. *At the End of an Age.* New Haven, CT: Yale University Press, 2002.

Luschei, Martin. *The Sovereign Wayfarer: Walker Percy's Diagnosis of the Malaise.* Baton Rouge: Louisiana State University Press, 1972.

Magee, Rosemary M., ed. *Conversations with Flannery O'Connor.* Jackson: University Press of Mississippi, 1987.

Makowsky, Veronica. *Caroline Gordon: A Biography.* New York: Oxford University Press, 1989.

Marcel, Gabriel. *Homo Viator: Introduction to a Metaphysic of Hope.* Chicago: Regnery, 1951.

———. *The Mystery of Being.* Chicago: Henry Regnery, 1950–1.

———. *The Philosophy of Existentialism.* Secaucus, NJ: Citadel, 1984.

Maritain, Jacques. *Art and Scholasticism, with Other Essays.* Trans. J. F. Scanlan. New York: Scribner's, 1930.

———. *The Dream of Descartes, Together with Some Other Essays.* Trans. Mabelle Andison. New York: Philosophical Library, 1944.

May, John R. *Toward a New Earth: Apocalypse and the American Novel.* Notre Dame, IN: University of Notre Dame Press, 1972.

Merton, Thomas. *The Courage for Truth: The Letters of Thomas Merton to Writers.* Ed. Christine M. Bochen. New York: Farrar, Straus and Giroux, 1993.

———. "The Other Side of Despair: Notes on Christian Existentialism." *Critic* 24 (October–November 1965): 12–22.

Miller, Randall M., and Jon L. Wakelyn, eds. *Catholics in the Old South: Essays on Church and Culture.* Macon, GA: Mercer University Press, 1983.

O'Connor, Flannery. *Collected Works of Flannery O'Connor.* Ed. Sally Fitzgerald. New York: Library of America, 1988.

———. *The Complete Stories.* Ed. Robert Giroux. New York: Farrar, Straus and Giroux, 1971.

———. *The Habit of Being: Letters of Flannery O'Connor.* Ed. Sally Fitzgerald. New York: Farrar, Straus and Giroux, 1979.

———. *Mystery and Manners: Occasional Prose.* Ed. Sally and Robert Fitzgerald. New York: Farrar, Straus and Giroux, 1969.

———. *Three by Flannery O'Connor.* New York: Penguin, 1983.

Percy, Walker. *Lancelot.* New York: Farrar, Straus and Giroux, 1977.

———. *The Last Gentleman.* New York: Farrar, Straus and Giroux, 1966.

———. *Lost in the Cosmos.* New York: Farrar, Straus and Giroux, 1983.

———. *Love in the Ruins.* New York: Farrar, Straus and Giroux, 1971.

———. *The Message in the Bottle.* New York: Farrar, Straus and Giroux, 1975.

———. *The Moviegoer.* New York: Alfred A. Knopf, 1961.

———. *The Second Coming.* New York: Farrar, Straus and Giroux, 1980.

———. *Signposts in a Strange Land.* Ed. Patrick Samway. New York: Farrar, Straus and Giroux, 1991.

———. *The Thanatos Syndrome.* New York: Farrar, Straus and Giroux, 1987.

Percy, William Alexander. *Lanterns on the Levee.* New York: Alfred A. Knopf, 1941.

Powell, Padgett. *Edisto: A Novel.* New York: Farrar, Straus and Giroux, 1984.

———. *Edisto Revisited.* New York: Henry Holt, 1996.

Quinlan, Kieran. *Walker Percy: The Last Catholic Novelist.* Baton Rouge: Louisiana State University Press, 1996.

Ragen, Brian Abel. *A Wreck on the Road to Damascus: Innocence, Guilt, and Conversion in Flannery O'Connor.* Chicago: Loyola University Press, 1989.

Rubin, Louis D., Jr. *A Gallery of Southerners.* Baton Rouge: Louisiana State University Press, 1982.

Rubin, Louis D., Jr., and Robert D. Jacobs, eds. *Southern Renascence: The Literature of the Modern South.* Baltimore: Johns Hopkins University Press, 1953.

Samway, Patrick H. *Walker Percy: A Life.* New York: Farrar, Straus and Giroux, 1997.

Settle, Mary Lee. Untitled memorial. In *Memorial Tributes to Walker Percy*. New York: Farrar, Straus and Giroux, 1990.

Simpson, Lewis P. *The Brazen Face of History: Studies in the Literary Consciousness of America*. Baton Rouge: Louisiana State University Press, 1980.

Singal, Daniel J. *The War Within: From Victorian to Modernist Thought in the South, 1919–1945*. Chapel Hill: University of North Carolina Press, 1982.

Sparr, Arnold. *To Promote, Defend, and Redeem: The Catholic Literary Revival and the Cultural Transformation of American Catholicism, 1920–1960*. New York: Greenwood Press, 1990.

Spivey, Ted. *Flannery O'Connor: The Woman, the Thinker, the Visionary*. Macon, GA: Mercer University Press, 1995.

———. *Revival: Southern Writers in the Modern City*. Gainesville: University of Florida Press, 1986.

Squires, Radcliffe. *Allen Tate: A Literary Biography*. New York: Pegasus, 1971.

Sullivan, Walter. *Requiem for the Renascence: The State of Fiction in the Modern South*. Athens: University of Georgia Press, 1976.

Tate, Allen. *Essays of Four Decades*. Chicago: Swallow, 1968.

———. *The Fathers and Other Fiction*. Baton Rouge: Louisiana State University Press, 1977.

———. *Memoirs and Opinions, 1926–1974*. Chicago: Swallow, 1975.

Tolson, Jay, ed. *The Correspondence of Shelby Foote and Walker Percy*. New York: Norton, 1996.

———. *Pilgrim in the Ruins: A Life of Walker Percy*. New York: Simon and Schuster, 1992.

Twelve Southerners. *I'll Take My Stand: The South and the Agrarian Tradition*. Baton Rouge: Louisiana State University Press, 1977.

Waldron, Ann. *Close Connections: Caroline Gordon and the Southern Renaissance*. New York: G. P. Putnam's, 1987.

Walker, Alice. *In Search of Our Mothers' Gardens*. New York: Harcourt Brace Jovanovich, 1983.

Walters, Dorothy. *Flannery O'Connor*. Boston: Twayne, 1973.

Welty, Eudora. Untitled memorial. In *Memorial Tributes to Walker Percy*. New York: Farrar, Straus and Giroux, 1990.

Wood, Ralph. *The Comedy of Redemption*. Notre Dame, IN: University of Notre Dame Press, 1988.

Wyatt-Brown, Bertram. *The House of Percy.* New York: Oxford University Press, 1994.

Zamora, Lois Parkinson. *Writing the Apocalypse: Historical Vision in Contemporary U.S. and Latin American Fiction.* New York: Cambridge University Press, 1989.

Zamora, Lois Parkinson, and Wendy B. Faris. *Magical Realism: Theory, History, Community.* Durham, NC: Duke University Press, 1995.

Index

Bonhoeffer, Dietrich, 136
Borges, Jorge Luis, 214
Bosworth, Sheila, 205, 205n13
Bourges, Camille, 20
Bradford, M. E., 55n6
The Bridge (Crane), 58, 130–31
Brinkmeyer, Robert, 3–4, 53n2, 57, 61
Brooks, Cleanth, 117
The Brothers Karamazov (Dostoyevsky), 30
Broun, Heywood, 71
Brown, Felix, 34
Brown, Larry, 212, 221–22
Brownson, Orestes, 109
Bruno, Giordano, 223n51
Buber, Martin, 136, 208
"The Buried Lake" (Tate), 91
Burke, James Lee, 205, 206, 206n16
Burns, Ken, 233
Burrell, David, 160n12

Caldwell, Erskine, 138, 212
Camus, Albert, 29–30, 43, 50, 76, 81, 97, 128
A Canticle for Leibowitz (Miller), 165
Capote, Truman, 89
Carlson, Thomas M., 228n59
Cash, W. J., 1, 23
"The Catholic Novelist in the Protestant South" (O'Connor), 114–15
Catholic Revival, 6, 10, 12, 17, 52, 53, 66, 67, 70–83, 90, 100–102, 107, 109–10, 115, 120, 129, 159, 195, 209, 235
Catholic theory of fiction: and realism, 6, 12, 105, 106–10, 116, 118–19, 123, 125, 129; Giles on, 64–66, 105–6, 108, 109, 127, 134n48; Gordon on, 67, 69, 86–87, 109, 116, 124–29, 125n32; and Percy, 103, 107–11, 116, 117, 120–24, 128–29, 146–49, 163; Labrie on, 104–5, 106, 108, 109, 112, 117–18; and O'Connor, 106–11, 114–15, 116, 122–24, 126–29, 132, 133, 146–48; and Maritain,

109–12, 112n11, 125, 125n32, 129, 132–33; and Tate, 109, 116, 117, 119–24, 129–33; and Lynch, 112–15, 135; distrust of abstraction, intuitive subjectivity, and romanticism, 116, 129–46; and language, 116, 118–24; literature as form of knowledge, 116; Deely on, 117–18n19; and postmodernism, 117, 117–18n19; Desmond on, 118; and New Criticism, 119; and flawed artists in fiction by O'Connor and Percy, 129, 137–46. *See also* Catholicism
Catholic Worker movement, 64, 66, 68
Catholicism: of O'Connor, 2–6, 10–13, 17, 40–41, 47–48, 50, 52–54, 70, 74–81, 100, 103, 104, 163, 164, 170, 195, 200–201, 201n2, 208, 213; of Percy, 2–6, 10–13, 17, 36, 42, 45, 50, 52–54, 53n2, 74–76, 74n50, 79n58, 86, 100, 163, 164, 195, 200–201, 201n2; and Gordon, 3, 5, 11, 17, 50, 52–54, 53n2, 55, 67–71, 74, 83, 85, 90, 92–94, 100, 101; of southern writers generally, 3–4; and Tate, 3, 5, 11, 50, 51, 52–67, 53n2, 69–70, 71, 73–74, 73n49, 83, 85, 90–94, 100, 101; and O'Connor family, 18, 19, 23–26; and Percy family, 18, 19, 21, 36, 36n42; in Georgia, 23–24; in Europe, 24, 66, 68–69, 71–83, 91, 102; in Birmingham, 28n28; and parochial schools, 30–31, 32, 38, 39; and vocation, 47; and desert monastic tradition, 49n65; R. Fitzgerald on, 51; Genovese on, 55n6; sacramental vision of, 58, 74, 104, 105, 106, 113, 146, 148, 225, 234; and transcendence and immanence, 58; and English Distributist movement, 64; and modernism, 64–65; Lowell's conversion to, 69, 71; in medieval Europe, 73; and Eucharist, 103, 104n1, 118n19, 204; and transubstantiation, 103–4, 118n19; and Jansenism, 104, 105; and Manicheanism, 104, 125, 126; and nature, 104–5; and Incarnation, 107n7; of Porter, 159–60; in postwar

America, 163, 164; and apocalypticism, 165; of Dillard, 207–9, 208n18, 209n20; of Settle, 221. *See also* Aquinas, Thomas; Catholic Revival; Catholic theory of fiction; Neo-Thomism; and names of Catholic writers

Cato, 54

Celebration (Settle), 221

Chandler, Raymond, 206

Charley Bland (Settle), 221

The Charterhouse (Percy), 12, 51–52, 86–87, 124–26

Cheney, Brainard, 51–52, 87

Chesnutt, Charles, 214

Chesterton, G. K., 64

Child of God (McCarthy), 207

Christ and Apollo (Lynch), 112, 113–14

Christian existentialism, 50, 52, 54n3, 72, 77–83, 99, 100–101, 107, 197, 201. *See also* Existentialism

Christian panentheism, 209

Christianity. *See* Catholicism; Protestantism

Civil War, 15–16, 16n1, 20, 25, 95–96, 148, 180, 190, 233

The Civil War: A Narrative (Foote), 148

Clark, Charlene Kerne, 206, 206n16

Clark, Dennis, 24

Clark, William Bedford, 206, 206n16

Cline, Herbert, 31

Cline, Margaret Ida Treanor, 24, 25

Cline, Nan O'Connor, 31

Cline, Peter James, 24, 25, 38

Cline, Regina, 25, 26, 31, 33

Cobb, James C., 36

Coindreau, Maurice, 84, 84n65

Coles, Robert, 39, 43

Collins, James, 79, 79n58, 80

Collins, Susannah, 19

Communism, 163, 164–65

The Confessions of Nat Turner (Styron), 96

Consumerism and materialism, 8, 155, 162, 163–67, 169–72, 177, 178, 180. *See also* Advertising

Copleston, Frederick, 79n58, 80

Corrington, John William, 205–6

Covington, La., 75, 86, 90, 232

Crane, Hart, 56, 57–58, 58n13, 130–32

Crime fiction, 205–6

"The Crop" (O'Connor), 137–38

Crowley, J. Donald, 156

"The Culture Critics" (Percy), 164

Dancing after Hours (Dubus), 204–5

Dante, 58, 59, 73, 91, 121, 131, 135, 144

Davidson, Donald, 56, 59, 60, 63, 176

Davis, Jefferson, 57, 66

Dawkins, Cecil, 75, 88

Dawson, Christopher, 72

Day, Dorothy, 64, 68, 69, 90, 91

"The Death of the Author" (Barthes), 117

DeBardeleben, Mary Pratt, 21

Deconstructionists, 123n30

Deely, John, 117–18n19

DeLillo, Don, 49n65, 200n1

Delta Wedding (Welty), 96

Derrida, Jacques, 105, 118n19

Descartes, René, 125, 133–34, 135

Desmond, John F., 118, 192n46, 204

"Diary of an African Nun" (Walker), 216n37

Dickey, James, 118

Dillard, Annie, 11, 207–9, 208n18, 209n20, 210

"The Displaced Person" (O'Connor), 112n11, 127, 148, 164, 164n21, 179, 183–85, 184n39, 193–94, 214, 217

The Divine Comedy (Dante), 58, 131

Dixie City Jam (Burke), 206

Dostoyevsky, Fyodor, 30, 43, 50, 76, 124, 136, 182, 201, 216n36

Douglass, Frederick, 215

"Dover Beach" (Arnold), 144, 146–47

Fortugno, Arthur, 74

Foucault, Michel, 105

France, 56, 57, 66, 71, 73*n*49, 75

Freud, Sigmund, 17, 144

Fugitive, 57

Fugitives, 23, 56, 60, 222

Fukuyama, Francis, 7*n*9

García Márquez, Gabriel, 157, 213, 214, 219

The Garden of Adonis (Gordon), 67

Genovese, Eugene, 55*n*6

"The Geranium" (O'Connor), 40, 40*n*49, 41, 49, 161

Germany, 71, 75, 81, 82*n*62, 197*n*52

Giannone, Richard, 49*n*65

Gibson, Etienne, 71

Giles, Paul, 11, 64–66, 65*n*30, 72–74, 92, 94, 102, 105–6, 108, 109, 127, 134*n*48, 159–60, 160*n*12

Gillespie, Michael Patrick, 4–5

Gilson, Étienne-Henry, 72, 75, 76, 79

The Glory of Hera (Gordon), 92

Go Down, Moses (Faulkner), 161–62

Godwin, Gail, 203, 203*n*8

"Good Country People" (O'Connor), 89, 128

"A Good Man Is Hard to Find" (O'Connor), 16*n*1, 148, 159, 178, 181–82, 192*n*46, 203, 207

A Good Man Is Hard to Find (O'Connor), 88, 180–86, 189, 193

Gordon, Caroline: and Catholicism, 3, 5, 11, 17, 50, 52–54, 53*n*2, 55, 67–71, 74, 83, 85, 92–94, 100, 101; as mentor to Percy and O'Connor, 5, 12, 17, 51–52, 53, 84–90, 89*n*83, 109, 115–16, 124–29, 135; and O'Connor's fiction, 12, 51–52, 86–87, 89, 104, 128; and Percy's *Charterhouse,* 12, 51–52, 86–87, 124–26; and Catholic Revival, 17, 53, 75, 83, 90, 100, 101, 115, 159; and Agrarian movement, 53, 68, 91; as literary modernist, 53, 67, 69, 94; marriage of, 56, 84; in New York, 56, 67, 84; and

Dorothy Day, 64, 68, 69, 90, 91; in Europe, 64, 67, 68–69; Guggenheim fellowship for, 64; and Catholic theory of fiction, 67, 69, 86–87, 109, 116, 124–29, 125*n*32; fiction by, 67–68, 69, 90–91, 92, 94, 96, 107; conversion of, to Catholic Church, 69–70, 71; Maritain's influence on, 71, 72, 90, 110, 125, 125*n*32, 135; decline of literary career of, 90–91, 92; and "School of the Holy Ghost," 90; on Tate's political involvement, 91; compared with O'Connor, 92–93, 94; death of, 92; literary criticism by, 92, 124; and reality of language, 116; on language, 122; on Protestantism, 124; and New Criticism, 128*n*35. *See also* specific works

Goyen, William, 214

Grace, 54, 178, 186, 219. *See also* Sacramental vision

The Gramercy Winner (Percy), 37–38, 87

Great Depression, 27, 30, 31–32

Green Centuries (Gordon), 67

Greene, Graham, 96–97*n*96, 125, 209*n*20

"Greenleaf" (O'Connor), 66*n*32, 127, 169, 185

Greenville, Miss., 20, 21, 34, 35, 36, 42

Grotesque, 48, 89, 95, 95*n*93, 98, 99, 112*n*11, 129, 160*n*12, 165*n*23, 179, 188, 201*n*2, 202, 210

Guardini, Romano, 3, 7, 53, 72, 75, 76, 77, 81, 81–82*n*62, 90, 158–60, 158*nn*9–10, 161*n*13, 182, 185, 193

Guinn, Michael, 9

Gulliver's Travels (Swift), 134, 134*n*47

Gurganus, Allen, 203

The Habit of Being (O'Connor), 22, 32, 33, 38, 45–46, 47, 49, 57, 79, 85*n*67, 88, 107, 111, 122, 127–28, 159

Haddox, Thomas, 69–70, 125*n*32, 128*n*35

Hannah, Barry, 212

"Hart Crane" (Tate), 57–58, 58*n*13, 130–32, 130*n*40, 135

Harty, Johannah, 24

Harty, Patrick, 24, 25

Havel, Václav, 7n9

Hawthorne, Nathaniel, 201, 231n65

Hegel, G. W. F., 44

Heidegger, Martin, 79, 122

Heller, Joseph, 166

Hemingway, Ernest, 56, 67, 125, 145n55

Hesse, Herman, 145n54

Hester, Betty, 88n79

The Hidden Persuaders (Packard), 164

Highsmith, Dixie Lee, 123n29

Hobson, Fred, 2n3, 10, 116–17, 123, 199, 212, 222, 235

Holman, C. Hugh, 2

Homer, 124

Honor, 177–78, 186–92

Hood, John Bell, 25

The House of Fiction (Tate and Gordon), 89, 92, 128

Housman, A. E., 141

"The Hovering Fly" (Tate), 120

"How to Be an American Novelist in Spite of Being Southern and Catholic" (Percy), 103, 107n7

How to Read a Novel (Gordon), 92, 124

Huff, Peter A., 57, 58, 61, 62n23, 66, 73, 119, 122

"Humanism and Naturalism" (Tate), 59

Humphreys, Josephine, 11, 200, 221, 222, 223–26, 223–24n52

Humphries, Jefferson, 221

Hurston, Zora Neale, 214

Husserl, Edmund, 79

Ignatius of Loyola, St., 124

I'll Take My Stand (Twelve Southerners), 60, 61

In Love and Trouble (Walker), 216n37

In the Electric Mist with Confederate Dead (Burke), 206

Intersubjectivity, 82

"The Intruder" (Dubus), 204–5

Invisible Man (Ellison), 215–16n36

Iowa Writers' Workshop, 39–40, 85, 137

Ireland and Irish immigrants, 23, 23n14, 24, 25, 26, 38

Irons, Susan H., 223n52

James, Henry, 89, 96, 124, 127–28

Jansenism, 104, 105

Jaspers, Karl, 79

Jayne, Mitchell F., 99

Jones, Madison, 201

Joyce, James, 4, 12, 39, 69, 125, 138

"Judgment Day" (O'Connor), 41, 161

K-Mart Realism, 212

Kafka, Franz, 39

Kant, Immanuel, 111, 119

Kelleher, Ray, 208n18, 209n20

Kenan, Randall, 11, 200, 216–20, 217n39, 235

Ketchin, Susan, 201n2

Keyes, Frances Parkinson, 71

Kierkegaard, Søren, 3, 43–44, 78, 79, 81, 82–83, 118n19, 136, 160n12, 161, 177, 191n45, 223n51

King, Richard, 54, 94

Kreyling, Michael, 2n3

Ku Klux Klan, 19, 20, 21, 23, 35, 163

Labrie, Ross, 104–5, 106, 108, 109, 112, 117–18

"The Lame Shall Enter First" (O'Connor), 179

Lancelot (Percy), 35n41, 80, 145–46, 151, 180, 188–93, 190n44, 192n46, 206

Language: in Catholic theory of fiction, 116, 118–19; and O'Connor, 116, 122–24, 123n29; and Percy, 116, 120–24, 123nn29–30; positivist view of, 119, 121; and Tate, 120, 124, 131–32; Gordon on, 122; Poe on, 135; in Powell's *Edisto*, 229

May, John R., 156

McCarthy, Cormac, 3, 206–7, 212

McCarthy, Mary, 104n1

McCorkle, Jill, 211

McKee, Kathryn B., 224

McLuhan, Marshall, 8n10, 167n26

McMillan, Terry, 216

Media, 8, 173, 180. *See also* Advertising

Medicine, 37–38, 42–43, 45, 84–85

Medieval Europe, 62, 63, 65, 72–73, 75, 77, 92

"The Mediterranean" (Tate), 64

Melville, Herman, 207

A Memoir of Mary Ann, 197n52

Memory, aesthetic of, 5, 98, 100

Merton, Thomas, 6n8, 47, 54, 54n3, 71, 77–78, 89n83, 100–101, 104, 208

"The Message in the Bottle" (Percy), 83, 88n79, 112n12, 192

The Message in the Bottle (Percy), 50, 120–21

"Metaphor as Mistake" (Percy), 121

Middle Ages. *See* Medieval Europe

Milbank, John, 7n9

Milledgeville, Ga., 22–25, 30, 32, 34, 38, 39, 45–49, 75, 85, 86, 163, 211

Miller, Walter M., Jr., 165

Modernism: definition of, 6–7, 7n9, 9; and Tate, 9, 53, 53n2, 55, 56, 57, 69, 73, 92, 94; and Gordon, 53, 67, 69, 94; examples of southern modernists, 54; and Fugitives, 56; and Catholicism, 64–65; and neo-scholasticism, 73; Lynch on, 113; and Foote, 129

Montaigne, Michel de, 102

Morgan, Berry, 205, 205n13

Morris, Willie, 207n17

Morrison, Toni, 195, 213, 214–15, 215n34, 216n36

The Moviegoer (Percy): father in, 29; science in, 37, 230; identity in, 41, 107–8; critics' responses to, 97, 162–63; Merton on, 101; Percy on, 107–8; "vertical" versus "horizon-

tal" search in, 108, 135, 141–44, 226–27; Lynch's influence on, 113; award for, 128, 153n3, 162; Maritain's influence on, 135; flawed artist in, 141–44; compared with O'Connor's fiction, 153–55, 170–76, 186; postwar themes of, 153–55, 162–63, 166, 171–76, 194–95; epigraph to, 161; O'Connor on, 171n31, 176; automobiles in, 173–74; apocalypticism in, 175; Catholic characters in, 176n34; honor code in, 177, 186–87; Ash Wednesday scene in, 186n41; allusion to, in Wells's fiction, 205; mystery in, 226–27, 231; compared with Powell's fiction, 229, 231–32

Mystery: Tate on, 65–66; and Percy, 74, 103, 108, 129, 147, 201n2, 226–27, 231, 235; and O'Connor, 108, 129, 147, 161, 201n2, 235; and language, 122; and Powell, 230

Mystery and Manners (O'Connor), 18, 50, 70, 74, 78, 106, 107, 108, 126, 127, 132, 133, 161, 178, 179

The Mystery of Being (Marcel), 82

"Naming and Being" (Percy), 122

"Narcissus on Narcissus" (Tate), 134–35n48

Naturalism, 106–7

Nature, 104–5, 112n11, 119–20, 169, 208, 209, 210

"The Nature and Aim of Fiction" (O'Connor), 126, 211

Nausea (Sartre), 79, 147

Nazism, 81, 82n62, 197n52, 215

Neo-scholasticism. *See* Neo-Thomism

Neo-Thomism, 66, 71, 72, 73, 79–80, 79n58, 83, 88, 90, 92, 107, 110, 125, 159. *See also* Aquinas, Thomas

New Criticism, 70, 83, 117, 119, 122, 128n35

"The New Provincialism" (Tate), 65n30

New South, 18, 28–29, 34, 133, 178n37

New York, 16, 37–38, 40–43, 56, 57, 58, 67, 69, 84, 85, 90, 94

Niebuhr, Reinhold, 119

Nietzsche, Friedrich, 54, 79, 144

Night Rider (Warren), 96

No Exit (Sartre), 82

None Shall Look Back (Gordon), 67, 96

Norton, Mary Ellen, 25

"Notes for a Novel about the End of the World" (Percy), 188

Notes from Underground (Dostoyevsky), 216n36

Notes toward the Definition of Christian Culture (Eliot), 60n17

Nouwen, Henri, 205n14

"Novel-Writing in an Apocalyptic Time" (Percy), 122n27

Nuclear warfare, 165, 175

Oates, Joyce Carol, 199n1

O'Connor, Edward Francis, 26

O'Connor, Edward Francis, Jr., 26, 30–34, 38, 47, 74

O'Connor, Flannery: birth of, 16, 26, 31; death of, 16, 85, 89; family history of, 16, 17–18, 22–26; and father's death, 16, 27, 33–34, 47, 74; illness of, 16, 32, 33, 35, 42, 45–49, 49n65, 85; in New York, 16, 40–41, 85; baptismal name of, 25; parents of, 25, 26–27, 30–34; childhood and youth of, 26–27, 31–34, 38; education of, 32, 33, 34–35, 38–40; travel and lectures by, 32; and writing vocation, 33, 34–35, 39–41, 45–50; and social sciences, 38–39, 41, 195–96; at Iowa Writers' Workshop, 39–40, 85, 137; at Yaddo writers' colony, 40–41, 85; personality of, 46; return to Milledgeville by, 46–49, 85; library of, 53, 79–80, 81–82n62, 82, 88n79, 112, 113; and race relations, 184n39; as writer-in-residence at Hollins College, 208

—philosophical and religious views: Catholicism of O'Connor, 2–6, 10–13, 17, 40–41, 47–48, 49n65, 50, 52–54, 70, 74–81, 100,

103, 104, 163, 164, 170, 195, 200–201, 201n2, 208, 213; Guardini's influence on, 3, 53, 72, 75, 76, 77, 81, 81–82n62, 158n9, 159, 160, 182, 193; aesthetic of revelation, 5, 98–99; existentialism, 6n8, 9, 50, 75–79, 158, 197, 201; postmodernism, 7–9, 7n9, 8n10, 97–98, 159–61, 160n12, 180–81, 193; Maritain's influence on, 53, 71–72, 75, 76–77, 109–12, 112n11, 129, 133; Catholic Revival, 75–83, 90, 100–102, 109, 115, 129, 195, 209, 235; Marcel's influence on, 78–79, 82, 158; on Eucharist, 103, 104n1; Catholic theory of fiction, 106–11, 114–15, 116, 122–24, 126–29, 132, 133, 146–48; Lynch's influence on, 112–15, 135; "anagogical vision," 123, 136; angelism, 135, 137–41; apocalypticism, 156, 157–59, 165–70, 175, 181–82, 192n46

—writings: essays on literature and language, 1, 15, 50, 114–15, 126, 132, 133, 179, 211; Gordon as mentor of O'Connor, 5, 12, 17, 51–52, 53, 84–90, 89n83, 109, 115–16, 124, 126–29; Tate as mentor of O'Connor, 5, 40, 52, 53, 84, 85, 109, 115–16; and realism, 6, 12, 107, 108–10, 196, 209–11, 214; influence of, on contemporary writers, 11–12, 199–220, 199–200n1, 234–35; on the South, 15–16, 16n1, 133; themes of, 38–39, 41, 91, 146, 154; grotesques in, 48, 89, 95, 98, 112n11, 129, 160n12, 188, 210; satire of, 49, 52, 109, 129, 137–41, 155, 168, 171, 180–81, 184n39, 186, 193, 202–3, 213; Percy on, 50, 115, 136, 146, 188, 220; book reviews by O'Connor for diocesan newspaper, 76–77, 113–14; Gordon's introduction of Percy to O'Connor, 86; and Percy's writings, 88, 95n95, 153–54, 153n3, 171n32, 176; correspondence between Percy and O'Connor, 89; on Gordon's *Malefactors*, 90–91; compared with Gordon, 92–93, 94; and end of Southern Renaissance, 94–102; Foote on, 97n96; on Emerson, 106; on natu-

201n2; existentialism, 2, 9, 29–30, 43–44, 50, 75–76, 79, 79n58, 88, 99, 101, 107, 122, 158, 160n12, 197, 201; Maritain's influence on, 3, 53, 71–72, 76, 88, 90, 109–12, 120, 129; aesthetic of revelation, 5, 98–99; postmodernism, 7–9, 7n9, 8n10, 98, 115, 148, 159–61; Guardini's influence on, 53, 72, 76, 81, 81–82n62, 90, 158nn9–10, 159, 160, 193; and Merton, 54n3, 89n83, 101; Catholic Revival, 75, 81, 83, 90, 100–102, 107, 109, 120, 129, 209, 235; Marcel's influence on, 78, 82, 90, 120–21, 158, 160n12; neo-Thomism, 79, 79n58, 80, 88, 107; Catholic theory of fiction, 103, 107–11, 116, 117, 120–24, 128–29, 146–49; on Incarnation, 107n7; Lynch's influence on, 112–15, 112n12; angelism, 114, 129, 135–36, 141–46; apocalypticism, 156, 157–59, 165, 170–76, 192–93, 192n46, 222

—writings: Gordon as mentor of Percy, 5, 12, 17, 51–52, 53, 84–90, 89n83, 109, 115–16, 124–26, 128–29, 135; Tate as mentor of Percy, 5, 40, 52, 53, 84–85, 87, 109, 115–16, 119–24; and realism, 6, 12, 107–10, 221; influence of, on contemporary writers, 11–12, 199–209, 199–200n1, 220–35; on the South, 15–16, 133; themes of, 39, 41, 44, 91, 95, 146, 154, 206; on mortality, 44, 50; satire of, 49, 52, 109, 129, 137, 141–46, 148, 155, 171, 179, 193, 202, 203; on O'Connor, 50, 115, 136, 146, 188; Gordon's introduction of O'Connor and Percy, 86; essays on literature and language, 87–88, 102, 103, 107n7, 116, 120–23, 123n30, 179, 188; philosophical essays, 87–88, 89, 112, 112n12; O'Connor's reading of Percy's works, 88, 95n95, 171n31, 176; correspondence with O'Connor, 89; and end of Southern Renaissance, 94–102; on writing process, 108; literature as form of knowledge, 116; flawed artists in, 129, 141–46; as influence on O'Connor, 153–54, 153n3, 220;

postwar themes of, 153–55, 160–66, 171–80, 186–97, 220; critique of South in, 177–80, 186–93; technology in, 193–97; Welty on, 196; O'Connor's influence on, 197n52; Betts on, 202; Percy as mentor to other southern writers, 205. *See also* specific works

Percy, William Alexander (mid-19th century), 20, 54

Percy, William Alexander (Walker Percy's uncle), 19, 20, 21, 22, 35–36, 36n42, 42, 43, 45, 84, 177

Percy family, 17–23, 23n14, 26–30

Phaedrus (Plato), 118n19

Phinizy, Martha Susan (Mattie Sue). *See* Percy, Martha Susan Phinizy (Mattie Sue).

"Physician as Novelist" (Percy), 102

Picard, Max, 75

Pickstock, Catherine, 118n19

Pilgrim at Tinker Creek (Dillard), 208

Pius XI, Pope, 73n49

Plato, 118n19

Playing in the Dark (Morrison), 215n34

Poe, Edgar Allan, 38, 75, 134–35

Poetry: and Tate, 56, 57, 58, 58n13, 61–62, 64, 65, 67, 91, 119–20, 127, 130–32; by Crane, 58, 130–32; Richards on, 119; O'Connor on, 122

Porter, Katherine Anne, 3, 54, 93, 159–60

A Portrait of the Artist as a Young Man (Joyce), 69

Positivism, 116, 119, 120, 121

Postmodernism: definition of, 6, 7–9; Guardini on, 7, 159; and O'Connor, 7–9, 7n9, 8n10, 97–98, 159–61, 160n12, 180–81, 193; and Percy, 7–9, 7n9, 8n10, 98, 115, 159–61, 161n13; Sullivan on, 97–98; Barthes on, 117; and Catholic theory of fiction, 117, 117–18n19; Deely on, 117–18n19; and McLuhan, 167n26; and Corrington, 205–6; and Burke, 206

Pound, Ezra, 55, 73

Powell, Padgett, 11, 200, 223, 227–34, 228n59

Prayer in Practice (Guardini), 77

"The Present Function of Criticism" (Tate), 119

Price, Reynolds, 202–3, 203n8

"The Profession of Letters in the South" (Tate), 65

Protestantism: in the South, 1–2, 23, 61–64, 98, 167–71, 178–79, 184–85, 200; and Percy family, 18, 19, 21, 28; and American literature, 51, 106; and Scopes trial, 60, 200; Weber on, 62n23; and Christian existentialism, 82–83; and romanticism, 106, 134n48; O'Connor on, 114–15; Gordon on, 124; and Reformation, 156; and anti-Catholicism, 163; and fundamentalism, 164, 178–79; in postwar America, 164; in O'Connor's fiction, 167–71, 178, 184–85

Proust, Marcel, 96

Psychiatry and psychoanalysis, 42, 43

Pynchon, Thomas, 156, 157, 166

Quinlan, Kieran, 10, 72, 79n58, 100, 121, 123n30

Rabbit, Run (Updike), 226

Race relations, 19, 21, 178n37, 184n39, 186, 186n41, 215, 217–19, 217n39

Radical Orthodoxy, 7n9

Rahner, Karl, 160n12

Rand, Ayn, 145n54

The Range of Reason (Maritain), 76–77

Ransom, John Crowe, 40, 56, 60, 61, 63, 117

Raper, Julius Rowan, 116–17

Reactionary Essays on Poetry and Ideas (Tate), 65

Real Presence (Bausch), 204

Realism, 105, 106–10, 116, 118–19, 123, 125, 129, 196, 209–12, 214, 221

Reformation, 59, 156

"The Regional Writer" (O'Connor), 1, 15, 50

Regionalist school, 37

Religion. *See* Catholicism; Protestantism

"Religion and Intellectuals" (*Partisan Review*), 73n49, 81

Religious literary criticism, 9–11

"Remarks on Southern Religion" (Tate), 61–64

"Retroduction to American History" (Tate), 58

"Revelation" (O'Connor), 112n11, 183, 184n39, 185, 194, 203, 214, 217

Revelation, aesthetic of, 5, 98–99

Richards, I. A., 119–20

Riesman, David, 164

"The River" (O'Connor), 169

The Robber Bridegroom (Welty), 96

Roberts, Terry, 205–6

Robinson, Douglas, 106

Roman Catholicism. *See* Catholicism

Romanticism, 106, 109, 113, 116, 124, 129–47, 134–35n48. *See also* Angelism

Rorty, Richard, 7n9

Rousseau, Jean-Jacques, 134

Rubin, Louis D., Jr., 2, 10, 93, 95, 179, 208, 212

Sacramental vision, 58, 74, 104, 105, 106, 113, 146, 148, 225, 234. *See also* Eucharist

The Sacred Wood (Eliot), 57

Samway, Patrick, 20, 37, 109, 112n12

Santa Fe, N.Mex., 165

Sartre, Jean-Paul, 43, 50, 76, 79, 81, 82, 97, 147

Savannah, Ga., 23, 25–26, 30, 31–32, 34

Saving Grace (L. Smith), 210

Sayers, Valerie, 221

Science fiction, 165, 222

Scientific disciplines, 6, 36–38, 41, 42–44, 53n2, 80, 101–2, 107, 120, 122, 129, 165n23, 193, 226–28, 230

Scopes trial, 60, 200

Scott, Sir Walter, 142